First World War
and Army of Occupation
War Diary
France, Belgium and Germany

41 DIVISION
Divisional Troops
84 Sanitary Section
29 March 1916 - 31 March 1917

WO95/2630/3

The Naval & Military Press Ltd
www.nmarchive.com
Published in association with The National Archives

Published by

The Naval & Military Press Ltd

Unit 10 Ridgewood Industrial Park,
Uckfield, East Sussex,
TN22 5QE England
Tel: +44 (0) 1825 749494

www.naval-military-press.com
www.nmarchive.com

This diary has been reprinted in facsimile from the original. Any imperfections are inevitably reproduced and the quality may fall short of modern type and cartographic standards.

Contents

Document type	Place/Title	Date From	Date To
Heading	WO95/2630/3 Mar 1916-Mar 1917 84 Sanitary Section		
Heading	No. 84 Sanitary Section 1916 Mar-1917 Mar To 2 Army		
Heading	No 84 San Sect. June 16 Dec 16		
War Diary	Chelsea	29/03/1916	29/03/1916
War Diary	Aldershot	29/03/1916	04/05/1916
War Diary	S Hampton	04/05/1916	04/05/1916
War Diary	Havre.	05/05/1916	07/05/1916
War Diary	Caestre	07/05/1916	07/05/1916
War Diary	Merris	08/05/1916	30/05/1916
War Diary	Nieppe	30/05/1916	02/06/1916
War Diary	Steenwerck	07/06/1916	07/06/1916
War Diary	Nieppe	08/06/1916	27/06/1916
Miscellaneous	Memorandum.	01/07/1916	01/07/1916
Heading	War Diary Of 8th Of January Section Jul 1916		
War Diary	Nieppe	01/07/1916	18/07/1916
Diagram etc	Main Dressing Station. Nieppe. New Forces Destructor		
Diagram etc	Faces Destructor. B.	17/07/1916	17/07/1916
War Diary	Nieppe	19/07/1916	31/07/1916
Heading	War Diary Of 84th Sanitary Section 1 August 1916 To 31st August 16 Volume 4		
War Diary	Nieppe.	01/08/1916	19/08/1916
War Diary	Meteren	19/08/1916	24/08/1916
War Diary	Ailly Lehaut Clocher	25/08/1916	25/08/1916
War Diary	Ailly	26/08/1916	31/08/1916
Heading	War Diary Of 84th Sanitary Section (41st Division) 1st September 16 To 30th September 16 (Volume V)		
War Diary	Ailly Le Haut Clocher	01/09/1916	01/09/1916
War Diary	Ailly	02/09/1916	06/09/1916
War Diary	Buire	07/09/1916	09/09/1916
War Diary	Bellevue Farm	10/09/1916	17/09/1916
War Diary	Ribemont	18/09/1916	30/09/1916
Heading	War Diary 84th Sanitary Section October 1916		
Heading	War Diary For Oct 1916 Sanitary Section 84 Volume VI		
War Diary	Ribemont	01/10/1916	04/10/1916
War Diary	N.E Of Mametz	05/10/1916	10/10/1916
War Diary	Fricourt	11/10/1916	12/10/1916
War Diary	Buire Sur L'Ancre	13/10/1916	13/10/1916
War Diary	Buire	14/10/1916	14/10/1916
War Diary	Buire Sur L'Ancre	15/10/1916	15/10/1916
War Diary	Hallencourt	16/10/1916	19/10/1916
War Diary	Fletre	20/10/1916	23/10/1916
War Diary	Reninghelst	23/10/1916	23/10/1916
War Diary	Reninghelst Belgium	24/10/1916	24/10/1916
War Diary	Reninghelst	25/10/1916	31/10/1916
Heading	41st Div 84th. Sanitary Section		
Miscellaneous	War Diary Of Sanitary Section 84 RAMCT B.E.F. H. Vickers (Capt RAM CT.)		
War Diary	Reninghelst.	01/11/1916	30/11/1916

Heading	War Diary Sanitary Section 84 B.E.F. December 1916		
War Diary	Reninghelst.	01/12/1916	31/12/1916
War Diary	War Diary January 1917 Sanitary Section 84 H.V Corps Capt Vol 9		
War Diary	Reninghelst.	01/01/1917	07/01/1917
War Diary	Fields. Reninghelst.	08/01/1917	08/01/1917
War Diary	Reninghelst.	09/01/1917	11/01/1917
War Diary	Field.	12/01/1917	31/01/1917
Miscellaneous Diagram etc	Syllabus Of Course Of Instruction.	04/01/1916	04/01/1916
Heading	War Diary 84th Sanitary Section Vol 10		
War Diary	War Diary Of Sanitary Section 84 From Feb 1.1917. To Feb 28.1917 Volume X		
War Diary	Reninghelst.	01/02/1917	01/02/1917
War Diary	Field	02/02/1917	28/02/1917
Heading	War Diary 84th Sanitary Section From 1st March 1917 To 31st March 1917 Vol XI		
War Diary	Field	01/03/1917	13/03/1917
War Diary	Field (Reninghelst.)	14/03/1917	14/03/1917
War Diary	Field	15/03/1917	15/03/1917
War Diary	Field (Reninghelst.)	16/03/1917	19/03/1917
War Diary	Field	21/03/1917	29/03/1917
War Diary	Reninghelst	30/03/1917	30/03/1917
War Diary	Field	31/03/1917	31/03/1917

(3)

WO95/2630

~~June~~ Mar 1916 - Mar 1917

84 Sanitary Section

41ST DIVISION

NO. 84 SANITARY SECTION

~~JUN - DEC 1916~~

1916 MAR ~~JUN~~ - 1917 MAR

TO 2 ARMY

41

(end of)
March
April
May
June
} 1916

No. 94 San. Sect.

June '16
Dec '16

Instructions regarding War Diaries and Intelligence Summaries are contained in F. S. Regs., Part II. and the Staff Manual respectively. Title pages will be prepared in manuscript.

WAR DIARY
or
~~INTELLIGENCE SUMMARY.~~
(Erase heading not required.)

84 Sanitary Sec

Army Form C. 2118.

May

Vol 1

Place	Date	Hour	Summary of Events and Information	Remarks and references to Appendices
CHELSEA	29/3/16	8 am	Lorry equipment with 2 MT ASC drivers & one NCO left Duke of Yorks School to proceed to Aldershot by road to join 41st Division.	H.V.
"	29/3/16	9 am	Remainder of San. Sec 84, viz 1 Officer, horse & 24 men left Duke of Yorks School Chelsea to entrain Waterloo 9.45 am for Aldershot to join 41st Division. (G.O.C. 41st Division inspected section after arrival at 11.45)	H.V.
ALDERSHOT	29/3/16	12 noon	Reported arrival of San Sec 84 complete to A.D.M.S. 41st Division.	H.V.
"	3/4/16	9 am	Started course of field sanitation. The object being to instruct Sanitary Squads from every unit in sanitation. This went on daily till 2 May 1st. Every unit of the 41st Division except the Divisional train sending its own complete sanitary squad & receiving instruction.	H.V.
"	5/4/16		Rehearsal for Kings Review on Laffans plain.	H.V.
"	6/4/16		Kings review. San Sec 84 did not take part in the review but helped to police the grounds around the Royal Pavillion.	H.V.
	11/4/16 to 12/4/16		1 NCO & 9 men were attached for 2 days each to the 3 Divisional Field ambulances for training in trench warfare.	H.V.

T2134. Wt. W708–776. 500000. 4/15. Sir J. C. & S.

Instructions regarding War Diaries and Intelligence Summaries are contained in F. S. Regs., Part II. and the Staff Manual respectively. Title pages will be prepared in manuscript.

WAR DIARY
or
~~INTELLIGENCE SUMMARY.~~
(Erase heading not required.)

Army Form C. 2118.

Place	Date	Hour	Summary of Events and Information	Remarks and references to Appendices
			3 ton Lorry proceeded S. Hampton by road on 3/5/16 according to orders.	
ALDERSHOT	4/5/16	1.30 am	Entrained @ ALDERSHOT government siding to proceed to Southampton	W.V.
S'HAMPTON	4/5/16	1.30 pm	arrived at S'HAMPTON to embark at 6.30 p.m.	W.V.
"	4/5/16	7.10 PM	Sailed on transport Hunscraft to HAVRE.	W.V.
HAVRE.	5/5/16	9.30 am	Disembarked from transport & proceeded to Camp No 2 SANVIC	W.V.
"	6/5/16	2 pm	Lorry equipment left by road to ABBEVILLE in charge of 1 NCO & 2 men. It was to receive further directions at Abbeville.	W.V.
"	7/5/16	1.30 pm	Entrained @ HAVRE.	W.V.
CAESTRE	8/5/16	1.10 am	Detrained at CAESTRE & proceeded on foot to HQ 41st Division at MERRIS	W.V.
MERRIS	9/5/16	2.30	Arrived at MERRIS found lorry just arrived & reported arrival of San Sec 84 complete to A.D.M.S. 41st Division.	W.V.
"	11/5/16	9 am	O.C. proceeded to NIEPPE & went round district to be taken over by 41st Division.	W.V.
"	11/5/16	9.30 am	10 men of San Sec 84 proceeded to NIEPPE to obtain information as to routine &c to be followed on taking over ground	

T2134. Wt. W708–776. 500000. 4/15. Sir J. C. & S.

Instructions regarding War Diaries and Intelligence Summaries are contained in F. S. Regs., Part II. and the Staff Manual respectively. Title pages will be prepared in manuscript.

WAR DIARY
or
~~INTELLIGENCE SUMMARY.~~

(Erase heading not required.)

Army Form C. 2118.

Place	Date	Hour	Summary of Events and Information	Remarks and references to Appendices
			from 9th Division.	H.V.
MERRIS	20/5/16	9.30am.	10 other men from this section replaced previous 10 men who returned to MERRIS. 2nd party returned on 24/5/16.	H.V.
"	29/5/16	11 am.	Advance party of this section proceeded to NIEPPE	
"	8/5/16 to 30/5/16.		San Sec 84 carried on Divisional duties amongst the 41st Divisional troops	H.V.
"	30/5/16.	12.30pm	Remainder of San. Sec. proceeded to NIEPPE to take over from San. Sec. 9th Division.	H.V.
NIEPPE	31/5/16	12.30PM.	Took over from San Sec 9th Division on arrival in NIEPPE	
"	31/5/16	9am.	1 NCO & 2 men of San Sec 84 attached to D.H.Q. NCO to be permanently in charge of H.Q. sanitation; 2 men to work districts round Steenwerck.	
"		9am.	Remainder of men detailed off to work Districts of Divisional area to supervise sanitation of 41st Div. troops & of troops in the Divisional area. Divisional area was divided up as follows:–	

T2131. Wt. W708–776. 500000. 4/15. Sir J. C. & S.

Instructions regarding War Diaries and Intelligence Summaries are contained in F. S. Regs., Part II. and the Staff Manual respectively. Title pages will be prepared in manuscript.

WAR DIARY
or
~~INTELLIGENCE SUMMARY.~~
(Erase heading not required.)

Vol 2

Army Form C. 2118.

84 San Sec

Place	Date	Hour	Summary of Events and Information	Remarks and references to Appendices
NIEPPE	May 31.		Districts: 1 Ploegsteert. 2 Le Bizet 3 Dondon Farm & Petit Pont 4. Papot. 5. NIEPPE 6 Along Bailleul Rd. 7. Les Arbres. 8. Between Dondon Farm & Bailleul Rd. 9. Steenwerck District. One man to be permanently on water duties.	
"	1 June		1 Foreman & 2 Civilian labourers had been engaged as no military fatigues were available. The civilian foreman to be retained permanently, other civilians to be retained only till military fatigues are available.	H.V.
NIEPPE	2 June		2 more civilian labourers engaged.	H.V.
STEENWERCK	7		Civilian labour employed until Military fatigues available.	H.V.
NIEPPE	8-20		General supervision of sanitary arrangements of troops in Division area.	
"	27		Problem of sterilisation of drinking water seen into, as it was found that water carts were not being used properly, & troops had been drinking water from unsterilized & even untested sources. A report was sent to	

T2134. Wt. W708-776. 500000. 4/15. Sir J. C. & S.

Army Form C. 2118.

Instructions regarding War Diaries and Intelligence Summaries are contained in F. S. Regs., Part II. and the Staff Manual respectively. Title pages will be prepared in manuscript.

WAR DIARY
or
~~INTELLIGENCE SUMMARY.~~

(*Erase heading not required.*)

Place	Date	Hour	Summary of Events and Information	Remarks and references to Appendices
			the A.D.M.S. 41st Division on the matter, together with suggestions for bringing about stricter water discipline.	
			H. Vecker Lt.	

84th ... SANITARY SECTION.
No. ....
Date 1/7/16.

T2134. Wt. W708–776. 500000. 4/15. Sir J. C. & S.

Harrison & Sons, Printers, St. Martin's Lane, W.C.
(M 4220) Wt. w. 13345–4182 2500M 2/16 Forms C. 348 / 61

Army Form C. 348.

MEMORANDUM.

From O/C San Sec 84	From
To D.A.G. 3rd Echelon Base.	To
	ANSWER.
______ 191 .	______ 191 .

I enclose War Diary for this unit for June 1916.

H. Vickers
Lt.

84th
SANITARY SECTION.
No. ......
Date 1/7/16

41 Division July
84 San Sec
- CONFIDENTIAL - vol 3

War Diary
of
84th Sanitary Section

Volume 3
July 1916

Instructions regarding War Diaries and Intelligence Summaries are contained in F. S. Regs., Part II. and the Staff Manual respectively. Title pages will be prepared in manuscript.

WAR DIARY

~~or~~

~~INTELLIGENCE SUMMARY.~~

(Erase heading not required.)

Army Form C. 2118.

Place	Date	Hour	Summary of Events and Information	Remarks and references to Appendices
July NIEPPE	July 1.		Complaints as to state of road drains at A.S.C. dump at STEENWERCK were being received by A.D.M.S. & O.C. San. Sec. 84. O.C. San. Sec. suggested that A.S.C. might keep their own grounds & adjoining drains clean as the principal cause of the bad state of affairs was presence of dump, and resulting accumulation & deposit of rubbish after each morning's dumps. Went over to STEENWERCK & had a general look round.	H.V.
	1.		O.C. San. Sec. sent application to A.A. & Q.M.G. for fatigue party to clear road ditch outside Div. H.Q. at STEENWERCK!	H.V.
	2.		Went over to STEENWERCK twice. Civilians in STEENWERCK were throwing rubbish into streets & throwing too much work on the few San. Sec. men there. (Clearance of STEENWERCK town rubbish, & clearance of streets & ditches in town was in charge of one San. Sec. man & 4 civilians. More civilians were not obtainable. A cart was being used for carting rubbish in town to	

Army Form C. 2118.

Instructions regarding War Diaries and Intelligence Summaries are contained in F. S. Regs., Part II. and the Staff Manual respectively. Title pages will be prepared in manuscript.

WAR DIARY

or

~~INTELLIGENCE SUMMARY.~~

(Erase heading not required.)

Place	Date	Hour	Summary of Events and Information	Remarks and references to Appendices
			incinerators. Gave instructions for another incinerator to be built. One of the civilians was continuously working on the incinerators.	H.V.
NIEPPE	July 3		Suggested to A.S.C. at STEENWERCK that they should try to obtain labour for cleaning ditches from a labour battalion, or I would send a San. Sec. man to supervise the cleaning of them. A.A.S.C. found that it was necessary to clear ditch all the way from Railway Station up to town & were doing this with their own labour. They then decided to clean out the same length of ditch on opposite side of ~~ditch~~ road, as no other labour was available.	H.V.
	July 4		About this time I received complaints that clothing of Div. baths at STEENWERCK returned from the laundry full of insects. Referred matter to A.D.M.S. as an M.O. was in charge of baths.	H.V.
	July 5		Reported inability to obtain necessary labour for carrying on cleaning of ditches @ Div. H.Q. at STEENWERCK. Supply of water for baths @ PAPOT was inspected by me, & I advised	

T2134. Wt. W708–776. 500000. 4/15. Sir J. C. & S.

Instructions regarding War Diaries and Intelligence Summaries are contained in F. S. Regs., Part II. and the Staff Manual respectively. Title pages will be prepared in manuscript.

WAR DIARY
or
~~INTELLIGENCE~~ SUMMARY.
(Erase heading not required.)

Army Form C. 2118.

Place	Date	Hour	Summary of Events and Information	Remarks and references to Appendices
			closing them as the water was very foul.	
			Work on A.S.C dump ditches at STEENWERCK was proceeding satisfactory	
			Received a note from O/C 140th F.A. that A.D.M.S. wished to have a pump installed @ their A.D.S.	
			As the H.Q. of 122 & 124 Brigades had very bad sanitary arrangements at their rest billets @ ROMARIN I wrote a report to A.D.M.S on the matter. The 122 & 124 shared the same billets or huts for their periods out of the trenches & what one brigade erected the other would pull down on "taking over". One of my men has spent a great deal of labour each week on setting the sanitary arrangements in order, only to find that they were broken down each time. The 2 brigade H.Q. did not have ~~[illegible]~~ sanitary squads for the work, & I suggested that they should have proper men told off to look after the sanitary work alone.	
			&	
			I had to complain of the filthy condition in which some men of the	

T2134. Wt. W708–776. 500000. 4/15. Sir J. C. & S.

Instructions regarding War Diaries and Intelligence Summaries are contained in F. S. Regs., Part II. and the Staff Manual respectively. Title pages will be prepared in manuscript.

WAR DIARY
or
~~INTELLIGENCE SUMMARY.~~
(Erase heading not required.)

Army Form C. 2118.

Place	Date	Hour	Summary of Events and Information	Remarks and references to Appendices
			2nd Army Intelligence Corps left their billet as the premises were being taken over by a Field Ambulance.	
			The 140th Field Ambulance sent in to ask if something could be done to the drains at their main dressing station. I inspected the drains as far as possible, for no plans were available	H.V.
NIEPPE	July 6		Sent in to ADMS a scheme for cleaning the drains at 140th Field Amb. main dressing station	
			I also asked the Camp Commandant for the services of temporarily unfit men for sanitary work at STEENWERCK, as he has a number of men who could be well employed by me in cleaning up generally.	
			The 3 ton lorry of this section was engaged in carting material for the new A.D.S. at PLOEGSTEERT. There was so much work being done by all units that the lorry was lent for 4 days a week to help the R.E. in carting. It was running between the R.E. yard at ARMENTIERES	

T2134. Wt. W708–776. 500000. 4/15. Sir J. C. & S.

Instructions regarding War Diaries and Intelligence Summaries are contained in F. S. Regs., Part II. and the Staff Manual respectively. Title pages will be prepared in manuscript.

WAR DIARY
or
~~INTELLIGENCE SUMMARY.~~
(Erase heading not required.)

Army Form C. 2118.

Place	Date	Hour	Summary of Events and Information	Remarks and references to Appendices
			& PLOEGSTEERT.	F.V.
NIEPPE.	July		It was decided to try & improve the water used for washing purposes at the PIGGERIES by installing a series of filter beds & settling pits. I obtained a dozen men from the unit then in rest billets at the PIGGERIES ~~started~~ on the work: my own men supervising the technical part of the work. The scheme which was made as simple as possible was to pump the water from its present source, ie a pond with thick vegetation - into a wooden lined pit: from here it would overflow into a gravel filter pit, & from this into a collecting pit from which it could be bailed or pumped out as required. The pits were arranged in series thus:-	
			Pump → A → B Gravel pit → C → 2nd pump → to ablution bench.	
			I had great difficulty in obtaining a party of men for the work, not only for this, but for every bit of work to be done anywhere.	Note F.V.

T2134. Wt. W708-776. 500000. 4/15. Sir J. C. & S.

Instructions regarding War Diaries and Intelligence Summaries are contained in F. S. Regs., Part II. and the Staff Manual respectively. Title pages will be prepared in manuscript.

WAR DIARY
or
~~INTELLIGENCE SUMMARY.~~
(Erase heading not required.)

Army Form C. 2118.

Place	Date	Hour	Summary of Events and Information	Remarks and references to Appendices
NIEPPE.	7.		The same applies to San. Squad men from the various units. I have over & over again found that San. Squad men are taken away from San. Duties & put to do other work. Constantly in doing rounds I have asked for the San. men, & have been told that none were available. This is the more surprising as while we were in training in Aldershot I had sanitary squads to instruct from all the units in the Division except one – the A.S.C. It has happened tho' that the A.S.C. are the least trouble gang in their sanitary arrangements, but this is no doubt due to the fact that their men are not scattered & isolated but are concentrated at LA CRECHE.	H.V.
"	July 8		As the baths at PAPOT seemed to be used a great deal by the units in camp there, I wrote ~~to the A.D.M.S.~~ suggesting that I might put in the same series of filter & settling pits to clear the water for the baths there. I proposed going direct to the O.C. of Unit there in & asking for labour, while I obtained the necessary materials from the R.E.	H.V.

T2134. Wt. W708–776. 500000. 4/15. Sir J. C. & S.

Instructions regarding War Diaries and Intelligence Summaries are contained in F. S. Regs., Part II. and the Staff Manual respectively. Title pages will be prepared in manuscript.

WAR DIARY

or

~~INTELLIGENCE SUMMARY.~~

(Erase heading not required.)

Army Form C. 2118.

Place	Date	Hour	Summary of Events and Information	Remarks and references to Appendices
NIEPPE.	9.		I again had occasion to complain to Mayor of STEENWERCK that the inhabitants were dumping rubbish in the streets & allowing dirty water to run all over the place. This the MAYOR promised to rectify.	
			~~The~~ The filter scheme for PIGGERIES was finished & kept in working order	
			Pump for 140th A.D.S. was fitted by one of San Sec men & put into working order	F.V.
"	10		The M.O. of unit in PAPOT had the channels for leading off the soapy water cleared out.	
			At Div H.Q. the Camp Commandant wished to have a bath house erected for H.Q. men only, & I submitted some simple plans. The work was started on these at once. he found the labour.	F.V.

T2134. Wt. W708–776. 500000. 4/15. Sir J. C. & S.

Instructions regarding War Diaries and Intelligence Summaries are contained in F. S. Regs., Part II. and the Staff Manual respectively. Title pages will be prepared in manuscript.

WAR DIARY
or
~~INTELLIGENCE SUMMARY.~~
(Erase heading not required.)

Army Form C. 2118.

Place	Date	Hour	Summary of Events and Information	Remarks and references to Appendices
NIEPPE.	11.		Work on drains was held up owing to inability to obtain labour: the only man who knew anything about the system of drains at the 2/1 F. Amb. Dressing station being occupied on other work. We started to clear the drains but A.D.M.S. ordered us to stop as the ambulance was moving very shortly & the work would not be finished in time.	H.V.
			The A.D.M.S. directed me to put 2 more of San. Sec. men on to water duties as the water carts were not being properly used by units. We only brought out one Horrock's box for water testing in the Section's equipment, & so have had to indent for another one. I think that each San. Sec. should have two, if not three Horrock's boxes in the Section equipment. There is no doubt that water carts are not properly used. On my rounds I have frequently found water carts being improperly used. The clarifier is rarely used, or if used the canvas is very rarely changed. Again alum is	

Instructions regarding War Diaries and Intelligence Summaries are contained in F. S. Regs., Part II. and the Staff Manual respectively. Title pages will be prepared in manuscript.

WAR DIARY
or
~~INTELLIGENCE SUMMARY.~~
(Erase heading not required.)

Army Form C. 2118.

Place	Date	Hour	Summary of Events and Information	Remarks and references to Appendices
NIEPPE	11		often omitted from the clarifier. Again the bleaching powder is not added to the cart properly. Men ~~totally~~ ignorant of the method of using the carts are put in charge of it – often defaulters as a matter of fact. Another point is that the water supplies are not tested often enough. Since coming on to this area I have found on testing waters, that the previous results of Horrocks's test no longer hold good. It is a bad practice to "post up" the no. of scoopfuls required at any given source, as the state of water varies with the weather condition, i.e. heavy rain flooding the well, & dry weather evaporating the water. Every M.O. of a unit ought to perform a daily test on the source from which his unit draws its water. If the a sample of the water were brought to him each morning, he could carry out the test while attending to his morning sick.	HV.

T2134. Wt. W708–776. 500000. 4/15. Sir J. C. & S.

Instructions regarding War Diaries and Intelligence Summaries are contained in F. S. Regs., Part II. and the Staff Manual respectively. Title pages will be prepared in manuscript.

WAR DIARY

or

~~INTELLIGENCE SUMMARY.~~

(Erase heading not required.)

Army Form C. 2118.

Place	Date	Hour	Summary of Events and Information	Remarks and references to Appendices
NIEPPE	[illegible]		I had occasion to report on irregular use of watercarts @ ROPOT	
			There is difficulty in dealing with ~~horse~~ manure. In dry weather most units manage to dispose of their manure by burning, but in wet weather they have difficulties. In many cases the farmers have more than they want & refuse to cart any more away. In these cases the only thing to do is to stack the manure tidily at least 400 yards from any camp or billet.	
			The horse lines vacated by the 9th Div. – from whom we took over – were left in a filthy condition & manure was thrown anywhere. Most of the 41st Div. units have cleared this up, but it has meant a great deal of extra work for our units – the time that ought to have been spent on our own work has had to be spent in clearing up what was left behind by our predecessors.	H.V.

Instructions regarding War Diaries and Intelligence Summaries are contained in F. S. Regs., Part II. and the Staff Manual respectively. Title pages will be prepared in manuscript.

WAR DIARY
or
~~INTELLIGENCE SUMMARY.~~
(Erase heading not required.)

Army Form C. 2118.

Place	Date	Hour	Summary of Events and Information	Remarks and references to Appendices
NIEPPE.	13		Saw C.O. of Unit at ARPOT & he at once gave me the necessary no. of men to carry out the filtration scheme for bath water. This scheme was to be similar to that at PIGGERIES.	W.V.
	14.		Spent a great deal of time in trying to work out water troubles. It would have simplified matters a great deal if there could have been definite refilling points for water carts. These carts fill at any & all places, & altho this is to be expected with an army on the move, yet with a stationary army it ought to be possible to fix up definite water stations. Again if units cannot use their water carts properly when they are stationary they are still less likely to use them properly & efficiently when on the move.	W.V.
	15.		It is found that the chief troubles arise in connection with cookhouse water & water from ablution benches & baths.	

Instructions regarding War Diaries and Intelligence Summaries are contained in F. S. Regs., Part II. and the Staff Manual respectively. Title pages will be prepared in manuscript.

WAR DIARY
or
INTELLIGENCE SUMMARY.
(Erase heading not required.)

Army Form C. 2118.

Place	Date	Hour	Summary of Events and Information	Remarks and references to Appendices
NIEPPE	15		Army cooks in the field appear to be the dirtiest & most insanitary ~~of~~ of all soldiers, & pay no regard to the dangers resulting from dirty cookhouses & inefficient disposal of kitchen refuse. Over & over again it is found that the cookhouse is absolutely neglected. Very feeble attempts if any are made to combat flies. The grease trap is usually in a filthy condition, however simple a contrivance it may be. A very simple grease trap is made out of 2 cresol drums fitting into one another, the inner being filled with hay, & the whole apparatus standing over a soakage pit. In clay soil such as is found in this area I have found it best to have a channel constructed & filled with clinkers & ashes; this carries off the water which can be then disposed of.	
			For ablution benches I have found that the best way to deal with the soapy water is to fix a large box to the end of the	

T2131. Wt. W708–776. 500000. 4/15. Sir J. C. & S.

Instructions regarding War Diaries and Intelligence Summaries are contained in F. S. Regs., Part II. and the Staff Manual respectively. Title pages will be prepared in manuscript.

WAR DIARY
or
INTELLIGENCE SUMMARY.
(Erase heading not required.)

Army Form C. 2118.

Place	Date	Hour	Summary of Events and Information	Remarks and references to Appendices
			bench. This box is perforated at the bottom. In the box are a few frames with canvas or sacking stretched over them. The soapy water then goes thro the canvas filters – between which may be placed straw or hay – out thro the bottom of the box into a wooden trough of a convenient length. In this trough at intervals of about 18" to 2 feet are perforated barriers against which straw is placed. This is a neat & tidy arrangement & is very efficient. I have not seen it outside this area, I have had many made by my carpenters for units.	T.V.
NIEPPE	16		Report on watercarts being not properly used still come in. Units do not understand that alum & bleaching powder (& disinfectants) can be obtained from A.S.C. train. Many watercarts are being used without either.	T.V.
			As a rule no trouble is experienced in dealing with	

T2134. Wt. W708–776. 500000. 4/15. Sir J. C. & S.

Instructions regarding War Diaries and Intelligence Summaries are contained in F. S. Regs., Part II. and the Staff Manual respectively. Title pages will be prepared in manuscript.

WAR DIARY
or
~~INTELLIGENCE SUMMARY.~~
(Erase heading not required.)

Army Form C. 2118.

Place	Date	Hour	Summary of Events and Information	Remarks and references to Appendices
			human excreta, & practically every unit is using pails & burning the excreta. A couple of units in the divisional area have long deep latrines, but in both cases these are well covered in & cared for & are perfectly clean & free from flies.	F.V.
			An issue of fly traps & butter muslin was ordered at the beginning of the month, but I have not found the traps very efficient, & believe that the best way to deal with flies is to keep all food covered up & all refuse burnt as soon as it collects.	F.V.
NIEPPE	17.		The A.D.M.S. asked me to erect an incinerator of a type suggested by D.D.M.S. V Corps. This was to serve as a model & was in a way purely experimental. I arranged with "B." Echelon D.A.C. at LEVEAU to erect this on the ground occupied by them as they had a large no. of men & horses.	

Instructions regarding War Diaries and Intelligence Summaries are contained in F. S. Regs., Part II. and the Staff Manual respectively. Title pages will be prepared in manuscript.

WAR DIARY
or
~~INTELLIGENCE SUMMARY.~~
(Erase heading not required.)

Army Form C. 2118.

Place	Date	Hour	Summary of Events and Information	Remarks and references to Appendices
			A sketch of this incinerator is enclosed. I do not however think it is as good & effective as the incinerator I am erecting at the new Main Dressing Station of the 38th F. Amb. at NIEPPE. This latter is more adaptable & can easily be enlarged by taking out the front. It is not so cumbersome & there is a shelf for drying excreta before it is actually put on the fire.	
			On going round today I found that more attention is being paid to water carts by units. Most of units do not pay sufficient attention to water.	
			I found that the ditches in & near STEENWERCK were gradually being cleared, but it is slow work. No civilians are available for the work, & no military fatigues.	
			Work on PAPOT baths is proceeding.	
			The units in LEBIZET are fairly satisfactory.	

T2134. Wt. W708—776. 500000. 4/15. Sir J. C. & S.

Instructions regarding War Diaries and Intelligence Summaries are contained in F. S. Regs., Part II. and the Staff Manual respectively. Title pages will be prepared in manuscript.

WAR DIARY
or
~~INTELLIGENCE SUMMARY.~~
(Erase heading not required.)

Army Form C. 2118.

Place	Date	Hour	Summary of Events and Information	Remarks and references to Appendices
NIEPPE	17.		The Camp Commandant ~~of~~ 41 21 Div. at STEERNWERCK is erecting under my supervision some baths for H.Q. troops alone. A portion of one of the large greenhouses is being paved & screened off. There is a fair water supply at hand, & the section is attending to the problem of disposal of soapy water. For this we are having a settling pit, & a long wooden gutter – of the type mentioned before – this will be about 30 feet at least, & I am hoping will prove effective. A complaint was made to the owner of DOUDOU FARM about his midden by the R.E's there. As the trouble arose because animals walked across the midden, I advised the R.E's to erect a light fence round the midden, & as the farmer was quite agreeable to having the midden emptied, I asked the R.E's to lend him a couple of men for a few days to clear the midden. In every case where animals – pigs chiefly – wander in &	

Instructions regarding War Diaries and Intelligence Summaries are contained in F. S. Regs., Part II. and the Staff Manual respectively. Title pages will be prepared in manuscript.

WAR DIARY
or
~~INTELLIGENCE SUMMARY.~~
(Erase heading not required.)

Army Form C. 2118.

Place	Date	Hour	Summary of Events and Information	Remarks and references to Appendices
			cause the midden to be a nuisance I have suggesting erecting a light fence around it.	H.V.
NIEPPE.	18		I discovered in my rounds today that No 9 Kite Balloon Section of the R.F.C. stationed near NIEPPE below the Railway, & attached to the 41st Div. were using a very old type of watercart. This had no clarifier at all, & was merely a tank on two wheels. The capacity of the tank was about 100 gallons. This Section came out from England without a watercart, & were using this old pattern cart which they found somewhere. There was an R.A.M.C. man in charge who had been adding bleaching powder, ~~a.c.c.~~ judging the cart to be of the capacity of a modern watercart. I have arranged with O/C 9 K.B. Section to lend him my portable clarifier until he can obtain a proper water-cart.	
			Owing to the unit in PAPOT requiring to pay more [illegible]	

T2134. Wt. W708—776. 500000. 4/15. Sir J. C. & S.

Instructions regarding War Diaries and Intelligence Summaries are contained in F. S. Regs., Part II. and the Staff Manual respectively. Title pages will be prepared in manuscript.

WAR DIARY
or
~~INTELLIGENCE~~ SUMMARY.
(Erase heading not required.)

Army Form C. 2118.

Place	Date	Hour	Summary of Events and Information	Remarks and references to Appendices
			the filter beds for the baths, work is proceeding rather slowly (a new unit took over on Monday). I hope to get them finished in a day or two now. My type of incinerator was to be put aside by the orders of A.D.M.S. who wishes the type submitted by D.D.M.S. V Corps to be erected if any other incinerators were required. I hope soon to be able to report on the merits & demerits of both types. Owing to the drier weather now camps – & especially horse lines are in a much more sanitary state, & if the weather keeps fine it ought to be possible at last to dispose of all the manure & refuse left behind by the 9th Division. It seems rather thoughtless on the part of those who are erecting large water tanks & laying large water pipes in	

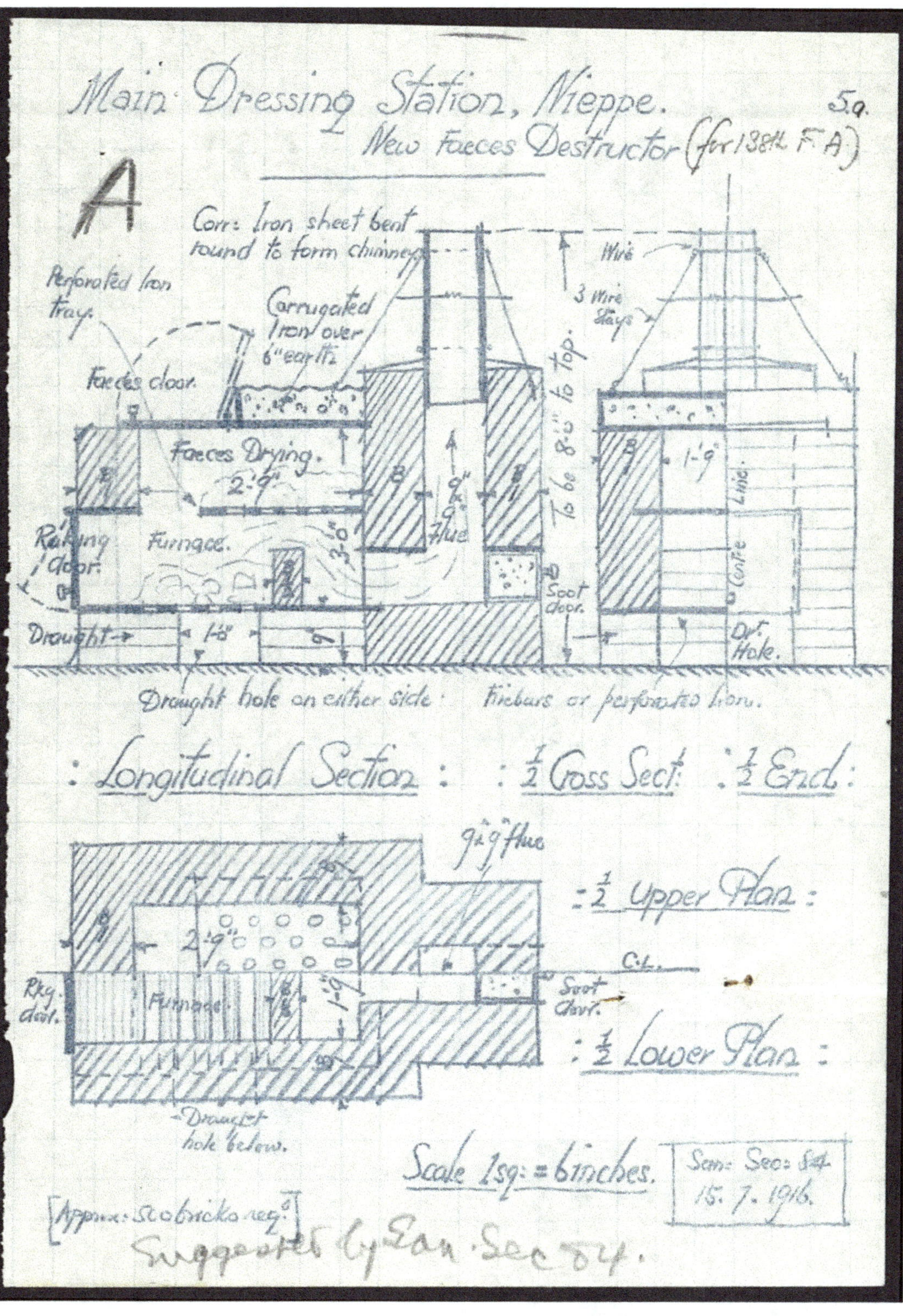
Main Dressing Station, Nieppe.
5a.
New Faeces Destructor (for 138th F.A.)
A
Corr: Iron sheet bent round to form chimney
Perforated Iron tray.
Corrugated Iron over 6" earth
Faeces door.
Faeces Drying.
2'-9"
Wire
3 Wire stays
To be 8'-0" to Top.
9" flue
1'-9"
Centre Line
Raking door.
Furnace.
3'-0"
Soot door.
Draught
1'-6"
9"
Drt. Hole.
Draught hole on either side   Firebars or perforated Iron.
: Longitudinal Section :
: ½ Cross Sect: : ½ End:
9"x9" flue
: ½ Upper Plan :
2'-9"
C.L.
Rkg. door.
Furnace.
Soot door.
: ½ Lower Plan :
Draught hole below.
Scale 1sq: = 6 inches.
San: Sec: 84
15. 7. 1916.
[Approx: 860 bricks reqd.]
Suggested by San. Sec 84.

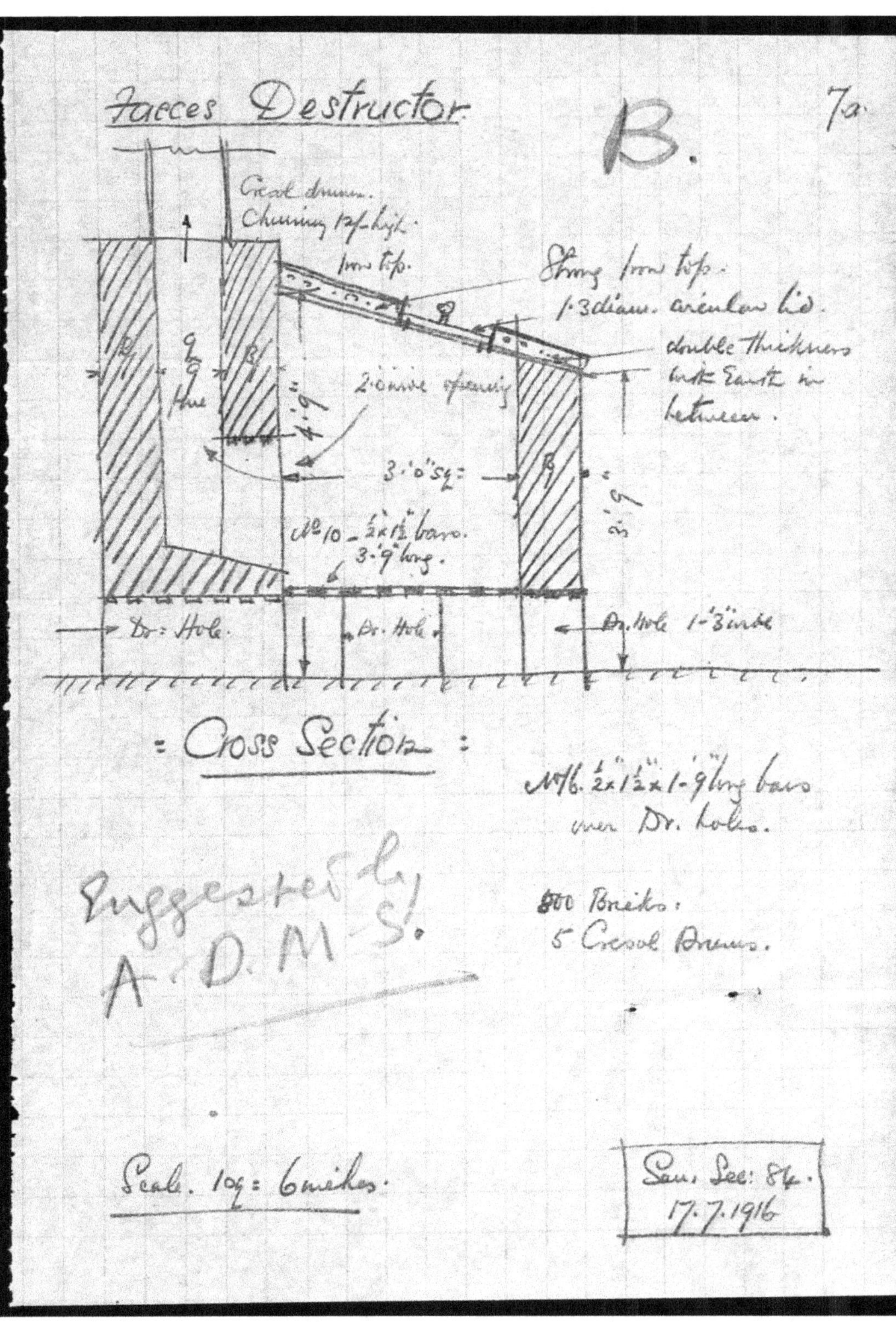

Faeces Destructor
B.
7a
Dr: Hole
Dr. Hole
Cross Section
800 Bricks.
5 Cresol Drums.
Suggested by A.D.M.S.
Scale. 1 sq = 6 inches.
San. Sec: 84.
17.7.1916

Instructions regarding War Diaries and Intelligence Summaries are contained in F. S. Regs., Part II. and the Staff Manual respectively. Title pages will be prepared in manuscript.

WAR DIARY
or
~~INTELLIGENCE SUMMARY.~~
(Erase heading not required.)

Army Form C. 2118.

Place	Date	Hour	Summary of Events and Information	Remarks and references to Appendices
			the Divisional area for supplying water for horses, that they did not at the same time erect tanks for supplying water carts. With proper care & efficient use of the water-carts this water ought to be quite fit for troops. These tanks are being erected at many places in the 41st Div. area. I want to try & obtain a proper set of refilling points for water carts in this area ~~on~~ the same lines as in other Divisional areas, & hope to be able to meet the O.C.s of neighbouring sanitary sections & discuss the matter with them.	H.V.
NIEPPE	19.		Work on the filter beds at PAPOT is @ a standstill owing to lack of labour. The approach road is being repaired, so it is impossible to take transport to the camp.	←
			Attached to this leaf are the two types of incinerators mentioned.	

T2134. Wt. W708—776. 500000. 4/15. Sir J. C. & S.

Instructions regarding War Diaries and Intelligence Summaries are contained in F. S. Regs., Part II. and the Staff Manual respectively. Title pages will be prepared in manuscript.

WAR DIARY
or
~~INTELLIGENCE SUMMARY.~~
(Erase heading not required.)

Army Form C. 2118.

Place	Date	Hour	Summary of Events and Information	Remarks and references to Appendices
			They are marked A & B. It will be seen that in A there is a tray on which the rubbish – in this case faeces – is dried before being dumped on to the fire. In "B" there is great likelihood of the incinerator being choked at once.	
			I am arranging for a full account of every watercart in the area to be inspected by my men & a report on the whole is being prepared by me.	
			One of the units is using very long huts for sleeping accommodation. These are very unhealthy & are now having windows – ventilators – fitted in the roofs. Huts at the best of times are stuffy & ill ventilated, & there seems to be a tendency among all units using huts to leave food lying about in the huts. There are very dirty canvas beds in most of the huts & these are not kept sufficiently clean & so harbour dirt.	F.V.

Instructions regarding War Diaries and Intelligence Summaries are contained in F. S. Regs., Part II. and the Staff Manual respectively. Title pages will be prepared in manuscript.

WAR DIARY
or
~~INTELLIGENCE SUMMARY.~~
(Erase heading not required.)

Army Form C. 2118.

Place	Date	Hour	Summary of Events and Information	Remarks and references to Appendices
NIEPPE	20.		Reports had reached me that certain units were not getting rid of manure by burning, but were dumping it behind hedges in ditches. Units in some cases are "slack" in their methods of disposing of manure, & in some cases "take it for granted" that the farmer carts it away.	
			The question of offensive middens was raised by a unit. It was found that the farm animals disturbed the midden which then became a nuisance. I have found that the ~~quer~~ "dealing with middens" by the military creates unpleasantness with the people. Where it is necessary to empty a midden the best thing to do is to clear away as much as possible of the rubbish, & cover over the rest with earth so that grass can grow on it. Where the midden may not be touched, fence it off & prevent any animals from walking over it.	
			M O's of units do not seem to be capable of thinking of such things for	

T2134. Wt. W708—776. 500000. 4/15. Sir J. C. & S.

Instructions regarding War Diaries and Intelligence Summaries are contained in F. S. Regs., Part II. and the Staff Manual respectively. Title pages will be prepared in manuscript.

WAR DIARY

or

~~INTELLIGENCE SUMMARY.~~

(Erase heading not required.)

Army Form C. 2118.

Place	Date	Hour	Summary of Events and Information	Remarks and references to Appendices
			themselves, & neglect to attend to these matters, the result is that the Sanitary section has a lot of extra work thrown on it.	
			With regard to the personnel of a Sanitary Section it would be a great help if they could have about a dozen labour men attached to the section permanently. This would enable the section to work more freely & they could then get thro' more work & in quicker time.	
			Then there should be in every section, a plumber, a mason, a carpenter in addition to others of course - by that I mean proper intelligent men. In this section - already one short of full strength I have the three above trades, & have found it necessary to get them to attend to the wants of small detached units. As it is my carpenter is continually engaged in doing work for even large units. Most units make attempts at carrying out the San Secs. suggestions, but there are units that have to have everything done for them.	

T2134. Wt. W708—776. 500000. 4/15. Sir J. C. & S.

WAR DIARY
or
~~INTELLIGENCE SUMMARY~~.
(Erase heading not required.)

Army Form C. 2118.

Instructions regarding War Diaries and Intelligence Summaries are contained in F. S. Regs., Part II. and the Staff Manual respectively. Title pages will be prepared in manuscript.

Place	Date	Hour	Summary of Events and Information	Remarks and references to Appendices
			I actually found one unit (attached only to this division) who were disposing of their urine by throwing it over the fields. They were on clayey soil, but that ought not to prevent them from attempting to build some form of urine hopper. Their water supply too was very bad, & they were prevented from using a good source by the O.C. of a neighbouring battalion in a different division.	H.V. H.V.
NIEPPE	21		I managed to get some "prisoners" to work on the ditches in STEENWERCK today. These I applied for from the Camp Commandant. I also applied to the A.P.M. that other prisoners might be handed to the San. Sec. for fatigue work.	
			The baths @ Div. H.Q. are nearly complete.	
			I inspected some of the clothing which has been washed @ the Div. baths @ Steenwerck, & I failed to find any traces of vermin in the	

T2134. Wt. W708—776. 500000. 4/15. Sir J. C. & S.

Army Form C. 2118.

Instructions regarding War Diaries and Intelligence Summaries are contained in F. S. Regs., Part II. and the Staff Manual respectively. Title pages will be prepared in manuscript.

WAR DIARY
or
~~INTELLIGENCE SUMMARY.~~
(Erase heading not required.)

Place	Date	Hour	Summary of Events and Information	Remarks and references to Appendices
			clean clothes. I found however that some dirty clothes, with vermin in, had been thrown amongst some clean clothes which were about to be issued. This is quite enough to cause contamination of the clean clothing. I paid this visit because I had received complaints that clothing issued out as clean contained vermin.	
			I had to spend the afternoon & evening of today looking for site for a new office & store house for the section, as our present place was being shelled.	H.V.
NIEPPE.	22		The M.O. of a unit attached to this Division came to see me with regard to his water supply for washing purposes. There was a large pond adjoining his camp, but the C.O. of a unit in the neighbouring Division refused to allow him to use the water. This pond was being used for bathing by men. I have applied to the A.D.M.S. to settle this question as it is out of my Division.	

T2134. Wt. W708–776. 500000. 4/15. Sir J. C. & S.

Instructions regarding War Diaries and Intelligence Summaries are contained in F. S. Regs., Part II. and the Staff Manual respectively. Title pages will be prepared in manuscript.

WAR DIARY
or
~~INTELLIGENCE SUMMARY~~
(Erase heading not required.)

Army Form C. 2118.

Place	Date	Hour	Summary of Events and Information	Remarks and references to Appendices
			Altho' every camp is supposed to have a sanitary area marked out, & each unit on vacating a site is supposed to leave the sanitary area marked out so that it can be easily recognised this is not done properly, and much ground is wasted. This is particularly the case in camps situated well up near the firing line.	
			There is also not enough cooperation between units sharing the same rest billets; grease traps, urinepits, ablution benches which one unit has left in good working condition are pulled down & others, generally not so effecient are erected. This means using extra ground, & it entails extra work for the San. Sec.	
			The incinerator or faeces destructor suggested by the San. Sec. for the Dressing station of the 138th F. Ambulance in NIEPPE.	

T2134. Wt. W708—776. 500000. 4/15. Sir J. C. & S.

Instructions regarding War Diaries and Intelligence Summaries are contained in F. S. Regs., Part II. and the Staff Manual respectively. Title pages will be prepared in manuscript.

WAR DIARY

or

~~INTELLIGENCE SUMMARY.~~

(Erase heading not required.)

Army Form C. 2118.

Place	Date	Hour	Summary of Events and Information	Remarks and references to Appendices
			has been finished & is in complete working order.	
			It would be a good thing if San. Secs. were allowed two more bicycles – four altogether. For one thing I have found that a cycle is much more convenient for covering the ground, espec. near the front line. It is easier to leave a bicycle than a horse, & the equipment of a San. Sec. only provides one horse – none for an orderly.	W.V.
NIEPPE	28		Sufficient use is not made of surface wells. Water is becoming very difficult to obtain, but more surface wells could easily be dug. The difficulty of obtaining water for one unit, who had only a dirty pond at hand, for instance, is easily solved by digging a surface well. If this had been done before a lot of unpleasantness might have been saved. The A.D.M.S. took me over	

Instructions regarding War Diaries and Intelligence Summaries are contained in F. S. Regs., Part II. and the Staff Manual respectively. Title pages will be prepared in manuscript.

WAR DIARY

or

~~INTELLIGENCE SUMMARY.~~

(Erase heading not required.)

Army Form C. 2118.

Place	Date	Hour	Summary of Events and Information	Remarks and references to Appendices
			to see the Special Coy 3rd Batt. R.E. of the BAILLEULRS who had difficulty because they would not use surface wells, & he advised ~~them~~ as the simplest way out of all difficulties. There is no reason why every unit should not obtain sufficient water for washing from these surface wells. I have been ordering these wells to be built in the area, tho' units do not seem to be willing to use the water.	
			I have been unable to see the DC. San Sec of 24th Div. but have found out that his area has definite water stations & that he receives reports from each station each day: ie results of tests, &c.	
			This system of having definite water stations I have found now is all very well for a stationary army, but with an army on the move, as we hope to be, it is essential that there should be	

Instructions regarding War Diaries and Intelligence Summaries are contained in F. S. Regs., Part II. and the Staff Manual respectively. Title pages will be prepared in manuscript.

WAR DIARY
or
~~INTELLIGENCE SUMMARY.~~
(Erase heading not required.)

Army Form C. 2118.

Place	Date	Hour	Summary of Events and Information	Remarks and references to Appendices
			proper water discipline. The methods of using the water carts are gradually improving, but there is still room for improvement.	
			I have seen nothing of the O/c Water patrols of the V. corps to which we are attached, but have written to him to try & arrange a meeting.	
			I am in need of a man to replace the casualty of 21/6/16. It is rather a long time to have to wait for a reinforcement – over a month.	H.V.
NIEPPE	24		I went into BAILLEUL this morning & saw the O/c Water patrols V. corps. He told me he did not know much of the water supply of this divisional area, but he gave me a good deal of information. A good deal however was of the "cut & dried" variety, & could only apply	

Instructions regarding War Diaries and Intelligence Summaries are contained in F. S. Regs., Part II. and the Staff Manual respectively. Title pages will be prepared in manuscript.

WAR DIARY
or
~~INTELLIGENCE SUMMARY.~~
(Erase heading not required.)

Army Form C. 2118.

Place	Date	Hour	Summary of Events and Information	Remarks and references to Appendices
			to a stationary army. I found out that 2 large water supplies for watercarts were being erected by the corps engineers in this divisional area. Each supply was to yield 10000 gals of pure water daily, & was to come from the Lys where it was to be chlorinated before being passed on to the tanks. I propose to put a water man of this section in charge of each supply & to keep a record of every watercart using the supply. Carts which are defective will not be supplied with water. By this means we shall be able to drill the watercart men into the proper way to use the carts & so ensure that water sterilising will be effective if it should be necessary to use doubtful sources at any time.	R.V.

WAR DIARY

or

~~INTELLIGENCE SUMMARY.~~

(Erase heading not required.)

Army Form C. 2118.

Instructions regarding War Diaries and Intelligence Summaries are contained in F. S. Regs., Part II. and the Staff Manual respectively. Title pages will be prepared in manuscript.

Place	Date	Hour	Summary of Events and Information	Remarks and references to Appendices
NIEPPE	26		We have at last been able to start work on erecting the incinerator suggested by the A.D.M.S. The delay was partly due to the fact that we had too much work in hand & also to the fact that we were unable to obtain material from the engineers. This was necessary as the A.D.M.S. wished it to be a "model."	
			The filter beds are not working satisfactorily. I can only say that this is due to the fact that the work was done in "bits" by odd men as I was not able to obtain men for the whole of the work. The pond from which the water was obtained is running dry too, & we shall have to obtain water from a different source.	
			Surface wells have been advised by me, but the suggestion doesn't appeal to units. In this clay soil it is possible to obtain fairly good water – a bit gritty – from any reasonably made well, but units won't make them.	H.D.
			(Note I was unable to do any visiting today on account of a severe attack of colic & general ague.)	

T2134. Wt. W708–776. 500000. 4/15. Sir J. C. & S.

Instructions regarding War Diaries and Intelligence Summaries are contained in F. S. Regs., Part II. and the Staff Manual respectively. Title pages will be prepared in manuscript.

WAR DIARY

or

~~INTELLIGENCE SUMMARY.~~

(Erase heading not required.)

Army Form C. 2118.

Place	Date	Hour	Summary of Events and Information	Remarks and references to Appendices.
NIEPPE	27.		I have had reports from one of my watermen today on the bad condition of watercarts. These reports go up to the A.D.M.S.	
			Units are shaping quite well in regard to sanitary arrangements. The chief trouble arises with some units which are only attached to the 41st Div.	W.V.
NIEPPE	28		I had a complaint this morning from the O/C N.Z. San Sec. one of the water carts of one of our units was being improperly filled in the NZ area, & from doubtful water altho' good water was available a few yards off. This matter was dealt with.	
			The type of grease trap I have been advising for all units is made of 2 creosol drums – one fitting inside the other, the inner one being filled with a filtering medium & easily removable for cleaning purposes. We have made a great many of these traps for	

T2134. Wt. W708—776. 500000. 4/15. Sir J. C. & S.

Army Form C. 2118.

Instructions regarding War Diaries and Intelligence Summaries are contained in F. S. Regs., Part II. and the Staff Manual respectively. Title pages will be prepared in manuscript.

WAR DIARY
or
~~INTELLIGENCE SUMMARY.~~
(Erase heading not required.)

Place	Date	Hour	Summary of Events and Information	Remarks and references to Appendices
			various units. A handle of hay wire is easily fixed to the inner movable drum, while the outer drum drains either into pit or filtration channel.	
			Work is proceeding on the A.D.M.S.' model incinerator, but it is slow as I can get no working men & have to take off my own "district" men to erect it. The original plans have had to be modified as they were not likely to allow proper ventilation to the fire. A door was put in the front & extra vent holes were put in while the base of chimney was made smaller. The feed hole too is made larger.	
			For the first time surface wells were found to yield no water — in the camp of unit which had had trouble with the water & in which the A.D.M.S. advised thinking dug.	

T2134. Wt. W708—776. 500000. 4/15. Sir J. C. & S.

Instructions regarding War Diaries and Intelligence Summaries are contained in F. S. Regs., Part II. and the Staff Manual respectively. Title pages will be prepared in manuscript.

WAR DIARY
or
~~INTELLIGENCE SUMMARY.~~
(Erase heading not required.)

Army Form C. 2118.

Place	Date	Hour	Summary of Events and Information	Remarks and references to Appendices
			The san arrangements of this unit are improving - they were of a very primitive kind before.	M.V.
NIEPPE	29.		I find that the water supply from the pond at PAPOT for the baths has dried up, & they are using water from an adjoining pond without passing it thro the filter beds: ~~the~~ [illegible] the work on these filter beds has thus been wasted. There is great trouble in making ~~[illegible]~~ men understand that sanitation has some object in view. I have found men complaining about the filthiness of a pond which is being used for washing water supply, while @ the same time they are contaminating it by throwing all sorts of dirty water in it. The ditches around H.Q. at STEENWERCK are gradually	

T2134. Wt. W708—776. 500000. 4/15. Sir J. C. & S.

Instructions regarding War Diaries and Intelligence Summaries are contained in F. S. Regs., Part II. and the Staff Manual respectively. Title pages will be prepared in manuscript.

WAR DIARY
~~or~~
~~INTELLIGENCE~~ SUMMARY.

(*Erase heading not required.*)

Army Form C. 2118.

Place	Date	Hour	Summary of Events and Information	Remarks and references to Appendices
			being cleared – using defaulters (for whom) could find any amount of work. Other San. Secs have had as many as one hundred extra men on their roll, these men being attached to them permanently. The result of this shortage is that my men are constantly doing fatigue work when they ought to be on their districts.	H.V.
NIEPPE	3[illegible]		The best way to sum up the work for the month would be to say that, camps & billets are being kept clean, tho' they need watching. The waggon lines are very good now in some parts. Precautions are taken against flies, food is kept in proper safes & not allowed to be kept in sleeping quarters (The type of fly traps from ordnance are not very effective & butter muslin is difficult to obtain). Excreta generally is burned: horse manure is properly	

T2134. Wt. W708–776. 500000. 4/15. Sir J. C. & S.

Army Form C. 2118.

Instructions regarding War Diaries and Intelligence Summaries are contained in F. S. Regs., Part II. and the Staff Manual respectively. Title pages will be prepared in manuscript.

WAR DIARY
or
~~INTELLIGENCE SUMMARY.~~
(Erase heading not required.)

Place	Date	Hour	Summary of Events and Information	Remarks and references to Appendices
			disposed of – old collections left by the previous Divisions are disappearing –	
			The water supply both for washing & drinking is getting bad, some of the wells deteriorating at the rate of ½ a scoopful of bleaching powder a day. The tanks of water from the engineers are not in working order yet; but are expected to be ready shortly.	
			The incinerator suggested by the A.D.M.S was used today for the first time & found satisfactory.	H.V.

T2134. Wt. W708–776. 500000. 4/15. Sir J. C. & S.

41st Div

Confidential

War Diary

of

54th Sanitary Section

Vol 4

Aug 1916

1st Aug 1916 to 31st Aug 16

Volume 1

8th Sanitary Section
41st Division.

Volume IV
1

Army Form C. 2118.

Instructions regarding War Diaries and Intelligence Summaries are contained in F. S. Regs., Part II. and the Staff Manual respectively. Title pages will be prepared in manuscript.

WAR DIARY
or
~~INTELLIGENCE SUMMARY.~~
(Erase heading not required.)

SECRET

Place	Date	Hour	Summary of Events and Information	Remarks and references to Appendices
NIEPPE.	Aug 1.		A great scarcity & shortage of water is beginning to be experienced owing to the dry weather. Wells are rapidly drying. The water supply from the Lys thro' tanks is not yet in working order, tho' the delay is likely to cause trouble.	
			One unit was found to have been allowing bathing in a stream, tho' this is contrary to D.R.O.	
			No attempt has been made by O/C Baths @ STEENWERCK to deal with the soapy water from the baths, which is allowed to run direct into a stream which ultimately flows thro' STEENWERCK.	
			Mosquitoes - anopheles & Culex - are becoming very troublesome, & large quantities of mineral oil will have to be utilised to spray the various ponds & breeding	

Instructions regarding War Diaries and Intelligence Summaries are contained in F. S. Regs., Part II. and the Staff Manual respectively. Title pages will be prepared in manuscript.

WAR DIARY

or

~~INTELLIGENCE SUMMARY.~~

(Erase heading not required.)

Army Form C. 2118.

IV/11

Place	Date	Hour	Summary of Events and Information	Remarks and references to Appendices
			breeding places. The procedure is to spray with fine sprayers (the disinfector sprays) the surface of pools &c the amount of oil being one tablespoonful to a square yard.	F.V.
NIEPPE	2		The A.D.M.S. gave me a couple of tubes with the larvae of Anopheles & Culex mosquitoes. These I have passed round the san. sec. men & have given orders for very strict watch to be kept for breeding places, which when found are to be freely & effectively sprayed with paraffin 3 oz to sq yd.	
			There are some very offensive drains round NIEPPE but I cannot obtain labour, either civilian or military to have them cleaned out.	F.V.

T2134. Wt. W708—776. 500000. 4/15. Sir J. C. & S.

Instructions regarding War Diaries and Intelligence Summaries are contained in F. S. Regs., Part II. and the Staff Manual respectively. Title pages will be prepared in manuscript.

WAR DIARY
or
INTELLIGENCE SUMMARY.
(Erase heading not required.)

Army Form C. 2118.

IV

Place	Date	Hour	Summary of Events and Information	Remarks and references to Appendices
NIEPPE	3.		Correspondence has arisen over the water supply of Oosthove Farm. The mobile laboratory claim that the water supply is bad & that tests by this section are not correct to date. These tests were however made nearly a month ago, & are quite likely to be wrong. The water sent over for testing was said to have passed thro' the water cart. In view of this some arrangements might be made that units should send a sample at regular periods to the O/C San Sec for being tested. This ought to be a regular routine procedure, & it is a very easy matter to arrange. I found a water cart of another Division today being improperly filled & have reported the matter to that Divisional Sanitary Officer.	

T2134. Wt. W708–776. 500000. 4/15. Sir J. C. & S.

1V / 1V

Army Form C. 2118.

Instructions regarding War Diaries and Intelligence Summaries are contained in F. S. Regs., Part II. and the Staff Manual respectively. Title pages will be prepared in manuscript.

WAR DIARY
or
~~INTELLIGENCE SUMMARY.~~
(Erase heading not required.)

Place	Date	Hour	Summary of Events and Information	Remarks and references to Appendices
NIEPPE.	4.		The Canadian Mobile Lab. tested a sample of water from a water-cart of the 9th Middlesex. The test showed that the water was insufficiently chlorinated, tho' the M.O's statement was to the effect that he had chlorinated the water according to my instructions after testing a sample sent me over a month ago. One of two things has obviously happened, either the water cart men have not been using the source from which the tested sample came or the water has deteriorated. I think the former will turn out to be the case. All the sources from which the watercart men of that unit draw water now have been thoroughly tested.	
			Soyers Farm is not in a satisfactory condition as regards sanitation. The difficulty continues to be that units & M.O's show no cooperation when exchanging billets, and until they do adverse report on the sanitation will	

T2134. Wt. W708—776. 500000. 4/15. Sir J. C. & S.

Instructions regarding War Diaries and Intelligence Summaries are contained in F. S. Regs., Part II. and the Staff Manual respectively. Title pages will be prepared in manuscript.

WAR DIARY

or

~~INTELLIGENCE SUMMARY.~~

(Erase heading not required.)

Army Form C. 2118.

Place	Date	Hour	Summary of Events and Information	Remarks and references to Appendices
			continue to be sent in	
			A case has arisen lately of an estaminet proprietor who refused to allow latrines & urinal to be erected for the use of troops using the estaminet. There was urgent need of this as the place was most insanitary. There were M Police billetted there & I reported the matter to the APM of this Division. Nothing was done as the estaminet ceased to be in our divisional area. I propose to see the place again & take the matter to the Of San. Sec. of the Division in whose area the estaminet now is.	H.V.
NIEPPE	5 Aug.		I have ordered a thorough cleaning & disinfection of Royer Farm & propose to see the MOs of all units using the place in turn & arrange for proper cooperation among them. We are using defaulters a great deal in this section for fatigue	

Instructions regarding War Diaries and Intelligence Summaries are contained in F. S. Regs., Part II. and the Staff Manual respectively. Title pages will be prepared in manuscript.

WAR DIARY

or

~~INTELLIGENCE SUMMARY.~~

(Erase heading not required.)

Army Form C. 2118.

Place	Date	Hour	Summary of Events and Information	Remarks and references to Appendices
			work, particularly ditch cleaning. The work is slow however as there are not many defaulters. With regard to San Sec equipment my own suggestion is that at least 3 pairs of thigh gum boots should be included in the equipment as there is always great need for them. The small set of baths erected @ H.Q. is working very well, & the soapy water is efficiently cleared before running away. The soapy water is passed first thro' a hay filter, then into a settling pit & on into a long box channel as I have previously suggested. In this case the channel is at least 40 feet long & it has perforated barriers every two or three feet. The 1st ¼ has hay in it, the next 2/4 coke breeze, & the rest is a closed drain. In addition there is an efficient & competent man to attend to it. This proves that soapy water can be properly dealt with if only someone is placed to see that	

T2134. Wt. W708—776. 500000. 4/15. Sir J. C. & S.

Instructions regarding War Diaries and Intelligence Summaries are contained in F. S. Regs., Part II. and the Staff Manual respectively. Title pages will be prepared in manuscript.

IV / VII

Army Form C. 2118.

WAR DIARY

or

~~INTELLIGENCE SUMMARY.~~

(Erase heading not required.)

Place	Date	Hour	Summary of Events and Information	Remarks and references to Appendices
			instructions are carried out.	
			As noted previously this box channel filter is being largely used now, & is easily portable, so that it can be easily cleaned & put up again.	
			I intend to institute a thorough & comprehensive system among my watermen whereby daily results are handed to me of water tests & watercart inspections. I will then deal with them daily & so have every water cart directly under my eye.	
			In spite of the fact that pure sterilized water is now available for water carts, there is still need for supervision as the cart tanks are not properly looked after.	H.V.

T2134. Wt. W708—776. 500000. 4/15. Sir J. C. & S.

Instructions regarding War Diaries and Intelligence Summaries are contained in F. S. Regs., Part II. and the Staff Manual respectively. Title pages will be prepared in manuscript.

WAR DIARY

or

~~INTELLIGENCE SUMMARY.~~

(Erase heading not required.)

Army Form C. 2118.

IV VIII

Place	Date	Hour	Summary of Events and Information	Remarks and references to Appendices
NIEPPE.	6.		Proceeding with cleansing of Soyer Farm in particular. I usually allow the San Sec men ½ day off on Saturday.	
			Plans of accomodation (estimated) for San Sec during the winter months were called for. A map 1-10000 is to be drawn showing all details of hutting, standing for vehicles, horse, duckboards &c. This will be sent in.	
			Plans for a new type of brazier were called for. As we have not been out one winter we could not ~~act~~ certify on the said defects of the existing type. The plans of new types however are being prepared & will be sent in.	H.V.

T2134. Wt. W708—776. 500000. 4/15. Sir J. C. & S.

IV/IX

Army Form C. 2118.

Instructions regarding War Diaries and Intelligence Summaries are contained in F. S. Regs., Part II. and the Staff Manual respectively. Title pages will be prepared in manuscript.

WAR DIARY

or

~~INTELLIGENCE SUMMARY.~~

(Erase heading not required.)

Place	Date	Hour	Summary of Events and Information	Remarks and references to Appendices
NIEPPE	8.		I spent the afternoon going round to units in the Div. area with the O/C Canadian Mobile Lab. We took samples from numbers of water carts & water supplies.	
			Goyer Farm is getting cleaner, tho' it will take some time. The O/C of the unit in refused to allow his men to do any more cleaning as he said he had done his share, & the next unit ought to do some cleaning. This is a most regrettable ~~[illegible]~~ attitude to place on things.	H.V.
NIEPPE	9		A reinforcement arrived for this section to day - after six weeks waiting.	
			Watercarts are not using the supply of good water @ the tanks altho' they are told to do so by DRO.	
			Nothing else to report, things are going on satisfactorily & the fine weather has enabled units to deal with manure	

T2134. Wt. W708—776. 500000. 4/15. Sir J. C. & S.

Instructions regarding War Diaries and Intelligence Summaries are contained in F. S. Regs., Part II. and the Staff Manual respectively. Title pages will be prepared in manuscript.

WAR DIARY

or

~~INTELLIGENCE SUMMARY.~~

(Erase heading not required.)

Army Form C. 2118.

Place	Date	Hour	Summary of Events and Information	Remarks and references to Appendices
			both accumulating & what was left behind by the last division.	W.
~~[illegible]~~ NIEPPE.	10.		Water reports showed that a source of inaccuracy had been found in the "measures" used to measure the Bleaching powder for sterilising water in carts. It was found that the full measure of B. Powder was not always being actually added as the measures were in many cases caked with old B Powder.	
			The M.O. of a unit refused to give my men any help to carry out their work @ Soyer farm as he said his unit would not be staying @ Soyer farm long. This is a disgraceful attitude for an M.O. to take. However we arranged matters satisfactorily. I note this instance	

Instructions regarding War Diaries and Intelligence Summaries are contained in F. S. Regs., Part II. and the Staff Manual respectively. Title pages will be prepared in manuscript.

WAR DIARY

or

~~INTELLIGENCE SUMMARY.~~

(Erase heading not required.)

Army Form C. 2118.

IV / ~~XI~~

Place	Date	Hour	Summary of Events and Information	Remarks and references to Appendices
			because it shows the difficulties a San. Sec. has to contend with, & also because it shows how difficult it is to fix responsibility on any unit; ~~[illegible]~~	[illegible]
NIEPPE	11		NIEPPE is nearly empty of soldiers billets now & I am considering the advisability of moving to some more central place. We still carry on the sanitation of the town with the aid of civilian labour.	
			The water from the water tanks erected by the engineers has a wretched taste, & in the case of the [illegible] tanks requires 2 1/2 scoopsful of B.P. The Trois Arbres tanks requires 1 scoop. The water of both sets of tanks is not agreeable to drink.	[illegible]

T2134. Wt. W708—776. 500000. 4/15. Sir J. C. & S.

Instructions regarding War Diaries and Intelligence Summaries are contained in F. S. Regs., Part II. and the Staff Manual respectively. Title pages will be prepared in manuscript.

WAR DIARY
or
~~INTELLIGENCE SUMMARY.~~
(Erase heading not required.)

Army Form C. 2118.

XII

Place	Date	Hour	Summary of Events and Information	Remarks and references to Appendices
NIEPPE	12		A complaint was sent in to the ADMS by me of the bad state in which working parties from 139 & 140 F. Ambulances had left billets they were using at Doudou Farm. I have noticed that when away from their main dressing station the RAMC personnel are more neglectful of sanitary arrangements than most units.	
			Return of steel helmets was called for.	
			Water for baths at PAPOT is fast running out. It is hoped to be able to tap the water mains near bye – which the R.E. have erected in this area – & so obtain a good inexhaustible supply. This ought to have been thought of & carried out before & a good deal of waste labour would have been ~~saved~~ spared. This section has had a great deal of difficulty in obtaining working parties to	

T2134. Wt. W708—776. 500000. 4/15. Sir J. C. & S.

Instructions regarding War Diaries and Intelligence Summaries are contained in F. S. Regs., Part II. and the Staff Manual respectively. Title pages will be prepared in manuscript.

WAR DIARY

or

~~INTELLIGENCE SUMMARY.~~

(Erase heading not required.)

Army Form C. 2118.

1V/XIII

Place	Date	Hour	Summary of Events and Information	Remarks and references to Appendices
			carry out their work. In many cases I have had to take the men away from their routine work & put them on to engineers work.	
			Secret orders were given to me today with regard to the moving of this Division from this area. This section will be attached to the 140th F Amb & will move to Steenwerck ~~—~~ Meteren area with it on the 18th. The movement to be completed by 8 a.m. on the 18th. We shall be attached to 140th F. Amb. from the 17th inst.	W.V.
NIEPPE	14		I had a mobilisation parade of section this morning, tho' no mention of a move was given to the men.	
			The general state of camps occupied by units in this divisional area is being kept satisfactory. No doubt	

IV
XIV

Instructions regarding War Diaries and Intelligence Summaries are contained in F. S. Regs., Part II. and the Staff Manual respectively. Title pages will be prepared in manuscript.

WAR DIARY

or

~~INTELLIGENCE SUMMARY~~

(Erase heading not required.)

Army Form C. 2118.

Place	Date	Hour	Summary of Events and Information	Remarks and references to Appendices
			cases will occur where billets are left dirty, but this always occurs. The lines adopted by this section have been to erect & suggest the simplest contrivances for dealing with refuse & for protection against flies &c. I have suggested to the 3 infantry brigades that I would attach an N.C.O. to them for the duration of the time they are on the move in order to keep an eye on their sanitation. 122 Brigade have refused my offer. 123 accepted. 124 accepted. I make this offer because ~~the~~ past experience has shown that the Brigade H.Q. do not have adequate San. arrangements – 122 in particular.	J.V.

T2134. Wt. W708–776. 500000. 4/15. Sir J. C. & S.

IV
XV

Army Form C. 2118.

Instructions regarding War Diaries and Intelligence Summaries are contained in F. S. Regs., Part II. and the Staff Manual respectively. Title pages will be prepared in manuscript.

WAR DIARY
or
~~INTELLIGENCE~~ SUMMARY.

(Erase heading not required.)

Place	Date	Hour	Summary of Events and Information	Remarks and references to Appendices
NIEPPE.	15.		I met the O/c San. Sec (VO) taking over from this Section & showed him round the divisional area. I explained various existing arrangements & handed over to him contracts (copies) of the agreements with mayors of STEENWERCK & NIEPPE. We went round the district in a car & so covered most of the ground. The office work was shown in detail.	
			I propose to hand over certain stores & apparatus to him & obtain his signature for them.	
			122 Brigade have accepted my offer of a san. man to be attached to them for the move. 3 men accordingly will report to the 122, 123 & 124 Brigades at 9.30 am tomorrow. One of my men will ~~be~~ move with Div. H.Q. ~~We~~	
			A reinforcement arrived today, making us one over	

T2134. Wt. W708–776. 500000. 4/15. Sir J. C. & S.

IV/XVI

Army Form C. 2118.

WAR DIARY
or
~~INTELLIGENCE SUMMARY.~~
(Erase heading not required.)

Instructions regarding War Diaries and Intelligence Summaries are contained in F. S. Regs., Part II. and the Staff Manual respectively. Title pages will be prepared in manuscript.

Place	Date	Hour	Summary of Events and Information	Remarks and references to Appendices
			strength. We shall therefore move at strength of one officer & 28 men, one lorry with equipment & one horse & 2 bicycles.	
			The ordinary work of San. Sec. men is to be carried on until actually evacuating the area.	H.V.
NIEPPE	16.		122nd Inf. Brigade has moved back early & as I was unable to trace them I decided to wait until this section moves back & then detail a man to accompany the Brigade. As this man I intended to send to 122 had been withdrawn from STEENWERCK I sent him round with the district men.	H.V.

T2134. Wt. W708—776. 500000. 4/15. Sir J. C. & S.

IV
XVIII

Army Form C. 2118.

Instructions regarding War Diaries and Intelligence Summaries are contained in F. S. Regs., Part II. and the Staff Manual respectively. Title pages will be prepared in manuscript.

WAR DIARY
or
INTELLIGENCE SUMMARY.
(Erase heading not required.)

Place	Date	Hour	Summary of Events and Information	Remarks and references to Appendices
NIEPPE.	17.		The O/C of the incoming San. Sec. came over & same to day, & I borrowed a car & took him round the principal parts of this Div. area, Papot, Romarin, Ploegsteert, Le Bizet, Pont de Nieppe, Le Leau. I also took him to the office & explained to him the contracts for keeping Steenwerck & Nieppe clean - contracts which were signed between "Q" branch of this Div & the respective Mayors. I also handed over the necessary maps, information as to water supply, disposal of civilian rubbish, etc, & explained things as much as I possibly could. We spent practically all the day @ this. He arranged to send some of his men over so that my district men could take them round the area & explain everything.	RV.

T2134. Wt. W708—776. 500000. 4/15. Sir J. C. & S.

IV / XVIII

Army Form C. 2118.

Instructions regarding War Diaries and Intelligence Summaries are contained in F. S. Regs., Part II. and the Staff Manual respectively. Title pages will be prepared in manuscript.

WAR DIARY
or
~~INTELLIGENCE SUMMARY.~~
(Erase heading not required.)

Place	Date	Hour	Summary of Events and Information	Remarks and references to Appendices
NIEPPE	18.		Eight men of the incoming San. Sec. came over & my district men ~~[illegible]~~ took them round the area.	
			I reported this section to O/C 140th Field Amb. as we were to be attached to them for the move — @ least the 1st part of it as far as METEREN. I arranged to meet the 140th F. Amb. with my men in marching order @ PONT D'ACHELLES at 6.30 am 19/8/16 as we were on our own ration strength till then 19th.	F.V.
NIEPPE.	17		A reinforcement arrived for this section today making us one over strength. I think it is due to an error that he has been sent to us.	F.V.
NIEPPE.	19		I received orders to take over a steam Foden waggon disinfector from the Div. baths at Pont de NIEPPE, & to	

T2134. Wt. W708—776. 500000. 4/15. Sir J. C. & S.

IV
XIX

Instructions regarding War Diaries and Intelligence Summaries are contained in F. S. Regs., Part II. and the Staff Manual respectively. Title pages will be prepared in manuscript.

WAR DIARY
or
~~INTELLIGENCE SUMMARY.~~
(Erase heading not required.)

Army Form C. 2118.

Place	Date	Hour	Summary of Events and Information	Remarks and references to Appendices
			attach it to this section & take it out of the Div. area.	
			I paid off all Civilian labourers until the evening of 18/8/16, & left no outstanding debts against us for the next section to pay. I also had all billeting vouchers filled in up to date of our departure. This was not done by the San. Sec. from whom we took over, & I had a couple of bills to pay in consequence.	
			I consider that the men in my section have worked very well & have left billets & camps in a very satisfactory condition. The amount of sickness in the Division has been very small indeed. The number of cases of typhoid & dysentery has been very small. A great deal of this I feel sure is due to the fact that practically all rubbish & latrine excreta, also manure, was burnt. Scabies	

T2134. Wt. W708—776. 500000. 4/15. Sir J. C. & S.

IV / XX

Army Form C. 2118.

Instructions regarding War Diaries and Intelligence Summaries are contained in F. S. Regs., Part II. and the Staff Manual respectively. Title pages will be prepared in manuscript.

WAR DIARY
or
~~INTELLIGENCE SUMMARY.~~
(Erase heading not required.)

Place	Date	Hour	Summary of Events and Information	Remarks and references to Appendices
			claimed some cases but at times the purification of soiled clothes @ the Div. baths was not very effective or complete.	
			I left NIEPPE at midday, @ least closed my office there & moved back to the farm where the San. Sec. men were billeted, so as to be more favourably situated both for arranging our move, & to be nearer the O/C. of the in-coming section, of which the officer decided to make STEENWERCK his headquarters. He came over to NIEPPE this afternoon, & I "handed over" to him, & got his receipt for certain stores we were leaving behind, eg. Corps road sweepers &c.	H.V.
NIEPPE.	19.		Reveillé 4 am. Section moved off @ 6.20 & arrived @ PONT D'ACHELLES exactly @ 6.30. am. The 140th F. Amb. had not arrived, & did not arrive till 7.20. We fell in behind them	

IV
XXI

Instructions regarding War Diaries and Intelligence Summaries are contained in F. S. Regs., Part II. and the Staff Manual respectively. Title pages will be prepared in manuscript.

WAR DIARY
or
~~INTELLIGENCE SUMMARY~~.
(Erase heading not required.)

Army Form C. 2118.

Place	Date	Hour	Summary of Events and Information	Remarks and references to Appendices
			& marched along the NIEPPE-BAILLEUL road. Halted just before entering BAILLEUL & then marched on to the École ASPUISNE, METEREN where we halted & were attached to the 140th F Amb. I put up my office there (in a tent) & went straight on to FLETRE & reported to the A.D.M.S. of arrival. I also reported arrival to 124th Brigade, in accordance with instructions in their order No 46, as the 140th F. Amb. was moving out with the 124 Brigade. (continued overleaf).	H.V.
			I instructed my men to "carry on" with their duties exactly as they had been doing, & visit camps & billets & look after water supplies. Altho' the units in this Division are more scattered now I have more men available as there is no necessity to keep men centred at my head quarters as there was at NIEPPE.	H.V.

T2134. Wt. W708–776. 500000. 4/15. Sir J. C. & S.

IV
XXII

WAR DIARY
or
~~INTELLIGENCE SUMMARY.~~
(Erase heading not required.)

Army Form C. 2118.

Instructions regarding War Diaries and Intelligence Summaries are contained in F. S. Regs., Part II. and the Staff Manual respectively. Title pages will be prepared in manuscript.

Place	Date	Hour	Summary of Events and Information	Remarks and references to Appendices
			The steam Foden disinfector I sent to BAILLEUL on 18/8/16, & instructed the men in charge of it to be ready to join me @ BAILLEUL at 8am on 19/8/16. I did this as I knew the roads would be crowded with troops & transport & horses, & the last might be disturbed by the Foden. We "picked up" the Foden without breaking line of march @ BAILLEUL, & it came on behind us to METEREN.	
			My men saw to the San. arrangements of the ambulance directly after arriving at METEREN. The outgoing amb. had left things in a very untidy state. I have found that on the move Field ambulances are among the worst in their sanitary arrangements.	
			It ought to be understood amongst formations that a San. Sec. is not a fatigue party, & it is not to be expected	

T2134. Wt. W708–776. 500000. 4/15. Sir J. C. & S.

Instructions regarding War Diaries and Intelligence Summaries are contained in F. S. Regs., Part II. and the Staff Manual respectively. Title pages will be prepared in manuscript.

WAR DIARY

or

~~INTELLIGENCE SUMMARY.~~

(Erase heading not required.)

Army Form C. 2118.

Place	Date	Hour	Summary of Events and Information	Remarks and references to Appendices
			that they should do the fatigue san. work of any unit. The O/C. 140th Field Ambulance asked me to erect the necessary latrines, urinals &c for his ambulance, but I politely said we would see that what his men erected were kept in order & in a clean state.	H.V.
METEREN	19.		The whole section had distributed themselves amongst the Divisional units by 8.30 am & spent the day at their regular duties. I have dispensed with the services of my clerk for a few days so as to enable him to go out & benefit by the "rest" the Division is now having. I am doing his work myself.	H.V.
METEREN	20	22	(Inclusive) I spent these three days during which the Division was in rest in going round the Divisional area & in sending out the men of the section over the Divisional	

T.2134. Wt. W708–776. 500000. 4/15. Sir J. C. & S.

IV
XXIV

Army Form C. 2118.

Instructions regarding War Diaries and Intelligence Summaries are contained in F. S. Regs., Part II. and the Staff Manual respectively. Title pages will be prepared in manuscript.

WAR DIARY
or
~~INTELLIGENCE SUMMARY.~~
(Erase heading not required.)

Place	Date	Hour	Summary of Events and Information	Remarks and references to Appendices
			area. We found that in many cases the sanitary squad man had been sent out with their units for route marches & training &c. On the whole however the sanitation was good. Watercarts were being properly used, & a fair amount of attention was paid to the general sanitation. It was found that one or two units, particularly the 140th Field Ambulance, left their temporary sites in a very dirty condition. The ambulance made no apparent attempt to clear out their latrines, grease traps, billets &c, & left their cookhouse covered with food refuse. They moved out of the area on the night of Aug. 22nd.	R.D.
METEREN	23	7.30am	I received orders to proceed with the section motor lorry & equipment & the Foden Steam Wagon Disinfector by road to the new area to be occupied by the Division in the Fourth Army area @ AILLY LE HAUT CLOCHER,	

T2134. Wt. W708—776. 500000. 4/15. Sir J. C. & S.

Instructions regarding War Diaries and Intelligence Summaries are contained in F. S. Regs., Part II. and the Staff Manual respectively. Title pages will be prepared in manuscript.

WAR DIARY
or
~~INTELLIGENCE SUMMARY.~~
(Erase heading not required.)

IV / XXV

Army Form C. 2118.

Place	Date	Hour	Summary of Events and Information	Remarks and references to Appendices
			near ABBEVILLE. I had to take with me the 4 ASC. MT. Drivers, my servant, & the D.A.D.M.S.'s servant. We proceeded thro' CAESTRE, ST OMER, MONTREUIL, where we had to stop as the Foden wagon could not go more than 8-9 miles per hour, & had to stop every few miles to pick up water. I reported to the Camp Commandant @ MONTREUIL, who told us what billets we were to occupy for the night.	
			I had left full instructions with the Staff Sergeant of the San Section, & put him in charge of the remainder of the Section & gave him full details as to entraining, & detraining in the new area. His times for the journey were to entrain @ BAILLEUL WEST station by train no 29 @ 6.18 am on 24/8/16. To report to the R.T.O. there on arrival @ the station. He was to report to the R.T.O. on detraining @	

T2134. Wt. W708—776. 500000. 4/15. Sir J. C. & S.

Instructions regarding War Diaries and Intelligence Summaries are contained in F. S. Regs., Part II. and the Staff Manual respectively. Title pages will be prepared in manuscript.

WAR DIARY
or
~~INTELLIGENCE SUMMARY.~~
(Erase heading not required.)

IV / XXVI Army Form C. 2118.

Place	Date	Hour	Summary of Events and Information	Remarks and references to Appendices
			PONT REMY & to proceed by road to join the ~~section~~ Division @ AILLY LEHAUT CLOCHER. This he did satisfactorily & arrived @ that place @ 7.20 PM on 24/8/16.	H.V.
MONTREUIL	24	7.50 am.	~~We~~ left MONTREUIL with section motor Lorry & Foden wagon & proceeded via ABBEVILLE to AILLY LEHAUT CLOCHER, where we arrived @ 12 noon. 24/8/16. The Foden could not have allowed us to complete the whole journey in one day. The remainder of section reported to me at AILLY the same evening.	H.V.
AILLY LEHAUT CLOCHER	25.		The whole section was set to work to clear up AILLY. Short trench latrines were found to be essential. There is a great scarcity of water, both for drinking & washing, only a few v. deep wells being available in the	

T2134. Wt. W708—776. 500000. 4/15. Sir J. C. & S.

IV / XXVII

Army Form C. 2118.

Instructions regarding War Diaries and Intelligence Summaries are contained in F. S. Regs., Part II. and the Staff Manual respectively. Title pages will be prepared in manuscript.

WAR DIARY
or
~~INTELLIGENCE~~ ~~SUMMARY.~~

(Erase heading not required.)

Place	Date	Hour	Summary of Events and Information	Remarks and references to Appendices
			place. What water there is requires @ least 2 scoopsful of B.P.	
			I arranged to have all the refuse from the troops carted to a central incinerator which we erected, & borrowed a civilian cart for the purpose. This will simplify matters v. considerably & save labour. Whatever troops were in here before left their sanitary arrangements in a v. bad state – in fact the conditions are worse than in any places we have been to.	
			I propose to erect a central latrine for use of troops (quite a temporary & portable ?? affair).	
			The arrangement of attaching this section to the 140th Field Ambulance did not work well, & they ~~made~~ did not arrange	

T2134. Wt. W708–776. 500000. 4/15. Sir J. C. & S.

IV
XXVIII

Army Form C. 2118.

Instructions regarding War Diaries and Intelligence Summaries are contained in F. S. Regs., Part II. and the Staff Manual respectively. Title pages will be prepared in manuscript.

WAR DIARY
or
~~INTELLIGENCE~~ ~~SUMMARY~~.
(Erase heading not required.)

Place	Date	Hour	Summary of Events and Information	Remarks and references to Appendices
			rationing properly. The A.S.C. separated us after a couple of days, and drew our rations & supplies separately.	
			It would be more satisfactory if a San. Sec were allowed to move "on its own", & remain detached always. For one thing the O/C. Field Ambulance tried to make this section do the sanitary fatigues; the section duties consist in seeing that units do their own work, not in doing it for others.	W.V.
AILLY.	26.		The San. Sec. men who were visiting the scattered units brought back very favourable reports.	
			Short trench latrines are being used: manure is disposed of either by burning or being scattered over the fields.	

T2134. Wt. W708—776. 500000. 4/15. Sir J. C. & S.

11/XXIX

Army Form C. 2118.

WAR DIARY

or

~~INTELLIGENCE SUMMARY.~~

(Erase heading not required.)

Instructions regarding War Diaries and Intelligence Summaries are contained in F. S. Regs., Part II. and the Staff Manual respectively. Title pages will be prepared in manuscript.

Place	Date	Hour	Summary of Events and Information	Remarks and references to Appendices
			Cookhouse refuse is being burned:—	
			Incinerators are being erected & used to burn all refuse.	
			Drinking water is rather scarce, but can be obtained; watercarts however in many cases are being filled with buckets. this is due to the fact that the water sources are deep wells - @ least 100 feet in many cases, & the water has to be drawn up in buckets.	
			Mostly the water requires @ least 2 scoops of B.P.	
			I have been unable to obtain labour to build the central latrine & urinal, & have no material: the R.E's have none.	
			The village itself requires so much supervision that	

T2134. Wt. W708—776. 500000. 4/15. Sir J. C. & S.

Instructions regarding War Diaries and Intelligence Summaries are contained in F. S. Regs., Part II. and the Staff Manual respectively. Title pages will be prepared in manuscript.

WAR DIARY
or
INTELLIGENCE SUMMARY.
(Erase heading not required.)

111 XXX Army Form C. 2118.

Place	Date	Hour	Summary of Events and Information	Remarks and references to Appendices
			have been unable to visit units outside.	
			I have a list of all water supplies - tested - available: this list however only contains sources in & around AILLY.	T.D.
AILLY.	27		By order of G.O.C. today was to be observed as a general holiday. The work of San squad men in this town was carried on however. I went for a tour round ABBEVILLE way.	T.D.
AILLY.	28		The latrine was erected in a central part of AILLY today, & is now in use. It is not as large as I intended it to be as sufficient labour & material were not available. It gives accomodation for 5 men & one officer, & is a canvas frame structure,	

T2134. Wt. W708—776. 500000. 4/15. Sir J. C. & S.

IV
XXXI Army Form C. 2118.

Instructions regarding War Diaries and Intelligence Summaries are contained in F. S. Regs., Part II. and the Staff Manual respectively. Title pages will be prepared in manuscript.

WAR DIARY
or
~~INTELLIGENCE~~ SUMMARY.
(Erase heading not required.)

Place	Date	Hour	Summary of Events and Information	Remarks and references to Appendices
			with iron roof. It is however portable, & can easily be placed in a fresh site when the large deep trench is full.	
			I went out round MOUFFLERS, BOUCHON, L'ETOILE, LONG & saw several units, which are fairly satisfactory. The district is too large to cover more than a very small part of it.	
			We disinfected some verminous blankets in the Foden today. Rain has made the fields & roads in a very muddy state, & hindered work.	W.V.
	Aug 29.		There has been a Divisional field day today, & most units have left v. little personnel behind to	

T2134. Wt. W708—776. 500000. 4/15. Sir J. C. & S.

IV
XXXII

Army Form C. 2118.

Instructions regarding War Diaries and Intelligence Summaries are contained in F. S. Regs., Part II. and the Staff Manual respectively. Title pages will be prepared in manuscript.

WAR DIARY
or
INTELLIGENCE SUMMARY.
(Erase heading not required.)

Place	Date	Hour	Summary of Events and Information	Remarks and references to Appendices
			carry on sanitary work.	
			D.R.O. 600, orders that sanitary squad men are not to be taken out on field training but are to remain behind to attend to their own sanitary duties.	
			The artillery brigades are quartered along the river between L'Etoile & Pont Remy. Horse lines are satisfactory, and the general sanitation is good. The billets are rather small, particularly with 183 Brigade.	[illegible]
AILLY.	30.		Some units have not obeyed D.R.O. 600, & have not left sanitary squad men behind when going on training. This is particularly referable to 139 F. Amb. & the 23rd Mx. Regt.	

T2134. Wt. W708–776. 500000. 4/15. Sir J. C. & S.

IV
XXXIII

Army Form C. 2118.

Instructions regarding War Diaries and Intelligence Summaries are contained in F. S. Regs., Part II. and the Staff Manual respectively. Title pages will be prepared in manuscript.

WAR DIARY
or
~~INTELLIGENCE SUMMARY.~~
(Erase heading not required.)

Place	Date	Hour	Summary of Events and Information	Remarks and references to Appendices
			One unit, 41st Signal Co R.E. have been using their water cart to carry ~~[illegible]~~ water for baths.	
			The ceaseless rain has put nearly everything to a standstill. I went down to PONT REMY myself, but everything was at a standstill. Billets were fairly clean.	
			~~[illegible]~~ The San. Sec. men who have been going round the area give fair reports.	
			Some clothing was sent up for disinfection - (lousy clothing from 10 R.W.K.). this was disinfected.	
			I arranged to have 25 extra men from the Pioneers (19th Mx) for the purpose of cleaning the gutters & roadsides of the principal streets. Middens from the houses	

T2134. Wt. W708—776. 500000. 4/15. Sir J. C. & S.

IV / XXXIV

Army Form C. 2118.

Instructions regarding War Diaries and Intelligence Summaries are contained in F. S. Regs., Part II. and the Staff Manual respectively. Title pages will be prepared in manuscript.

WAR DIARY

or

~~INTELLIGENCE SUMMARY.~~

(Erase heading not required.)

Place	Date	Hour	Summary of Events and Information	Remarks and references to Appendices
	August.		has been overflowing into the streets, & urine & other unsanitary refuse was being washed all over the place by the rain.	H.V.
AILLY	31.		The Middlesex pioneers are working at the road cleaning altogether I have obtained 37 men who are now all on the work which I hope to complete today. I am having a small "gutter" dug each side of the road, & the mud & rubbish is being carted away.	
			The two latrines I have erected are satisfactory.	
			A supply of notice boards referring to the kind & quality, quantity & amount of chlorination necessary for water is in hand now, & will be available for issue to units who require them.	

Instructions regarding War Diaries and Intelligence Summaries are contained in F. S. Regs., Part II. and the Staff Manual respectively. Title pages will be prepared in manuscript.

WAR DIARY
or
~~INTELLIGENCE SUMMARY.~~
(Erase heading not required.)

IV / XXXV

Army Form C. 2118.

Place	Date	Hour	Summary of Events and Information	Remarks and references to Appendices
			I found that the watercart belonging to Div. H.Q. was out of order. It had got out of order in travelling, & tho we have been here a week it has not been put right: this shows that the cart has not been ~~put~~ used properly in spite of what the H.Q. ~~water~~cartman has said!	
			Orders have been received from 4th Army, that the position of all permanent structures, e.g. latrines, incinerators erected in our area, are to be notified to them before we leave the area.	
			A good many of the units have been infected with lice: I suspect a source of infection in the cattle & horse trucks in which the division was conveyed from the 2nd to the 4th Army area.	

IV / XXXVI

Army Form C. 2118.

Instructions regarding War Diaries and Intelligence Summaries are contained in F. S. Regs., Part II. and the Staff Manual respectively. Title pages will be prepared in manuscript.

WAR DIARY

or

~~INTELLIGENCE SUMMARY.~~

(Erase heading not required.)

Place	Date	Hour	Summary of Events and Information	Remarks and references to Appendices
			The permanent structures erected by us are 1. 1. Latrine, for 5 men or 1 officer near the Mairie. 2. 1 Latrine for 1 officer - behind the Mairie. 3. 1. Round beehive type incinerator in a field just off the main street. It is to be noted that this section has been able to get thro' more actual work since we have had the use of fatigue & working parties. The work of the section is chiefly supervisory; it is not meant to do the sanitation for units (vide back), but if the men of the section are to be called upon to do this, the work of the whole section suffers.	H.V.

Sept. 1916

140/1815

Vol 5

War Diary

of

8th Sanitary Section

(41st Division)

from

1st September 16 to 30th September 16

(Volume V)

Volume V

Instructions regarding War Diaries and Intelligence Summaries are contained in F. S. Regs., Part II. and the Staff Manual respectively. Title pages will be prepared in manuscript.

84th SANITARY SECTION. No. ... Date ...

WAR DIARY
or
~~INTELLIGENCE SUMMARY.~~
(Erase heading not required.)

84th SANITARY SECTION. No. ... Date ...

Army Form C. 2118.

Place	Date	Hour	Summary of Events and Information	Remarks and references to Appendices
AILLY LE HAUT CLOCHER	Sept 1.		I have found that sufficient cleanliness is not been exercised by the officers & N.C.O's messes. The disposal of kitchen refuse & precautions against flies, e.g. keeping food covered, are neglected.	
			One unit in this division were using their water cart to carry water for baths: this was stopped @ once, & action taken.	
			I had my water man stationed at points on the area, & near water stations so that they could test carts after being filled. Several carts were found which were not being used properly.	
			I visited units myself around YAUCOURT-BUSSUS & BUSSUS, tho' the men were all out training, a few	

T2134. Wt. W708–776. 500000. 4/15. Sir J. C. & S.

Instructions regarding War Diaries and Intelligence Summaries are contained in F. S. Regs., Part II. and the Staff Manual respectively. Title pages will be prepared in manuscript.

WAR DIARY
or
~~INTELLIGENCE SUMMARY.~~
(Erase heading not required.)

Army Form C. 2118.

Place	Date	Hour	Summary of Events and Information	Remarks and references to Appendices
			sanitary men had been left behind & conditions were fair.	
			The Foden disinfector had been sent off to the German Prisoners of war camp at PICQUIGNY ~~to~~ disinfect clothing of Prisoners &c, & was not available for our use today.	[initials]
AILLY	Sept. 2		Foden returned early this morning & proceeded to disinfect clothes.	
			There is difficulty in obtaining coal for the Foden.	
			Visited the district around BOIGNY L'ABBE & VAUCHELLES & FRANCIERES today. There are very few troops there, & find I cannot cover the ground as I should like to on the horse.	

Instructions regarding War Diaries and Intelligence Summaries are contained in F. S. Regs., Part II. and the Staff Manual respectively. Title pages will be prepared in manuscript.

WAR DIARY

or

~~INTELLIGENCE SUMMARY.~~

(Erase heading not required.)

Army Form C. 2118.

Place	Date	Hour	Summary of Events and Information	Remarks and references to Appendices
			The artillery have moved up & left their area in a very satisfactory condition	
			I have decided to leave @ railhead or convenient dump a good deal of the unnecessary Equipment of this section: some of it has never been used, & from what I have seen of other San. Secs is not likely to be used. eg. flagpoles – box disinfectors, which are only useful for parking purposes – no section I know of has used them, & they have been sent back to base as useless.	P.V
AILLY.	Sept 3.		Very little work was done today owing to the Divisional Horse show.	P.V

T2134. Wt. W708–776. 500000. 4/15. Sir J. C. & S.

Instructions regarding War Diaries and Intelligence Summaries are contained in F. S. Regs., Part II. and the Staff Manual respectively. Title pages will be prepared in manuscript.

WAR DIARY

or

~~INTELLIGENCE SUMMARY.~~

(Erase heading not required.)

Army Form C. 2118.

Place	Date	Hour	Summary of Events and Information	Remarks and references to Appendices
AILLY	Sept 4		Orders were issued to prepare to move @ very short notice from here to XV corps area.	
			The Section men were all out on their rounds, ~~but~~ I did not recall them in at once, but proceeded to prepare to move with the couple of men round H.Q.	
			I was unable to go out visiting today, as for the 1st part of morning I was taking sick parade of Div. H.Q. & later on was out with the Field Ambulances at their manoeuvres which however were stopped @ 11 a.m. owing to anticipated move. Several minor matters prevented me from going out in the afternoon.	

T2131. Wt. W708–776. 500000. 4/15. Sir J. C. & S.

Army Form C. 2118.

Instructions regarding War Diaries and Intelligence Summaries are contained in F. S. Regs., Part II. and the Staff Manual respectively. Title pages will be prepared in manuscript.

WAR DIARY
or
~~INTELLIGENCE SUMMARY.~~
(Erase heading not required.)

Place	Date	Hour	Summary of Events and Information	Remarks and references to Appendices
			In accordance with X corps orders I sent in to A.D.M.S. a list of the permanent & semi permanent structures erected by this section in this area. They were, 2 latrines erected near Mairie at AILLY LE HAUT CLOCHER & an incinerator in the field of farm of "Cantrell Hamel" at AILLY.	
			It has again happened that ~~the~~ steam has been "got up" in the disinfector & the unit who asked to have clothes disinfected has failed to turn up. It was the 23rd Middlesex in the case today. Yesterday it was the 39th Field Ambulance. This means a great waste of coal each time.	H.V.
			Rain is again making the place waterlogged, & middens & cesspits are overflowing into the streets again.	H.V.

T2134. Wt. W708—776. 500000. 4/15. Sir J. C. & S.

Instructions regarding War Diaries and Intelligence Summaries are contained in F. S. Regs., Part II. and the Staff Manual respectively. Title pages will be prepared in manuscript.

WAR DIARY
or
~~INTELLIGENCE~~ SUMMARY.
(Erase heading not required.)

Army Form C. 2118.

Place	Date	Hour	Summary of Events and Information	Remarks and references to Appendices
AILLY	Sept 5		The great heavy rain of last evening & night has made things very dirty & the ditches &c are full of dirty "washings" from middens &c. I have tried to construct drains along the principal streets in this place, but they are quite inadequate.	
			I sent my horse in charge of a Sergeant to the new area along with the transport of Div H.Q. which is proceeding by road.	
			The disinfector was borrowed by 138th F. Amb. this morning.	
			The men of section confined their rounds to the neighbourhood of AILLY, as most troops are on the move today, & as H.Q. san detachment have gone	

T2134. Wt. W708—776. 500000. 4/15. Sir J. C. & S.

Instructions regarding War Diaries and Intelligence Summaries are contained in F. S. Regs., Part II. and the Staff Manual respectively. Title pages will be prepared in manuscript.

WAR DIARY
or
~~INTELLIGENCE~~ SUMMARY.
(Erase heading not required.)

Army Form C. 2118.

Place	Date	Hour	Summary of Events and Information	Remarks and references to Appendices
			It is very necessary to attend to sanitation, & leave the place in a tidy condition. I think it may be helpful if I place on record a series of sanitary rules sent out by X Corps. These have been in force in the 5th Corps area from which we came. The rules apply to cookhouses & messes. 1. Servants, cooks &c are not to sleep in mess kitchens. 2. No clothing or equipment is to be kept in kitchens. 3. Personal washing materials, eg hairbrushes, towels, soap, shaving brushes &c, must not be kept in the kitchens. 4 The hands of all those handling food must be kept clean, a bowl of water with soap & towel should be kept outside each kitchen for this purpose.	

T2134. Wt. W708—776. 500000. 4/15. Sir J. C. & S.

Instructions regarding War Diaries and Intelligence Summaries are contained in F. S. Regs., Part II. and the Staff Manual respectively. Title pages will be prepared in manuscript.

WAR DIARY
or
~~INTELLIGENCE~~ SUMMARY.
(Erase heading not required.)

Army Form C. 2118.

Place	Date	Hour	Summary of Events and Information	Remarks and references to Appendices
			5. All clothing used by cooks must be ~~kept~~ washed once a week; all cooks will wear dungaree clothing when cooking.	
			6 Washing up cloths must be boiled in boiling water & thoroughly washed @ least once a day. They must not be kept in the kitchen, but hung up outside to dry when not in use.	
			7. All refuse tins & boxes used for refuse must be provided with a lid & must be kept closed.	
			8. All food must be kept under cover & protected from flies @ all times, even when placed on the table.	
			9. The gauze for windows &c should be fitted to a proper frame, & not tacked up to the windows.	
			10 All food should be stored in a cool dark place.	
			11 This notice is to be hung up in every officers, NCOs & men's kitchen & cookhouse.	H.V.

Instructions regarding War Diaries and Intelligence Summaries are contained in F. S. Regs., Part II. and the Staff Manual respectively. Title pages will be prepared in manuscript.

WAR DIARY

or

~~INTELLIGENCE~~ SUMMARY.

(Erase heading not required.)

Army Form C. 2118.

Place	Date	Hour	Summary of Events and Information	Remarks and references to Appendices
AILLY	Sept 6.	8.20am	The lorry & Foden disinfector of this section left AILLY LE HAUT CLOCHER at 8.20am in charge of an NCO to proceed by road to the XV Corps area.	
		10am	Remainder of Section 84 left AILLY at 10am & marched to Pt LONGPRE to entrain & to proceed to XV. Corps area & Div. H.Q which was to be at BUIRE SUR L'ANCRE. Detraining station was MERICOURT, from where we marched to BUIRE. The riding horse of this section proceeded by road with the transport of Div. H.Q. on Sept 5th	
			On arrival at BUIRE we found the lorry & Foden just arrived; horse arrived at 7pm. We pitched 3 tents & accomodated the men in them. It was too late to do any sanitation tonight.	R.V.

Instructions regarding War Diaries and Intelligence Summaries are contained in F. S. Regs., Part II. and the Staff Manual respectively. Title pages will be prepared in manuscript.

WAR DIARY
or
INTELLIGENCE SUMMARY.
(Erase heading not required.)

Army Form C. 2118.

Place	Date	Hour	Summary of Events and Information	Remarks and references to Appendices
BUIRE	Sept 17		I sent out as many as possible of this section to Divisional units as usual, & kept back a certain number to see to the sanitation of the area around Div H.Q. The whole place was ~~in~~ a v. dirty state: flies swarmed in every tent & hut, hedge & ditch, & on all heaps of uncovered food litter & refuse. I had to spend a lot of time using cresol sprayers, & had to have 2 men permanently doing nothing ~~but~~ but spraying huts & offices of Div H.Q. The whole area is in a dirty condition, & sanitation appears to have been neglected for a long time. I had short trench latrines dug for N.C.O's & men, & efficient incinerators & grease traps erected to burn everything. Strict attention was directed by this section to provide efficient & sufficient covered storage for food. I myself went out round the district but was unable to find any units in the limited time available	

T2134. Wt. W708–776. 500000. 4/15. Sir J. C. & S.

Instructions regarding War Diaries and Intelligence Summaries are contained in F. S. Regs., Part II. and the Staff Manual respectively. Title pages will be prepared in manuscript.

WAR DIARY
or
~~INTELLIGENCE SUMMARY~~.
(Erase heading not required.)

Army Form C. 2118.

Place	Date	Hour	Summary of Events and Information	Remarks and references to Appendices
BUIRE	Sept 8.		I went over to VIVIER MILL this morning on order from ADMS in order to look over some Corps Baths which we were told we were to take over. The rest of the section were out at their district work as usual. I had occasion to report the Camp Commandant for the untidy state of H.Q. horse lines.	RV.
BUIRE	Sept 9.		I rode over to BELLEVUE FARM this morning to see the O/C San. Sec. from whom we were taking over. He gave me the necessary particulars & details as to distribution of San. Sec. Personnel. His section were not working as an advisory body @ all, but were doing fatigue work, with the result that San work in the Division was neglected. I have not seen such a filthy state of affairs in any area I have seen yet. We continued on our usual work; seeing that all rubbish, manure	

T2134. Wt. W708–776. 500000. 4/15. Sir J. C. & S.

Instructions regarding War Diaries and Intelligence Summaries are contained in F. S. Regs., Part II. and the Staff Manual respectively. Title pages will be prepared in manuscript.

WAR DIARY
or
~~INTELLIGENCE SUMMARY.~~
(Erase heading not required.)

Army Form C. 2118.

Place	Date	Hour	Summary of Events and Information	Remarks and references to Appendices
			was burnt, trench latrines used & properly filled in, grease traps kept clean & covered: food covered properly. cookhouses continually supervised.	
			The Foden Disinfector was used for disinfection.	F.V.
BELLEVUE FARM	10.		I took over from O/c San. Sec. 55th Division @ 3.30 PM. 3 men of this section were sent in to BECORDEL (2 for water duties,) & 4 were sent to FRICOURT (-2 for water duties) The remainder were put on @ once to attend to this area which was in a filthy condition. I applied for a fatigue party to clean up: this was promised for tomorrow morning @ 10 am.	F.V.
BELLEVUE FARM	Sept. 11		Fatigue party of 20 men were sent to Camp Commandant for purposes of cleaning the Camp. as he has not arrived	

T2134. Wt. W708–776. 500000. 4/15. Sir J. C. & S.

Instructions regarding War Diaries and Intelligence Summaries are contained in F. S. Regs., Part II. and the Staff Manual respectively. Title pages will be prepared in manuscript.

WAR DIARY
or
~~INTELLIGENCE~~ SUMMARY.
(Erase heading not required.)

Army Form C. 2118.

Place	Date	Hour	Summary of Events and Information	Remarks and references to Appendices
			took charge of them & proceeded to try & clean the place. We cleared all tents, huts & shelters thoroughly & removed dirty septic bivouacs & burnt them. Tents & huts &c were also sprayed. Old manure was swept up & arrangements made for clearing the farm premises from old longstanding collections of manure. This last will take a long time, & I doubt whether in view of the present military situation we shall be able to finish it before we leave this area. The civil owners of the farm raise a great deal of obstruction in our work of clearing up. The Midden alongside the H.Q. is v. offensive & the farmers fowls stir it up & scratch it as fast as we attempt to stack it & spray it.	
			We are attempting to create some sort of order in the camp. Previously horselines &c were placed anywhere	

T2134. Wt. W708—776. 500000. 4/15. Sir J. C. & S.

Instructions regarding War Diaries and Intelligence Summaries are contained in F. S. Regs., Part II. and the Staff Manual respectively. Title pages will be prepared in manuscript.

WAR DIARY
or
~~INTELLIGENCE SUMMARY.~~
(Erase heading not required.)

Army Form C. 2118.

Place	Date	Hour	Summary of Events and Information	Remarks and references to Appendices
			& everywhere between sleeping tents & alongside messes. All horse lines have been removed some distance from the camp & no horses are allowed to enter the camp now.	
			Deep trench latrines & urinals have been erected for the use of officers & men	
			The indiscriminate distribution of cookhouses among the tents has been stopped, & dirty bivouacs have been pulled down.	
			The water supply is very bad, only one deep well with no proper means of drawing water being available at this camp. The water only requires one scoopful per cart	
			Foden steam disinfector was in use today.	H.V.

T2134. Wt. W708—776. 500000. 4/15. Sir J. C. & S.

Instructions regarding War Diaries and Intelligence Summaries are contained in F. S. Regs., Part II. and the Staff Manual respectively. Title pages will be prepared in manuscript.

WAR DIARY
or
~~INTELLIGENCE SUMMARY.~~
(Erase heading not required.)

Army Form C. 2118.

Place	Date	Hour	Summary of Events and Information	Remarks and references to Appendices
BELLEVUE FARM	12.		On instructions from A.D.M.S. I recalled the men of this section who were posted with the Infantry Brigades of this division.	
			The men who are doing water duty at BECORDEL & FRICOURT are very urgently needed for work amongst our own divisional troops. I understand that these two water stations ~~at~~ are Corps Stations, & I wrote to the Town Majors of these 2 places saying that I intend to withdraw the men from water duties tomorrow night, & advising them to apply to the XV Corps for watermen.	
			I visited the advanced dressing stations at the QUARRIES & DELVILLE WOOD in company with the A.D.M.S. The places are very filthy – food lying about everywhere, flies swarming: no adequate latrines or urinals &c. I propose to send 2 men of this section up there to supervise matters, &	

T2134. Wt. W708–776. 500000. 4/15. Sir J. C. & S.

Instructions regarding War Diaries and Intelligence Summaries are contained in F. S. Regs., Part II. and the Staff Manual respectively. Title pages will be prepared in manuscript.

WAR DIARY
or
~~INTELLIGENCE SUMMARY.~~
(Erase heading not required.)

Army Form C. 2118.

Place	Date	Hour	Summary of Events and Information	Remarks and references to Appendices
			understand that a fatigue party of 100 men will be available for work there. DELVILLE WOOD is very filthy & insanitary, & it would be better if it were entirely left alone until a proper body of men can be obtained later on to clear it & bury the dead there.	
			Continual spraying of huts & tents is necessary to fight against flies, & I am even having to work incinerators myself as all my available men are out on rounds.	
			Some public latrines – said to be kept in order by the RE of 55th Division were in a filthy condition, & I had to complain to the 55th Div. RE.	
			The difficulty with public latrines in this state of things is that it is difficult to fix responsibility for keeping them in order: everyone uses them, but no one will keep	

T2134. Wt. W708–776. 500000. 4/15. Sir J. C. & S.

Instructions regarding War Diaries and Intelligence Summaries are contained in F. S. Regs., Part II. and the Staff Manual respectively. Title pages will be prepared in manuscript.

WAR DIARY
or
~~INTELLIGENCE SUMMARY.~~
(Erase heading not required.)

Army Form C. 2118.

Place	Date	Hour	Summary of Events and Information	Remarks and references to Appendices
			them in order. I have decided that the unit nearest to them shall be responsible for their upkeep.	
			According to XV Corps circular of 8/9/16 the town majors of places in the XV Corps area are authorised to demand 1 nco & 10 men for sanitary work from the nearest unit. This gets over the difficulty of fatigue men.	W.
BELLEVUE FARM	13		I reported the fact that my men were doing Corps work @ BECORDEL & FRICOURT & he is going to bring the matter up to the Corps. The O/C XV Corps water column asked me to arrange to have my men on duty @ the water station at FRICOURT all night on 12-13th Sept. in order to facilitate a special convoy of water which was going to take water up the line on important work. I gave my men orders to do	

T2134. Wt. W708—776. 500000. 4/15. Sir J. C. & S.

Instructions regarding War Diaries and Intelligence Summaries are contained in F. S. Regs., Part II. and the Staff Manual respectively. Title pages will be prepared in manuscript.

WAR DIARY
or
~~INTELLIGENCE SUMMARY.~~
(Erase heading not required.)

Army Form C. 2118.

Place	Date	Hour	Summary of Events and Information	Remarks and references to Appendices
			this.	
			The A.D.M.S. has ordered me to refer such matters to him in future.	
			The camp round H.Q. is ~~[illegible]~~ being well cleaned up.	
			I have to report the bad state of the sanitary arrangement of Ordnance belonging to this Division. They have made no attempt to erect or clean up anything, & have utilised an old filthy house as a cookhouse & dining room while the tents are scattered round a filthy bit of field. These men have always given a great deal of trouble ever since the Division came overseas & have never attempted to do anything for themselves. They complain that they have no men for sanitation. Their state of affairs can be deduced when it is said that the [illegible] warrant officer has scabies	

Instructions regarding War Diaries and Intelligence Summaries are contained in F. S. Regs., Part II. and the Staff Manual respectively. Title pages will be prepared in manuscript.

WAR DIARY
or
~~INTELLIGENCE SUMMARY.~~
(Erase heading not required.)

Army Form C. 2118.

Place	Date	Hour	Summary of Events and Information	Remarks and references to Appendices
BELLEVUE FARM.	14		Sanitation before removal in our own division.	
			The two water men at BECORDEL were withdrawn by orders from XV Corps, & I left 2 men [illegible] on water duties at FRICOURT.	
			I have been ordered to report for medical work at the Advanced Dressing station at the Quarries @ night, to help the ~~[illegible]~~ Field Ambulances. I have left my Staff Sergeant in charge of the work in my absence.	[illegible]
"	16		I returned to the Section after 48 hours continuous duty @ the Advanced Dressing Station. My Staff Sergeant reported that in my absence the Foden Disinfector had been ordered to proceed to baths belonging to XV Corps at HEILLY, & also that the motor	

T2134. Wt. W708—776. 500000. 4/15. Sir J. C. & S.

Instructions regarding War Diaries and Intelligence Summaries are contained in F. S. Regs., Part II. and the Staff Manual respectively. Title pages will be prepared in manuscript.

WAR DIARY
or
~~INTELLIGENCE SUMMARY.~~
(Erase heading not required.)

Army Form C. 2118.

Place	Date	Hour	Summary of Events and Information	Remarks and references to Appendices
			Lorry of this section has been used to help the 20th F. Amb. of this division to move from BELLEVUE FARM to the neighbourhood of MONTABAN. I mentioned this latter because every unit with a motor car or lorry has to send in a weekly return of petrol consumption. The lorry was 4 hours coming a distance of about six miles & as this was done with the engine running all the time in slowly moving traffic the petrol consumption is enormous, & a low mileage is inevitable. This might be put down as due to wastefulness on the driver's part if the true circumstances of the cases were not known.	N.V.
BELLEVUE FARM.			The section taking over from us sent up men this afternoon to take over FRICOURT water station. The O.C. of the San. Sec. also came over & looked over. We are to go back in to rest tomorrow at RIBEMONT.	N.V.

Instructions regarding War Diaries and Intelligence Summaries are contained in F. S. Regs., Part II. and the Staff Manual respectively. Title pages will be prepared in manuscript.

WAR DIARY
or
~~INTELLIGENCE SUMMARY.~~
(Erase heading not required.)

Army Form C. 2118.

Place	Date	Hour	Summary of Events and Information	Remarks and references to Appendices
RIBEMONT	Sep 18.		This section was relieved by San. Sec. of 55th Div & proceeded to RIBEMONT. I had to send the lorry back to BELLEVUE FARM for a second load. We found RIBEMONT in a filthy condition. A certain number of Public latrines & urinals had been erected, in accordance with ARMY ORDER, & there were some public incinerators. There was also a manure dump outside the town. The billets however were very filthy & were left by the outgoing division in a disgusting condition & they required a great deal of cleaning. The H.Q. messes in particular were disgusting, & no attempt seems to have been made to take the simplest precautions against ~~and~~ dumping kitchen refuse, empty ration tins &c in every conceivable place. The usual procedure has to be gone thro', & I have to get extra fatigue men from all over the place to clean up.	

T2131. Wt. W708–776. 500000. 4/15. Sir J. C. & S.

Instructions regarding War Diaries and Intelligence Summaries are contained in F. S. Regs., Part II. and the Staff Manual respectively. Title pages will be prepared in manuscript.

WAR DIARY
or
~~INTELLIGENCE~~ SUMMARY.
(Erase heading not required.)

Army Form C. 2118.

Place	Date	Hour	Summary of Events and Information	Remarks and references to Appendices
			The water supply is not bad, one scoop per cart. I obtained a plan from the Town Major showing positions of public structures &c, & am insisting on their being used & kept in order by the nearest unit.	
			We erected a Public Latrine near the mill at RIBEMONT, & a latrine for Officers behind the chateau.	
			I have cleaned up all the billets & messes occupied by units of this Division, & have approached the Town Major with regard to units of other Divisions.	
			There is a good deal that requires to be done, & it will take some time. I am going to see the Town Major personally tonight.	H.V.
RIBEMONT.	19 Sept		My section distributed itself over the Divisional area, 19 Sept	

T2134. Wt. W708—776. 500000. 4/15. Sir J. C. & S.

Instructions regarding War Diaries and Intelligence Summaries are contained in F. S. Regs., Part II. and the Staff Manual respectively. Title pages will be prepared in manuscript.

WAR DIARY
or
~~INTELLIGENCE SUMMARY.~~
(Erase heading not required.)

Army Form C. 2118.

Place	Date	Hour	Summary of Events and Information	Remarks and references to Appendices
			back a few men to take in hand the clearing up of RIBEMONT.	
			One of my men reported to me that he had been refused permission to inspect one of our Div. F. ambulances. I mention this because the ambulance in question have never given us any assistance at all, & on one occasion at least have left behind them a dirtier set of billets than any I have seen in the Division. It appears that ambulances are outside the sphere of the San. Secs. work tho' this is wrong. They need as much looking after as any other units.	
			There were several private latrines in RIBEMONT, these I ordered to be taken down according to XV Corps order & Public Latrines used.	
			In addition [to] our Div H.Q. here there is a brigade of	

Instructions regarding War Diaries and Intelligence Summaries are contained in F. S. Regs., Part II. and the Staff Manual respectively. Title pages will be prepared in manuscript.

WAR DIARY
or
~~INTELLIGENCE SUMMARY.~~
(Erase heading not required.)

Army Form C. 2118.

Place	Date	Hour	Summary of Events and Information	Remarks and references to Appendices
			the 24th Division, & they have been rather neglected & put in filthy billets.	
			Some baths for our own Div. H.Q. were erected by the mill at RIBEMONT	
			We have done a good deal of spraying of billets in RIBEMONT to keep down flies. The cresol does not seem to be very effective tho', & has to be done repeatedly.	
			There is still a lack of covered receptacles for keeping food.	
			We have been ordered to re-equip to full inventory and then move.	W.V.
RIBEMONT	Sept 21.		I received orders this morning to send one N.C.O. to XV Corps	

T2134. Wt. W708—776. 500000. 4/15. Sir J. C. & S.

Instructions regarding War Diaries and Intelligence Summaries are contained in F. S. Regs., Part II. and the Staff Manual respectively. Title pages will be prepared in manuscript.

WAR DIARY
or
INTELLIGENCE SUMMARY.
(Erase heading not required.)

Army Form C. 2118.

Place	Date	Hour	Summary of Events and Information	Remarks and references to Appendices
			H.Q. at HEILLY to superintend the san. arrangements by Corps H.Q. There is a good deal of minor sickness amongst units due to drinking improperly chlorinated water. I have noticed that water carts of other divisions are not properly used & the man in charge of carts knows nothing of chlorinating. The fact that it is necessary to have water duty men at places like BECORDEL & FRICOURT, whose sole duty is to chlorinate water proves what I have just stated.	
RIBEMONT	Sept 22		I have had several interviews with the Town Major & he is of the same opinion as I that it is absolutely essential to have a ~~full~~ large no. of men to supervise & keep the town & billets clean. The arrangement that we have come to is this, that his fatigue men shall keep the public latrines, billets & public incinerators in [illegible]	

Instructions regarding War Diaries and Intelligence Summaries are contained in F. S. Regs., Part II. and the Staff Manual respectively. Title pages will be prepared in manuscript.

WAR DIARY

or

~~INTELLIGENCE SUMMARY.~~

(Erase heading not required.)

Army Form C. 2118.

Place	Date	Hour	Summary of Events and Information	Remarks and references to Appendices
			proper working & clean condition. I shall ~~see~~ look after my own divisional units messes, & also supervise the sanitation of the town & if anything requires attending to outside my own divisional units I shall report to him & he will attend to it.	
			In a number of the billets the XV Corps are erecting series of bunks, composed of wirenetting on wooden frames. Altho' these are cleaner than any other system could be I believe that they will prove too draughty & cold during the winter months.	F.V.
RIBEMONT.	23.		I have had a number of men of this section erecting public latrines in the Village today. The village is not so full of troops, & it is possible to work with a freer hand. It is much cleaner now than it was when we	

T2134. Wt. W708—776. 500000. 4/15. Sir J. C. & S.

Instructions regarding War Diaries and Intelligence Summaries are contained in F. S. Regs., Part II. and the Staff Manual respectively. Title pages will be prepared in manuscript.

WAR DIARY
or
INTELLIGENCE SUMMARY.
(Erase heading not required.)

Army Form C. 2118.

Place	Date	Hour	Summary of Events and Information	Remarks and references to Appendices
			came in a few days ago. The Camp Commandant of our division has erected some baths for H.Q. troops alongside the stream: they were very badly needed. My section have been @ work amongst the rest of the division as usual with the exception of three or four men whom I have had to put on light duty because of colic & severe colds. The water round here is from the same stream as we used @ BUIRE, & only requires one scoop. per cart.	R.V.
RIBEMONT	Sept. 24		Wherever possible box seats over deep trenches are being used as latrines instead of short shallow trenches in this division. ~~Clearance~~ Units throw their rubbish into shell holes & any other	

Instructions regarding War Diaries and Intelligence Summaries are contained in F. S. Regs., Part II. and the Staff Manual respectively. Title pages will be prepared in manuscript.

WAR DIARY
or
~~INTELLIGENCE SUMMARY.~~
(Erase heading not required.)

Army Form C. 2118.

Place	Date	Hour	Summary of Events and Information	Remarks and references to Appendices
			hole & leave it there instead of burning it up. Any odd hole is used as a latrine too by some units & it is v. difficult & almost impossible trace those responsible for this form of nuisance	R.V.
RIBEMONT. 25.			The 123rd Inf. Brigade have remained behind near BECORDEL & I have been unable to visit them myself: they are reported to be in good order by my NCOs. & using large deep trench latrines with box seats. The San. Squads of units complain that the recently arrived "drafts" know nothing about keeping their areas clean. With the help of the fatigue party of the Town Major we have succeeded in erecting 4 more public latrines for officers & men & in collecting rubbish &c from nearly all the billets. As there are v. few troops in RIBEMONT this has been done fairly easily.	R.V.

T2134. Wt. W708—776. 500000. 4/15. Sir J. C. & S.

Instructions regarding War Diaries and Intelligence Summaries are contained in F. S. Regs., Part II. and the Staff Manual respectively. Title pages will be prepared in manuscript.

WAR DIARY
or
~~INTELLIGENCE SUMMARY.~~
(Erase heading not required.)

Army Form C. 2118.

Place	Date	Hour	Summary of Events and Information	Remarks and references to Appendices
RIBEMONT	Sept. 26/9/27		There is a certain amount of diarrhoea about amongst the troops, & even in officers messes where only boiled water is drunk.	
			I should like to get the water analysed both before & after boiling.	
			The A.D.M.S. asked me to indent for material to build a large filter bed for the bath water @ the Corps rest station @ BUIRE, & also for material for 2 large incinerators. I sent these indents in to his office.	
			The public latrines &c in RIBEMONT require more careful attention: I have seen the Town Major on the subject. The 10 men of M.O. which form the fatigue party for the sanitary work of RIBEMONT are not sufficient.	

T2134. Wt. W708—776. 500000. 4/15. Sir J. C. & S.

Instructions regarding War Diaries and Intelligence Summaries are contained in F. S. Regs., Part II. and the Staff Manual respectively. Title pages will be prepared in manuscript.

WAR DIARY
or
~~INTELLIGENCE~~ SUMMARY.
(Erase heading not required.)

Army Form C. 2118.

Place	Date	Hour	Summary of Events and Information	Remarks and references to Appendices
			There are 4 horsefall destructors & one pelgin incinerators each requiring 1 man to look after them, & this leaves only 6 men to look after the place, which is not enough, & of these 6 men only 4 are available for work as one is required to cook the men's meals & one acts as a quartermaster.	WV
RIBEMONT	28 Sept.		A brigade of the 55th Division came in to RIBEMONT today & altho they have been in only a few hours they have already got their billets in a filthy condition. There is no attempt apparently @ sanitation & empty food tins &c are thrown everywhere with food refuse. The troops appear to have no idea of cleanliness. I have complained to the Town Major & advised him to write to the respective O/C's units on the matter.	

T2134. Wt. W708—776. 500000. 4/15. Sir J. C. & S.

Instructions regarding War Diaries and Intelligence Summaries are contained in F. S. Regs., Part II. and the Staff Manual respectively. Title pages will be prepared in manuscript.

WAR DIARY
or
~~INTELLIGENCE SUMMARY.~~
(Erase heading not required.)

Army Form C. 2118.

Place	Date	Hour	Summary of Events and Information	Remarks and references to Appendices
			The civilians in a few cases are responsible for a great proportion of the insanitary conditions, & are just as bad after they have promised to rectify matters. It is impossible to clear up their rubbish as well as that of the troops. There ought to be a contract for keeping the place clean between the Town Major & the Mayor as we had at NIEPPE & STEENWERCK between the Mayors & "Q" of this Division.	
			Sanitation of this division units is fair, but needs constant supervision.	H.V.
RIBEMONT	29.		Rain has again made everything in a fearful mess. Found that the corps engineers were building filter beds for the baths @ the corps rest station. I am collecting material for incinerators however,	

Instructions regarding War Diaries and Intelligence Summaries are contained in F. S. Regs., Part II. and the Staff Manual respectively. Title pages will be prepared in manuscript.

WAR DIARY
or
INTELLIGENCE SUMMARY.
(Erase heading not required.)

Army Form C. 2118.

Place	Date	Hour	Summary of Events and Information	Remarks and references to Appendices
			hopes to build one like the one erected for the D.A.C. near NIEPPE.	
			It has been reported to me by one of my men that men are still taken off San. work to go on to other work. One unit – the 74th Inf. Brig. H.Q. has allowed this to occur, & they had applied to me to have one of my men attached permanently to them for san. work as they found it necessary to have someone. I cannot spare one of my men, nor is it necessary if the san. man is kept only for his work. I reported this to the A.D.M.S.	H.V.
RIBEMONT	30 Sept.		Nothing to note today: war diary has been sent in by this afternoon.	H.V.

T2134. Wt. W708—776. 500000. 4/15. Sir J. C. & S.

War Diary

82nd Sanitary Section

October 1916

41st Div.

Oct. 1916

VOLUME VI

War Diary for
Oct 1916

Sanitary Section 84.

H. Vickers
O.C. Capt

Instructions regarding War Diaries and Intelligence Summaries are contained in F. S. Regs., Part II. and the Staff Manual respectively. Title pages will be prepared in manuscript.

WAR DIARY
or
~~INTELLIGENCE~~ SUMMARY.
(Erase heading not required.)

Army Form C. 2118.

84th SANITARY SECTION. No. ... Date 1/10/16.

VOL VI SHEET 1

Place	Date	Hour	Summary of Events and Information	Remarks and references to Appendices
	1916			
RIBEMONT	Oct 1.		123 Inf. Brigade moves out of our area & so are not within reach of this section. The 41st Div artillery stayed behind in the line after the Division moved out a fortnight ago, & so have also not been within reach of this section.	
			I arranged with our Camp Commandant to send 2 men up to our new Div. H.Q. tomorrow morning & superintend a fatigue party @ FRICOURT who were to clean up the place.	A.V.
RIBEMONT	2.		2 men of this section left for the new advanced Div. H.Q. @ FRICOURT. The fatigue party of 50 men arranged by the Camp Commandant did not arrive. One man of this section with 8 fatigue men from Div. H.Q. was left @ FRICOURT to proceed with the cleaning	

T.2134. Wt. W708—776. 500000. 4/15. Sir J. C. & S.

Instructions regarding War Diaries and Intelligence Summaries are contained in F. S. Regs., Part II. and the Staff Manual respectively. Title pages will be prepared in manuscript.

WAR DIARY

or

~~INTELLIGENCE SUMMARY.~~

(Erase heading not required.)

Army Form C. 2118.

2

Place	Date	Hour	Summary of Events and Information	Remarks and references to Appendices
			the new advanced HQ.	
			The V Corps rest station @ BUIRE was ~~[illegible]~~ supplied c̄ 2 large "covered in" incinerators by this section & attempts were made to clean up the place.	
			The plans submitted by me for a large fixed tank for the ~~incinerators~~ washhouse @ V Corps Rest Stn were refused & the Corps engineers installed their own soakpit &c.	
			I had occasion to report to the Town Major @ RIBEMONT on the dirty state of some of the billets under his care. The no of men at his disposal for sanitary work is quite inadequate for keeping the place in a sanitary condition.	
			I have had to dispose of some more of the superfluous	

T2134. Wt. W708–776. 500000. 4/15. Sir J. C. & S.

Instructions regarding War Diaries and Intelligence Summaries are contained in F. S. Regs., Part II. and the Staff Manual respectively. Title pages will be prepared in manuscript.

WAR DIARY
or
~~INTELLIGENCE SUMMARY.~~
(Erase heading not required.)

Army Form C. 2118.

3

Place	Date	Hour	Summary of Events and Information	Remarks and references to Appendices
			equipment of this section, & ~~handed~~ sent it over to ordnance railhead this morning. We have now reduced our sectional equipment to the minimum as far as I can see. The A.D.M.S. has been utilising the lorry of this section for his office staff. This has necessitated two journeys for the lorry wherever we have moved, & tho' it works all right now that we are moving only short distances it would be impossible if the Div. had to move any considerable distance. The lorry has also been utilised by the Field Ambulance of this Division to replenish their stores, & on 30/9/16 it was sent to DOULLENS on work for the V Corps.	
			Note: A weekly petrol consumption has to be sent in to the Div. Supply Column. Lately the mileage return has been very low: this is due to the frequent congestion	

Instructions regarding War Diaries and Intelligence Summaries are contained in F. S. Regs., Part II. and the Staff Manual respectively. Title pages will be prepared in manuscript.

WAR DIARY
or
~~INTELLIGENCE SUMMARY.~~
(Erase heading not required.)

Army Form C. 2118.

4

Place	Date	Hour	Summary of Events and Information	Remarks and references to Appendices
			& stoppages of traffic on the roads, when the motor has to be kept running all the time.	
			There is a certain amount of diarrhoea & dysentery amongst the troops. One cause is that estaminets sell drinks made from impure water: these estaminets are to be placed "out of bounds" for troops.	?P.
RIBEMONT	Oct. 3		I sent half a dozen more men of this section to FRICOURT this morning to superintend the work of cleaning up Div. H.Q.	
			I received orders to have this section ready to move @ 7 am 4/10/16.	
			I sent some of the equipment of this section on to the new "B" Echelon of Div. H.Q. near BECORDEL & left it there in	

Instructions regarding War Diaries and Intelligence Summaries are contained in F. S. Regs., Part II. and the Staff Manual respectively. Title pages will be prepared in manuscript.

WAR DIARY
or
~~INTELLIGENCE SUMMARY.~~
(Erase heading not required.)

Army Form C. 2118.

5

Place	Date	Hour	Summary of Events and Information	Remarks and references to Appendices
			charge of two men of this section.	
RIBEMONT	Oct. 4		Main portion of this section left RIBEMONT at 7 am & marched to MEDICAL DUMP N.E. of MAMETZ, & its new position.	
			Remainder of section left in lorry at 8.45. am.	
			The lorry is being largely used by the A.D.M.S. for moving his office material & that of his mess. This causes great inconvenience & extra work, & is not the use for which the lorry was intended.	
			We "bivouaced" at new position: erected our own latrines &c & set out @ once to carry on the usual sanitary work amongst our own Div troops.	
			With so many troops around the work is very difficult, & the whole area is in a disgusting condition.	
			Shell holes are used for as depositories for all Sorts	

T2134. Wt. W708–776. 500000. 4/15. Sir J. C. & S.

Instructions regarding War Diaries and Intelligence Summaries are contained in F. S. Regs., Part II. and the Staff Manual respectively. Title pages will be prepared in manuscript.

WAR DIARY
or
INTELLIGENCE SUMMARY.
(Erase heading not required.)

Army Form C. 2118.

6

Place	Date	Hour	Summary of Events and Information	Remarks and references to Appendices
			of rubbish & refuse, & even as latrines. I intend to make units in this division cover in all shell holes in their area.	W.V.
N.E. of MAMETZ.	October. 5		I ~~have~~ sent off 2 men to each of the A.D.S. at FLAT IRON COPSE & THISTLE DUMP to attend to the sanitation. They came back, after going over these places, & proceeded to make box latrine seats which were to be sent up with the ration carts.	
			The MEDICAL DUMP here (c of [illegible] F Amb of this division) has a no. of old trenches & shell holes in its area which are filled c̄ rubbish & excreta. I was told by the D.A.D.M.S. some time ago to leave the Field Ambs. alone & so have done so, tho' at this medical dump the insanitary conditions are v. bad.	
			Some attempt ought to be made to erect public latrines	

T2134. Wt. W708–776. 500000. 4/15. Sir J. C. & S.

Instructions regarding War Diaries and Intelligence Summaries are contained in F. S. Regs., Part II. and the Staff Manual respectively. Title pages will be prepared in manuscript.

WAR DIARY
or
INTELLIGENCE SUMMARY.
(Erase heading not required.)

Army Form C. 2118.

4

Place	Date	Hour	Summary of Events and Information	Remarks and references to Appendices
			in these areas. I have no men to spare to do this tho', & see no prospect of getting any. As far as we have been able to trace our own Div. units, they have been visited, & are fairly satisfactory. The wet weather of the last few days has prevented the burning of manure, & in many cases it has been buried in shell holes & well covered over. There is a good deal of dysentery about, & one cause is said to be the drainage of foul surface water into springs & wells. Two men of this section have been left behind at "A" Echelon. Div H.Q. at FRICOURT to supervise there. Three men of this section are with "B" Echelon near BECORDEL. There is in addition ~~the~~ one man of this	

T2134. Wt. W708–776. 500000. 4/15. Sir J. C. & S.

Instructions regarding War Diaries and Intelligence Summaries are contained in F. S. Regs., Part II. and the Staff Manual respectively. Title pages will be prepared in manuscript.

WAR DIARY
or
~~INTELLIGENCE SUMMARY.~~
(Erase heading not required.)

Army Form C. 2118.

8

Place	Date	Hour	Summary of Events and Information	Remarks and references to Appendices
			section permanently attached to Div. H.Q.	W.V.
N.E. of MAMETZ	Oct. 6.		I have put 3 men on water duties to test frequently all water stations in this area & to test samples of water from water carts & see that the water is efficiently chlorinated. These tests & all particulars are to be kept in duplicate, one copy being for my own reference & the other for the A.D.M.S. according to instructions.	
			All units in this Div. have been visited by one or other of this section & fairly satisfactory reports are given.	W.V.
N.E. of MAMETZ.	Oct. 7.		I found that drinking water @ Y Corps station @ MONTAUBAN was insufficiently chlorinated by the men on duty there.	

T2134. Wt. W708—776. 500000. 4/15. Sir J. C. & S.

Army Form C. 2118.

Instructions regarding War Diaries and Intelligence Summaries are contained in F. S. Regs., Part II. and the Staff Manual respectively. Title pages will be prepared in manuscript.

WAR DIARY
or
~~INTELLIGENCE SUMMARY.~~
(Erase heading not required.)

9

Place	Date	Hour	Summary of Events and Information	Remarks and references to Appendices
			I have been insisting on units in this Div filling in all shell holes &c.	
			I have suggested to the A.D.M.S. that water cart men of this Div should chlorinate their own water carts, & not leave it to water station men, as the chlorination is not always done efficiently.	
			We have been making large nos. of box seats for latrines & urinals & grease traps for the units in this Div. – obtaining boxes & wood from the D.A.C.	
			Altogether this is the most favourable position we have been in as regards being near the various units. Two of my men are still on light duty as convalescents.	

T2134. Wt. W708–776. 500000. 4/15. Sir J. C. & S.

Instructions regarding War Diaries and Intelligence Summaries are contained in F. S. Regs., Part II. and the Staff Manual respectively. Title pages will be prepared in manuscript.

WAR DIARY
or
~~INTELLIGENCE SUMMARY~~.
(Erase heading not required.)

Army Form C. 2118.

10

Place	Date	Hour	Summary of Events and Information	Remarks and references to Appendices
			We have labelled up any hitherto untested water supplies.	N.V.
N.E. of MAMETZ	Oct. 9		I had to go to the A.D.S. at FLAT IRON COPSE for duty yesterday: leaving section in charge of my Staff Sergeant. The ordinary work of section was carried on as usual in my absence.	N.V.
N.E. of MAMETZ	Oct. 10.		I received information this morning that this Div was moving down from this area, & have given the necessary instructions: we are to move to FRICOURT.	
			The R.E. of this Division were using short trench latrines in disobedience to D.R.O. & Corps order. The M.O. refused to have deep trenches & box seats, as he said they	

T2134. Wt. W708—776. 500000. 4/15. Sir J. C. & S.

Instructions regarding War Diaries and Intelligence Summaries are contained in F. S. Regs., Part II. and the Staff Manual respectively. Title pages will be prepared in manuscript.

WAR DIARY
or
~~INTELLIGENCE~~ SUMMARY.
(Erase heading not required.)

Army Form C. 2118.

Place	Date	Hour	Summary of Events and Information	Remarks and references to Appendices
			were a source of infection. They may be but need not be if they are looked after properly & cleaned frequently.	
			Filling in of shell holes is a difficult matter in some cases as there is no loose earth with which to fill them.	
			More public latrines & urinals, & incinerators are required amongst such large bodies of troops. I can not get anybody to build them, & a large amount of ground is being fouled in consequence.	H.V.
FRICOURT Oct 11.	Oct 11		The section left their location N.E. of MAMETZ on orders from the A.D.M.S. & proceeded to FRICOURT. As the 30th Div. had taken over all the camp at FRICOURT I bivouaced just South of FRICOURT & reported my arrival to the A.D.M.S.	

Instructions regarding War Diaries and Intelligence Summaries are contained in F. S. Regs., Part II. and the Staff Manual respectively. Title pages will be prepared in manuscript.

WAR DIARY
or
~~INTELLIGENCE SUMMARY.~~
(Erase heading not required.)

Army Form C. 2118.

12

Place	Date	Hour	Summary of Events and Information	Remarks and references to Appendices
			I endeavoured to find out the units of this Div, but without success as no notification of their location had been given to me.	H.T.
FRICOURT	Oct 12.		I went to see the A.D.M.S. at H.Q. at BUIRE CAMP & was told that I had to proceed c̄ section to BECORDEL adjoining 124 Inf. Brigade; no orders to this effect had reached me altho it was said that orders had gone on to me to move. Some of the Div. units had been found & visited by men of this section.	
			Later orders came thro from A.D.M.S. to proceed to BUIRE Camp & bivouac c̄ Div. H.Q.	H.T.
BUIRE [illegible]	13 [?]			

T2134. Wt. W708—776. 500000. 4/15. Sir J. C. & S.

Instructions regarding War Diaries and Intelligence Summaries are contained in F. S. Regs., Part II. and the Staff Manual respectively. Title pages will be prepared in manuscript.

WAR DIARY
or
~~INTELLIGENCE SUMMARY.~~
(Erase heading not required.)

Army Form C. 2118.

13

Place	Date	Hour	Summary of Events and Information	Remarks and references to Appendices
BUIRE Sur Ancre	Oct 13		Section complete moves off from FRICOURT at 8.30 am. Lorry proceeded to BUIRE with sectional equipment: men of section marched to BUIRE. Bivouaced c Div. H.Q. at BUIRE. Proceeded to find units of this Div. at once. No information as to their location was given to me. Found BUIRE camp in a v. dirty condition: particularly around the H.Q. messes. Section is now at full strength within except for one of the permanent N.C.O.s at XV Corps H.Q. at HEILLY.	H.V.
			I sent the men out to the various units immediately after arriving @ BUIRE this morning.	H.V.
BUIRE	Oct. 14		I found it necessary to replace the latrines which were in existence @ BUIRE with better ones. No	

T2134. Wt. W708—776. 500000. 4/15. Sir J. C. & S.

Instructions regarding War Diaries and Intelligence Summaries are contained in F. S. Regs., Part II. and the Staff Manual respectively. Title pages will be prepared in manuscript.

WAR DIARY
or
~~INTELLIGENCE SUMMARY~~.
(Erase heading not required.)

Army Form C. 2118.

14

Place	Date	Hour	Summary of Events and Information	Remarks and references to Appendices
			attempts appear to be made ~~to~~ in laying out camps to study the sanitation & order of things. This occurs wherever we go. Tents are pitched anywhere & anyhow, messes are placed anywhere, cookhouses are allowed amongst sleeping tents, latrines & urinals & grease traps are likewise put anywhere, & the men's tents are intermingled c̄ the officers. We made an attempt to alter these things @ BUIRE but there is no cooperation on the part of various sections; a sanitary section's work is laughed at & its advice is ignored. The result is there is v. little to show for their labour, & on top of it all the A.D.M.S. or G.O.C. blames the sanitary section.	H.V.
BUIRE. sur l'Ancre	Oct	15	One battalion were found to be using short shallow latrines in disobedience to orders. (18 K.R.R.)	

T2134. Wt. W708—776. 500000. 4/15. Sir J. C. & S.

Instructions regarding War Diaries and Intelligence Summaries are contained in F. S. Regs., Part II. and the Staff Manual respectively. Title Pages will be prepared in manuscript.

WAR DIARY
or
~~INTELLIGENCE SUMMARY~~
(Erase heading not required.)

Army Form C. 2118.

15

Place	Date	Hour	Summary of Events and Information	Remarks and references to Appendices
			Every infantry unit in the Division has been visited by me or the section since coming out from the line this last time. I think that in nearly all cases where an insanitary state of affairs exists it is caused by men of Drafts, who know little & care little for sanitation. While continually moving about it is very difficult to follow the units & to insist on their observing Div orders with regard to sanitation. Water supply is good, & there are large numbers of water stations which have been erected by the Corps & Army engineers. Flies are not so bad as when we were in this place 5 weeks ago. The N.C.O. belonging to this section who was attached to XV Corps H.Q. at HEILLY reported back to me this eve. Section is now full strength. Warning order has been issued that we are to move back out of XV Corps area tomorrow. No entraining orders or times of trains have come thro' yet, tho' it is 10 p.m.	[illegible]

2149 Wt. W14957/M90 750,000 1/16 J.B.C. & A. Forms/C.2118/12.

Instructions regarding War Diaries and Intelligence Summaries are contained in F. S. Regs., Part II. and the Staff Manual respectively. Title Pages will be prepared in manuscript.

WAR DIARY
or
~~INTELLIGENCE SUMMARY~~
(Erase heading not required.)

Army Form C. 2118.

16

Place	Date	Hour	Summary of Events and Information	Remarks and references to Appendices
HALLENCOURT	Oct 16		Orders came thro' @ 2 am this morning that main body of San sec was to entrain at EDGEHILL @ 14 hours 16/10/16. Detraining station to be AIRAINES. I left BUIRE camp in Lorry @ 9 hours & proceeded via AMIENS, PICQUIGNY & AIRAINES & arrived at HALLENCOURT at 13-40 hours. Nothing & no one was available to put on to Sanitary work & erect latrines &c. I could not get on with anything altho' I proceeded to draw out a working table for everyone in the section in order that they might start 1st thing in the morning. I had been given a list showing billets of every unit in the Division so that I knew exactly where to send men & what to do. This billeting list has been handed to me in advance for the 1st time since we have been abroad. I have had to ask for it every time before; the result being that much valuable time has been lost in hunting for units. Up till 11 p.m. nothing was known as to when the section would arrive, & it was @ any rate not expected tonight. This will upset all my plans of getting to work 1st thing in the morning.	R.V.

2449 Wt. W14957/M90 750,000 1/16 J.B.C. & A. Forms/C.2118/12.

Army Form C. 2118.

14

Instructions regarding War Diaries and Intelligence Summaries are contained in F. S. Regs., Part II. and the Staff Manual respectively. Title Pages will be prepared in manuscript.

WAR DIARY

or

~~INTELLIGENCE SUMMARY~~

(Erase heading not required.)

Place	Date	Hour	Summary of Events and Information	Remarks and references to Appendices
HALLENCOURT	Oct 17		I had to try & erect some latrines with the help of one of my lorry drivers - the other one I had to send to fetch rations. The section did not arrive till 3.45 P.M. having taken from 2 P.M. the previous day to come by train - a distance of not more than 40 miles. The result of this was that there were only two hours at the most available of daylight to do some work, & in this I was further handicapped by not being able to find any suitable material to build proper structures. This state of affairs is most unsatisfactory: everyone demands everything from the sanitary section & no one will help himself: units are supposed to build their own latrines & look after them & it is the work of the sanitary section to see that sanitation is in good order, not to do the work for other people. In many cases we do erect structures &c for units but each unit is primarily responsible for its own area, & it is only ~~[illegible]~~ we can spare the time that we have helped units in this respect. Moving frequently as the Division has been doing for the	

2449 Wt. W14957/M90 750,000 1/16 J.B.C. & A. Forms/C.2118/12.

Instructions regarding War Diaries and Intelligence Summaries are contained in F. S. Regs., Part II. and the Staff Manual respectively. Title Pages will be prepared in manuscript.

WAR DIARY
or
~~INTELLIGENCE SUMMARY~~

(Erase heading not required.)

Army Form C. 2118.

18

Place	Date	Hour	Summary of Events and Information	Remarks and references to Appendices
			Last two months there's a lot ~~[illegible]~~ work on the San Sec, for without a doubt sanitation is greatly neglected by units. Everywhere one finds heaps of refuse & dirt left behind by previous units. Our units dump their rubbish on the existing scrap heaps & then declare that they "thought that was the place for rubbish". Sanitation ought to be part of an O/C's work, whereas it is nearly always left to the most junior NCOs & men who are defaulters & men who are "no good for anything else".	
			NOTE I would like to make a note again here that the lorry of this section is used too much for carrying the office material of the A.D.M.S. & the mess kit. In this last move fully 1/4 of the lorry load was made up of boxes & office matter belonging to the A.D.M.S. & mess. We have had to cast a large amount of our war establishment equipment, including the 2 box disinfectors, Clamper cans, tent poles &c in order to make it possible to make it possible to move in anything like reasonable time. The San Sec lorry was meant	

2449 Wt. W14957/M90 750,000 1/16 J.B.C. & A. Forms/C.2118/12.

Army Form C. 2118.

19

Instructions regarding War Diaries and Intelligence Summaries are contained in F. S. Regs., Part II. and the Staff Manual respectively. Title Pages will be prepared in manuscript.

WAR DIARY
or
~~INTELLIGENCE SUMMARY~~
(Erase heading not required.)

Place	Date	Hour	Summary of Events and Information	Remarks and references to Appendices
			for the use of the San. Sec. We have been allotted practically no disinfectants & material for erecting Latrines, grease traps &c, in this last move owing to the amount of material which we have had to carry & which does not belong to the San Sec.	
			I have made out a working table for the men of this section for tomorrow, & will start off at the earliest possible moment.	
			Latrines &c do not exist in the place altho it has been used for troops before.	H.V.
HALLENCOURT	Oct 19.		I sent out the majority of the men on their usual patrols, & also the 3 water duty men, to the units of this Division.	
			A difficulty has arisen with regard to rationing of this section. The Div Train have allotted the 12[illegible] Brigade Dump to us for some time, & this has caused great inconvenience.	

2449 Wt. W14957/M90 750,000 1/16 J.B.C. & A. Forms/C.2118/12.

Instructions regarding War Diaries and Intelligence Summaries are contained in F. S. Regs., Part II. and the Staff Manual respectively. Title Pages will be prepared in manuscript.

WAR DIARY
or
~~INTELLIGENCE~~ SUMMARY
(Erase heading not required.)

Army Form C. 2118.

20

Place	Date	Hour	Summary of Events and Information	Remarks and references to Appendices
			21 also means using the Lorry to draw 30 rations from a distant point, altho' we are Div troops attached @ Div. H.Q.	
			The Lorry went off to draw rations at a place about 7 miles away @ 10 am today & has not returned @ 12 midnight.	
			The A.S.C. train will not give us a limber for the purpose.	
HALLENCOURT	Oct 19		Lorry returned at 1.30 am with rations for section, & also for the whole of a battalion. I had orders to proceed to LONGPRE by 4 am to join convoy of 17th Div Supply Column & proceed with it to new area. Lorry was ready loaded with San Sec equipment & A.D.M.S. office equipment & luggage from mess by 2.35 am. I left HALLENCOURT in Lorry at 3 am. & proceeded to LONGPRE, arrived there 3.50 am & joined the 17th Div A.S.C. which left LONGPRE at 6.45 am, & proceeded to VIGNACOURT, then via DOULLENS, ST POL, AIRE, HAZEBROOK & FLETRE, arriving at last place @ 10 PM.	

2449 Wt. W14957/M90 750,000 1/16 J.B.C. & A. Forms/C.2118/12.

Instructions regarding War Diaries and Intelligence Summaries are contained in F. S. Regs., Part II. and the Staff Manual respectively. Title Pages will be prepared in manuscript.

WAR DIARY
or
~~INTELLIGENCE SUMMARY~~
(Erase heading not required.)

Army Form C. 2118.

21

Place	Date	Hour	Summary of Events and Information	Remarks and references to Appendices
			The rest of section were to leave HALLENCOURT on night of 20th, entrain at LONGPRE at 10.11 PM. Detraining station CAESTRE.	W.V.
FLETRE	Oct 20.		I proceeded to work with San. Squad from Div. H.Q. to clean up & erect the necessary latrines. I had no materials & had to ~~make~~ improvise as best I could.	W.V.
FLETRE	Oct 21.		I left @ 8.30 am with ADMS. for the new area, H.Q. at RENINGHELST. I went over details of area with O/C San. Sec. from whom we are taking over. I arranged with him to send an ~~advance~~ advance party of this section on 22/10/16, & take over from him the routine work, which is exactly on the same lines as we were working on in the PLOEGSTEERT area. There are 2 carts for carting refuse in RENINGHELST, & I hope to get horses from the F. Amb. as before. They are handing over to us a Clayton Sulphur disinfector & ~~sundry~~ maps & plans of the area.	

2449 Wt. W14957/M90 750,000 1/16 J.B.C. & A. Forms/C.2118/12.

Instructions regarding War Diaries and Intelligence Summaries are contained in F. S. Regs., Part II. and the Staff Manual respectively. Title Pages will be prepared in manuscript.

WAR DIARY

or

~~INTELLIGENCE SUMMARY~~

(Erase heading not required.)

Army Form C. 2118.

22

Place	Date	Hour	Summary of Events and Information	Remarks and references to Appendices
			There are a number of P.B. men at work in the (town of) RENINGHELST, & I have asked the A.D.M.S. for the services of some P.B. men. There is a large refuse dump & some incinerators. Box seat latrines & deep trenches are used nearly every where, & in some cases pails are used & excreta burnt.	
			The section arrived about midday, & the FODEN steam lorry disinfector also arrived about midday, having come up from VIVIER MILL via VIGNACOURT, ABBEVILLE, DOULLENS, ST OMER & HAZEBROUCK alone: no definite orders were given to the drivers as to where to go after going to VIGNACOURT, & they came up here with no escort. They ran short of coal & had to obtain it from an R.T.O. at some railhead.	R.P.
FLETRE	Oct 22		The affair about using the lorry to draw rations has been settled — for good I hope. The rations for this section ~~have been~~ are to be drawn by ordy	

Army Form C. 2118.

23

Instructions regarding War Diaries and Intelligence Summaries are contained in F. S. Regs., Part II. and the Staff Manual respectively. Title Pages will be prepared in manuscript.

WAR DIARY
or
~~INTELLIGENCE SUMMARY~~
(Erase heading not required.)

Place	Date	Hour	Summary of Events and Information	Remarks and references to Appendices
			the H.Q. wagons. Advance party of 10 men in charge of Staff Sergeant leaves for new area tomorrow morning. The patrol men of this section were out all day on their rounds, but found very few of our Div. units, as most of them had moved up into the new area. Note. The following is extract from 41st Div. RAMC. orders with regard to moving into new area; concerning this section. "Officer Commanding Sanitary Section will make arrangements as to detail of Sanitary work with officer Commanding Sanitary Section 41st. Div., & the sending forward of an advance party. O.C. Sanitary Section will have his H.Q. at RENINGHELST." I arranged to have one man from H.Q. sent up with the advance party of this section in the morning. I have started to have a stove made from specifications given me at HALLENCOURT. It will be necessary to modify	

2449 Wt. W14957/M90 750,000 1/16 J.B.C. & A. Forms/C.2118/12.

Army Form C. 2118.

Instructions regarding War Diaries and Intelligence Summaries are contained in F. S. Regs., Part II. and the Staff Manual respectively. Title Pages will be prepared in manuscript.

WAR DIARY
or
~~INTELLIGENCE SUMMARY~~
(Erase heading not required.)

Place	Date	Hour	Summary of Events and Information	Remarks and references to Appendices
			these plans, as they are not perfect.	H.V.
FLETRE	Oct 23	8am	Advance party of 9 men in charge of Staff Sergeant & one man of H.Q. Sanitary squad, left here at 8 a.m. this morning, taking with them the greater part of sections equipment.	
			Rest of men are out on patrol work as far as possible. Two men are making the "type" stove.	
			An "area" Commandant has been appointed for the new area. He will deal with all questions of accomodation huts, accomodation, transport lines &c. This is a useful institution, for it ought now to be able to fix responsibility regarding the condition of sanitary matters in the area.	H.V.
RENINGHELST BELGIUM	Oct 24.		Section left FLETRE at 8.30 am. & proceeded to RENINGHELST. arrived there 9.15 am. FODEN Steam lorry accompanied sanitary Section lorry.	

2449 Wt. W14957/M90 750,000 1/16 J.B.C. & A. Forms/C.2118/12.

Army Form C. 2118.

Instructions regarding War Diaries and Intelligence Summaries are contained in F. S. Regs., Part II. and the Staff Manual respectively. Title Pages will be prepared in manuscript.

WAR DIARY
or
~~INTELLIGENCE SUMMARY~~
(Erase heading not required.)

25

Place	Date	Hour	Summary of Events and Information	Remarks and references to Appendices
			We found that civilian "cabinets" were being used by the troops. There were practically no military latrines or urinals. The existing incinerators were half broken down. Human excreta was being buried, or trench latrines were being used. There was no proper system for compelling the civilians to dispose of their rubbish in a sanitary manner, & the streets were in a very dirty state in Reninghelst.	
			We took over 2 carts for collecting rubbish in RENINGHELST, one "Clayton" disinfector.	
			I at once put men on to cleaning out billets in this town, while I sent some men out on patrol duty on the Div. area	
			I have asked the R.E. to supply me with material to build a number of latrines for the various messes, & for "Public Latrines".	[illegible]
RENINGHELST	Oct 25.		I arranged for horses for the rubbish carts with the Field Ambulance in RENINGHELST.	

2449 Wt. W14957/M90 750,000 1/16 J.B.C. & A. Forms/C.2118/12.

Instructions regarding War Diaries and Intelligence Summaries are contained in F. S. Regs., Part II. and the Staff Manual respectively. Title Pages will be prepared in manuscript.

WAR DIARY
or
~~INTELLIGENCE SUMMARY~~
(Erase heading not required.)

Army Form C. 2118.

26

Place	Date	Hour	Summary of Events and Information	Remarks and references to Appendices
			I applied to "Q" for fatigue men – 1 NCO & 10 men to report here daily @ 8 am.	
			Some of my own section are @ work making incinerators both for manure & refuse. I have found that small quantities of excreta can be burned without nuisance on an ordinary open incinerator.	
			I started work on the cleaning of roads in the place.	
			Various men of the section have been out amongst the Div troops all day.	
			Three men of the section have been out on water duties all day.	
			(A good deal of time is lost by ~~having~~ to employ the section carpenter in constructing "mess" furniture. He could be better employed in putting together latrines &c.)	
~~Oct~~ RENINGHELST.	Oct 26.		I have divided up the Div. area into 3 districts for the purpose of sanitary work, & have placed one N.C.O. & three men to take charge of each	

2449 Wt. W14957/M90 750,000 1/16 J.B.C. & A. Forms/C.2118/12.

Instructions regarding War Diaries and Intelligence Summaries are contained in F. S. Regs., Part II. and the Staff Manual respectively. Title Pages will be prepared in manuscript.

WAR DIARY
or
~~INTELLIGENCE SUMMARY~~
(Erase heading not required.)

Army Form C. 2118.

24

Place	Date	Hour	Summary of Events and Information	Remarks and references to Appendices
			district. In addition there is one waterman allotted to each district, which are called W. E. & S. As all the Div. troops are ~~not~~ in yet, these divisions of the area will be altered.	
			Constructional work is delayed owing to the delay of the R.E. in supply timber &c.	
			The water tanks in the Divisional area are in charge of 2 water wardens from the field ambulances, & my watermen go round testing the water supplies & water carts where they can catch them.	
			I arranged with "Q" "A" for 1 N.C.O. & 10 men to be supplied to me daily to act as a fatigue party in RENINGHELST. These men to come from the brigade in rest.	
			Owing to the number of bucket latrines being erected, a large ~~[illegible]~~ amount of extra work is thrown on Sanitary men. More destructors are required, & also more incinerators.	
			The sodden nature of the ground in the area necessitates	

Instructions regarding War Diaries and Intelligence Summaries are contained in F. S. Regs., Part II. and the Staff Manual respectively. Title Pages will be prepared in manuscript.

WAR DIARY
or
~~INTELLIGENCE SUMMARY~~
(Erase heading not required.)

Army Form C. 2118.

28

Place	Date	Hour	Summary of Events and Information	Remarks and references to Appendices
			great care in the construction of pits for absorbing urine & greasy water from the kitchens	
			The R.E. supplied me with "trench revetment frames" for constructing latrines. These are very heavy structures & are very wasteful, as a great amount of good timber is used in the construction of the frames, & it is impossible to break up the frames for timber as the lengths are too short.	
			I will get men on to the work in the morning.	
			I have also obtained the necessary material for constructing [illegible] latrines in the officers' messes in RENINGHELST.	
RENINGHELST.	Oct 27.		We erected a public latrine in RENINGHELST for use by the military.	
			The camps are in a very dirty state. Latrines are of the trench type this is to be abolished, & all excreta is to be burnt, latrines being of the fly proof, seat & pail type.	
			Efficient incinerators have to be built; there is a large amount of dirt & rubbish in the camps left behind by	

Instructions regarding War Diaries and Intelligence Summaries are contained in F. S. Regs., Part II. and the Staff Manual respectively. Title Pages will be prepared in manuscript.

WAR DIARY
or
~~INTELLIGENCE SUMMARY~~
(Erase heading not required.)

Army Form C. 2118.

29

Place	Date	Hour	Summary of Events and Information	Remarks and references to Appendices
			the last Division Manure is either to be burnt or carted away by the farmers. The following are rules to be enforced in the Div. area. 1. All cookhouses, washing benches & latrines are to be covered in, & to be provided with screens on the weather side & connected with the huts or tents by duckboarded walks. 2. Cookhouses & other places where food is cut up or handled must be provided with tables or shelves. On no account must any food be kept on the floor of huts or on the ground. 3. Constant attention to be paid to camp drains to see that they are not choked up with rubbish. 4. There must be a complete system of duck boards in every camp, & duckboarded walks from camps to roads. These roads require constant attention. In nearly all the camps recently taken over the walks require relaying & general overhauling & repair.	

2349 Wt. W14957/M90 750,000 1/16 J.B.C. & A. Forms/C.2118/12.

Instructions regarding War Diaries and Intelligence Summaries are contained in F. S. Regs., Part II. and the Staff Manual respectively. Title Pages will be prepared in manuscript.

WAR DIARY

or

~~INTELLIGENCE SUMMARY~~

(Erase heading not required.)

Army Form C. 2118.

30

Place	Date	Hour	Summary of Events and Information	Remarks and references to Appendices
			5. All latrines to be on the bucket system & excreta to be burned & not buried. Incinerators & destructors for this purpose to be erected without delay. Urinals for use @ night time to be provided outside the men's huts. Cookhouses to be provided with receptacles for refuse. All such refuse to be burnt.	
			6. In every camp a small permanent party will be told off & will be responsible for keep the precincts of camps clear & tidy, keeping duckboards & pathways in order & seeing that drains are kept clear of rubbish.	
			Sawdust for sanitary purposes can be obtained from R.E. workshops.	H.V.

2449 Wt. W14957/M90 750,000 1/16 J.B.C. & A. Forms/C.2118/12.

Army Form C. 2118.

31

Instructions regarding War Diaries and Intelligence Summaries are contained in F. S. Regs., Part II. and the Staff Manual respectively. Title Pages will be prepared in manuscript.

WAR DIARY
or
~~INTELLIGENCE SUMMARY~~

(Erase heading not required.)

Place	Date	Hour	Summary of Events and Information	Remarks and references to Appendices
RENINGHELST	Oct 28.		I went over to STEENVOORDE ~~today~~ with the A.D.M.S to see about the sanitary arrangements of the town. The town is in a very dirty condition. The Town Major has no fatigue men, & street cleaning is entirely neglected. There are no military latrines or incinerators. There are 3 Divisional supply columns in the town, & no provision is made for latrine accomodation refuse is thrown anywhere; kitchen refuse is not burnt, & I could see no grease traps to cookhouses I sent in a report to the A.D.M.S. suggesting improvements on the following lines: a. adequate public latrines, pail & box seat type. b. incinerators for burning excreta & refuse. c. adequate fatigue parties for working the incinerators, & cleaning the streets d. arrangements with the mayor for provision of horse & cart for street cleaning & refuse carting.	

2149 Wt. W14957/M90 750,000 1/16 J.B.C. & A. Forms/C.2118/12.

Instructions regarding War Diaries and Intelligence Summaries are contained in F. S. Regs., Part II. and the Staff Manual respectively. Title Pages will be prepared in manuscript.

WAR DIARY
or
~~INTELLIGENCE SUMMARY~~
(Erase heading not required.)

Army Form C. 2118.

32

Place	Date	Hour	Summary of Events and Information	Remarks and references to Appendices
			I also promised to send over a few men from this section to put the sanitary arrangements in order & to superintend the construction of latrines, & incinerators, if the R.E. would deliver the necessary material. The labour would be found by men of the ambulance section in STEENVOORDE.	
			We erected more latrines in RENINHELST, & the patrol men did their rounds as usual.	
			I have to take men off their patrol work tho' to help in constructional work in RENINGHEST, & thus the work amongst the troops is handicapped.	
			An outbreak of what was diagnosed as measles was supposed to have occurred. Means of disinfection, & isolation were @ once adopted.	
			Fatigue party of men @ work in RENINGHELST.	H.V.
			I am preparing schemes for dealing with the soapy water from the baths @ RENINGHELST, CHIPPEWA &	

2449 Wt. W14957/M90 750,000 1/16 J.B.C. & A. Forms/C.2118/12.

Instructions regarding War Diaries and Intelligence Summaries are contained in F. S. Regs., Part II. and the Staff Manual respectively. Title Pages will be prepared in manuscript.

WAR DIARY
or
~~INTELLIGENCE SUMMARY~~
(Erase heading not required.)

Army Form C. 2118.

33

Place	Date	Hour	Summary of Events and Information	Remarks and references to Appendices
			LA CLYTE. At present there is no method of pumping the soapy water before it runs into the streams, in one case the water is more impure after passing thro' the existing settling chamber than before it enters.	H.V.
RENINGHELST	Oct. 29.		~~[illegible]~~	
			The Foden-thresh disinfector is to be used for disinfecting men's tunics & trousers. I have always considered that it is insufficient to provide clean underclothes to a lousy man: every stitch of his clothing must be disinfected.	
			I sent in plans to A.D.M.S. for dealing with bath & laundry effluent at RENINGHELST, CHIPPEWA & LA CLYTE. An attempt has been made to instal a proper set of sedimentation tanks & filter bed at the ~~laundry~~ @ RENINGHELST, but the plant shows no signs of ever having been used. It was built wrongly too, & could not have been utilised as it stands.	
			The Div. units are gradually cleaning up their camp sites & installing latrines &c of a sanitary & approved type.	

2149 Wt. W14957/M90 750,000 1/16 J.B.C. & A. Forms/C.2118/12.

Instructions regarding War Diaries and Intelligence Summaries are contained in F. S. Regs., Part II. and the Staff Manual respectively. Title Pages will be prepared in manuscript.

WAR DIARY
or
~~INTELLIGENCE SUMMARY~~
(Erase heading not required.)

Army Form C. 2118.

34

Place	Date	Hour	Summary of Events and Information	Remarks and references to Appendices
RENINGHELST.	Oct 30.		The A.D.M.S. asked me to get into communication with the area Commandants at BOESCHEPE & STEENVOORDE & submit a report to him on the treatment of the soapy effluent from the military baths there. I have arranged to visit these places tomorrow, & then submit a report to him on these baths, together with plans for the efficient treatment of the effluents there. 123rd Brigade H.Q. have been neglecting their sanitary arrangements. The brigades HQ have always been neglectful & insanitary. They should have a proper san. squad. A man is supposed to be detailed for san work, but he is nearly all the time on other work. A great deal of work is being done in constructing winter camps for the Div troops. It has been decided to build proper structures as Cookhouses, ablution sheds, latrine sheds, &c. This is a step in the right direction, for these structures are always dumped down in any odd corner. No attention	

2449 Wt. W14957/M90 750,000 1/16 J.B.C. & A. Forms/C.2118/12.

Instructions regarding War Diaries and Intelligence Summaries are contained in F. S. Regs., Part II. and the Staff Manual respectively. Title Pages will be prepared in manuscript.

WAR DIARY

or

~~INTELLIGENCE SUMMARY~~

(Erase heading not required.)

Army Form C. 2118.

35

Place	Date	Hour	Summary of Events and Information	Remarks and references to Appendices
			usually being paid to avoid placing latrines adjoining sleeping quarters. &c.	V.V.
RENINGHELST	Oct 31.		Visited the baths @ BOESCHEPE & STEERNVOORDE this morning, & submitted statement on the treatment of soapy water effluent there. In the former case the effluent is mixed with water from a stream & passes over a weir.	
			More latrines are being erected by this section.	
			Note. In order to do the necessary sanitary work in this new area I find I have quite an insufficient number of men. The men who are doing patrol work are trying to get each camp they visited in a clean condition. This is slow work, but I am of opinion that it is the only way to get things in a satisfactory state. i.e. to: ie	

2449 Wt. W14957/M90 750,000 1/16 J.B.C. & A. Forms/C.2118/12.

Instructions regarding War Diaries and Intelligence Summaries are contained in F. S. Regs., Part II. and the Staff Manual respectively. Title Pages will be prepared in manuscript.

WAR DIARY
or
~~INTELLIGENCE SUMMARY~~
(Erase heading not required.)

Army Form C. 2118.

35

Place	Date	Hour	Summary of Events and Information	Remarks and references to Appendices
			Each man concentrates his attention on a particular site, & works there till it is clean. The men doing district work do not only supervise, they do a great deal of actual labour. There is always something in the form of hoppers, grease traps &c being made by the men @ our workshops. ~~[illegible]~~ The proper way to clean up the camps in this area would be to have a fatigue party of @ least 20 men in charge of an N.C.O. from this section for each camp, & to concentrate & clean up each camp in this way. The O/C San. Sec. should be supplied beforehand when moves are taking place with a list of locations of units. Then with a fatigue party he could clear up & get things in to a sanitary state in very little time.	S.V

2449 Wt. W14957/M90 750,000 1/16 J.B.C. & A. Forms/C.2118/12.

Nov. 1916

41st Div.

140/194 3

84th Sanitary Section.

Vol 7

Secret

War Diary of
Sanitary Section 84. RAMCT.
B.E.F.

H. Vickers
(Capt RAMCT.)

Army Form C. 2118.

WAR DIARY
or
~~INTELLIGENCE SUMMARY~~
(Erase heading not required.)

Instructions regarding War Diaries and Intelligence Summaries are contained in F. S. Regs., Part II. and the Staff Manual respectively. Title Pages will be prepared in manuscript.

Place	Date	Hour	Summary of Events and Information	Remarks and references to Appendices
RENINGHELST.	[illegible] 1		I have readjusted the division of the three districts into which this area was divided for sanitary work. There are 3 districts W, Central & East. One N.C.O. & 3 men are in charge of each district, & one water duty man is alloted to each district.	
			Since we have settled down in this area I have returned to the routine I adopted at PLOEGSTREET, i.e., district men start on their daily rounds at 8.30am. stay out all day, coming in about 4.30 P.M. Each man then gives his report to his own N.C.O. who after noting points in each report, passes them to me.	
			Incinerators are not to be lighted east of a line drawn from KEMMEL brook with Eclusette, so that nothing can be burnt in areas to the east of this line.	
			I am fixing up a room at the Baths here to be used as a disinfecting room for the Clayton disinfector.	
			I gave the A.D.M.S. a general report on the sanitary state of this	

2449 Wt. W14957/M90 750,000 1/16 J.B.C. & A. Forms/C.2118/12.

Army Form C. 2118.

Instructions regarding War Diaries and Intelligence Summaries are contained in F. S. Regs., Part II. and the Staff Manual respectively. Title Pages will be prepared in manuscript.

WAR DIARY
or
~~INTELLIGENCE SUMMARY~~
(Erase heading not required.)

Place	Date	Hour	Summary of Events and Information	Remarks and references to Appendices
			area as we found it. It was briefly thus: Latrines – long deep trench – a few flyproof seats. Incinerators – non existent for the most part: bad generally Urine pits – poor Drying sheds – none Grease traps – a few – non efficient. Cookhouses – indifferent. Manure – dumped ~~or~~ carted by farmers	H.V.
RENINGHELST	Nov 2.		I went over to BOESCHEPPE today to report on the sanitary conditions there. These were very bad. No latrines for troops, no incinerators: no means of cleaning & scavenging. No P.B. men for sanitary work. In my report I recommended the necessary improvements. One of the men of this section is proceeding to STEENVOORDE to take charge of the sanitary arrangements there, & to	

2449 Wt. W14957/M90 750,000 1/16 J.B.C. & A. Forms/C.2118/12.

Army Form C. 2118.

WAR DIARY

or

~~INTELLIGENCE SUMMARY~~

(Erase heading not required.)

Instructions regarding War Diaries and Intelligence Summaries are contained in F. S. Regs., Part II. and the Staff Manual respectively. Title Pages will be prepared in manuscript.

Place	Date	Hour	Summary of Events and Information	Remarks and references to Appendices
			see that the improvements suggested by us are carried out.	
			We are erecting some public latrines in DICKEBUSH, where no provision is made for the troops billeted there.	
			WE disinfected some huts at CHIPPEWA camp which were lousy.	
			Watermen are always out to inspect watercarts & test water & to watch the waterwardens at the water stations. So far we have found very little wrong with the chlorination of water.	
			I sent in a memorandum to the A.D.M.S. suggesting that a party of pioneers, consisting of bricklayers & carpenters & 15-20 in number, be attached to this section for a time, so that we could go thro the various camps & build efficient durable incinerators & other necessary sanitary structures. I proposed going thro the camps methodically & surely. The scheme for building winter quarters for the troops in this area made no provision for the erection of incinerators, Soakage pits & urinals, & these are absolutely necessary.	H.V.

Army Form C. 2118.

Instructions regarding War Diaries and Intelligence Summaries are contained in F. S. Regs., Part II. and the Staff Manual respectively. Title Pages will be prepared in manuscript.

WAR DIARY
or
~~INTELLIGENCE SUMMARY~~
(Erase heading not required.)

Place	Date	Hour	Summary of Events and Information	Remarks and references to Appendices
RENINGHELST.	Nov 15		I was on leave from Nov 4 to 14th, & the following notes were made by the Staff Sergeant of this section & by the M O who was acting as locum for me.	
			Notes by Staff Sergeant.	
RENINGHELST.	Nov 4.		General inspection of the town revealed several dirty areas which will be scavenged, & rubbish incinerated. An extra public latrine was found necessary. The existing latrine at the Y.M.C.A was repaired & covered in & enlarged to form a public one. The existing urinals demolished, & trough urinals substituted. There are now two good public latrines in the village, but only one public urinal: indents have gone in for material for more urinals.	
			Latrine accomodation at "G" office found insufficient & rectified. Approaches to some messes need duckboarding.	

2449 Wt. W14957/M90 750,000 1/16 J.B.C. & A. Forms/C.2118/12.

Army Form C. 2118.

WAR DIARY
or
~~INTELLIGENCE SUMMARY~~
(Erase heading not required.)

Instructions regarding War Diaries and Intelligence Summaries are contained in F. S. Regs., Part II. and the Staff Manual respectively. Title Pages will be prepared in manuscript.

Place	Date	Hour	Summary of Events and Information	Remarks and references to Appendices
RENINGHELST.	Nov 5.		Water supply from DICKEBUSCH LAKE was inspected. All the tanks were inspected & water wardens seen. Certain complaints re the water were dealt with. DICKEBUSCH VILLAGE was inspected. There was only one Public Latrine recently put up by this section, trench latrines were found behind numerous billets. Two further public latrines have been installed & accomodation for officers is being seen to. Incinerators are being erected there.	
"	6.		Visited STEENVOORDE to see area commandant with regard to San. arrangements of the Town. No sanitation existed. The following are urgently needed: (1). Three 6 seater Public latrines & urinals (2). Two two seater Latrines for officers at the station. (3). Two well built incinerators for incineration of refuse & excreta. We supplied estimates for above to area commandant, who will notify us when the materials come to hand. We have offered	

2449 Wt. W14957/M90 750,000 1/16 J.B.C. & A. Forms/C.2118/12.

Instructions regarding War Diaries and Intelligence Summaries are contained in F. S. Regs., Part II. and the Staff Manual respectively. Title Pages will be prepared in manuscript.

WAR DIARY
or
~~INTELLIGENCE SUMMARY~~
(Erase heading not required.)

Army Form C. 2118.

Place	Date	Hour	Summary of Events and Information	Remarks and references to Appendices
			our advice & assistance in this construction	
			The water supply was gone into & found unsatisfactory. Water is supplied from a stream by a pump. Owing to the nature of the ground there is likely to be great surface contamination. The use of this supply should be discontinued, & excellent water should be drawn from 3 wells. The water officer Xth Corps says the latter give one of the best supplies in France.	
RENINGHELST	Nov 7.		Visited BOESCHEPE to interview area commandant. For the present sanitary arrangements suffice, but when extra troops arrive present arrangements will be inadequate. The area commandant had no sanitary squad, & consequently there is no supervision. A man from this section has been sent there for supervision, but without a sanitary squad little can be done.	
			The water supply has been tested by us, & necessary water boards erected. Some supplies were found to be unfit for drinking or cooking.	

2449 Wt. W14957/M90 750,000 1/16 J.B.C. & A. Forms/C.2118/12.

Army Form C. 2118.

WAR DIARY
or
~~INTELLIGENCE~~ SUMMARY
(Erase heading not required.)

Instructions regarding War Diaries and Intelligence Summaries are contained in F. S. Regs., Part II. and the Staff Manual respectively. Title Pages will be prepared in manuscript.

Place	Date	Hour	Summary of Events and Information	Remarks and references to Appendices
RENINGHELST.	Nov 8.		Today I visited the rest billets of Ontario, Alberta & Quebec. These camps were found to be in a deplorable condition, & each requires immediate attention. These camps should be first drained, & all key points protected, & any barrages removed from adjoining streams & ditches. Duckboarding is needed in large quantities. A well built brick incinerator suitable for excreta & rubbish should be built in each camp. Latrine accomodation should be increased, leaky huts should receive attention, & also kitchens & drying rooms. The area commandant & CRE have been approached & arrangements have been made to start with Alberta camp.	
"	9.		In accordance with instructions received I inspected the various estaminets & cafes etc in RENINGHELST. The cleansing of all drinking "materials" was ordered.	
"	10		MICMAC CAMP was visited today. Bde Transport lines are	

2449 Wt. W14957/M90 750,000 1/16 J.B.C. & A. Forms/C.2118/12.

Instructions regarding War Diaries and Intelligence Summaries are contained in F. S. Regs., Part II. and the Staff Manual respectively. Title Pages will be prepared in manuscript.

WAR DIARY
or
~~INTELLIGENCE SUMMARY~~
(Erase heading not required.)

Army Form C. 2118.

Place	Date	Hour	Summary of Events and Information	Remarks and references to Appendices
			being built here. Much time & attention should be given to drainage The units are working hard to get things in a respectable state.	

2449 Wt. W14957/M90 750,000 1/16 J.B.C. & A. Forms/C.2118/12.

Army Form C. 2118.

WAR DIARY
or
~~INTELLIGENCE~~ SUMMARY

(Erase heading not required.)

Instructions regarding War Diaries and Intelligence Summaries are contained in F. S. Regs., Part II. and the Staff Manual respectively. Title Pages will be prepared in manuscript.

Place	Date	Hour	Summary of Events and Information	Remarks and references to Appendices
			NOTES by M.O. acting i/c 9 SS 84 in my absence.	
RENINGHELST	Nov 3.	7 p.m.	Capt. Vickers left at 7 p.m on leave and I assumed charge of San Sec 84 41st Div. Nothing was handed over.	
"	4th		Inspected RENINGHELST this morning and found that the general condition of the place is very dirty. The question of incinerator and latrine accommodation should be gone into as some of the existing latrines are very bad - particularly those known as the Public Latrines, situated near the Y.M.C.A. Hut. The incinerators run by the Sanitary Section are working all right, but their surroundings are bad; only time & weather conditions will improve them. I visited the kitchens in connection with the Officers Messes and several were dirty; the cooks were warned. The approach to R.Es kitchen behind 'B Mess' is very bad and duck boards are urgently required; also the structure used as the kitchen is poor, very small, and contains no arrangement for storing of food etc. The storage of water at Y.M.C.A. Hut requires attention and a man has been detailed for this purpose. At present there are 42 pails to be cleared & cleaned before 9 a.m and the labour at my disposal is inadequate for carrying out this, and in a very short time further latrines will be erected	

2449 Wt. W14957/M90 750,000 1/16 J.B.C. & A. Forms/C.2118/12.

Army Form C. 2118.

Instructions regarding War Diaries and Intelligence Summaries are contained in F. S. Regs., Part II. and the Staff Manual respectively. Title Pages will be prepared in manuscript.

WAR DIARY
or
INTELLIGENCE SUMMARY
(Erase heading not required.)

Place	Date	Hour	Summary of Events and Information	Remarks and references to Appendices
RENINGHELST	9 Nov 4th		increasing our number to 53. I went through the Reports of the different Inspectors i/c of Districts none of which called for my personal attention as the points raised are being dealt with and further reports will be sent to me Correspondence 1 letter received from M.O. 10th Queens re quality of water issued to his battalion. Instructions given in connection with this and M.O. written to (See S. 249) 2 Letter from Water & Salvage Officer POPERINGHE re Water Wardens' Reports - re question of water the OC let me have daily copies of Water Wardens' Reports. (S. 250)	
	Nov. 5th		All ranks of San. Sec 84 were paraded this morning at 8.15 a.m. Box Respirators, Iron Rations First Field Dressings, and Identity Discs were inspected. None of the men or NCOs had Iodine Ampules and several men are short of First Fd Dressing. Fire notices have been issued and are posted in mens' huts. I find no guards are posted in this unit and have not been since its formation, so I presume it is not required to do so. The road into the camp is in a deplorable condition and it is almost impossible to get the motor lorry in or out. A new stand must be arranged for Conference in A.D.M.S office re report from Gen. Porter as to Diphtheria infection being conveyed via drinking utensils in Estaminets, Canteens etc OCs Fd Ambs. to arrange for inspection of all Estaminets etc in their areas Notes on above Report. (1) All Estaminets which are not approved of by inspecting M.O on account of want of cleanliness, will be placed out of bounds to British Troops	

Army Form C. 2118.

Instructions regarding War Diaries and Intelligence Summaries are contained in F. S. Regs., Part II. and the Staff Manual respectively. Title Pages will be prepared in manuscript.

WAR DIARY
or
INTELLIGENCE SUMMARY
(Erase heading not required.)

Place	Date	Hour	Summary of Events and Information	Remarks and references to Appendices
RENINGHELST.	Nov 5th		(II) Steps to be taken for ensuring the disinfection of all drinking utensils by boiling water or solution of Pot: Permang: (III) Areas in which Diphtheria has occurred: ~~Wulverghem~~, ~~Bailleul~~ WULVERGHEN, BAILLEUL, CAESTRE, VIEUX BERQUIN. (IV) No unboiled milk to be used either in Tea, Coffee Cocoa etc. (V) Re Circular ~~[illegible]~~ letter S.G. 881/181/16. It was decided by A.D.M.S. that the Sanitary Section Officer of Division should assist when time permitted Correspondence 1, Report to ADMS on inspection of Water cart of 15th Hants - 8/253 water under chlorinated. 2, Re letter to M.O. 26th Fus. re Ablution Benches and Latrines 8/252 3, Letter to A.D.M.S. re error in P.B men - 5251 Went to DICKEBUSH ~~Dickebusch~~ and inspected the village - Sanitary condition extremely bad the only system of latrines being numerous shallow trenches scattered indiscriminately over the area. There is now one military latrine erected by San Sec 84 This is not sufficient & another must be started. The disposal of ~~[illegible]~~ refuse is unsatisfactory depending as it does upon haphazard burying no incinerator being in the village. There seems to be a doubt whether an incinerator	

2449 Wt. W14957/M90 750,000 1/16 J.B.C. & A. Forms/C.2118/12.

Instructions regarding War Diaries and Intelligence Summaries are contained in F. S. Regs., Part II. and the Staff Manual respectively. Title Pages will be prepared in manuscript.

Army Form C. 2118.

WAR DIARY
or
INTELLIGENCE SUMMARY

(Erase heading not required.)

Place	Date	Hour	Summary of Events and Information	Remarks and references to Appendices
RENINCHELST	Nov 5th		should be erected here on military grounds. But according to our instructions it may (letter ADMS on the above) I proceeded to DICKEBUSCH LAKE and investigated arrangements of a water supply to RIDGEWOOD and trenches. It is an excellent plan. The water in Tank 18 was underchlorinated. I wrote M.O 10th Queens (see letter 255) The method employed for the testing of water at these tanks is not quite clear and certainly the access to chlorinate is difficult. I was unable to definitely place who was responsible for the proper carrying out of the necessary testing but presume it is O.C. 139 F.A.	
	Nov 6th		Visited STEENVOORDE today and had consultation with Area Commandant with regard to improving existing conditions as to sanitation. It is necessary to at once put up 3 military latrines + urinals – sites agreed upon for these. One good destructor is also required immediately. I arranged to send a specification of material required for erecting these + to send a man to superintend the building. There is a sanitary squad of P.B men 13 in number for labour. The water supply as used at present does not seem satisfactory being drawn from the stream by pumping. There is an excellent supply of potable water in 3 wells in the village (authority 2nd Army) which should be used (chlorination being attended to) The question of disposal of urine is difficult + if discharged into the stream it must pass through chloride of lime.	

2449 Wt. W14957/M90 750,000 1/16 J.B.C. & A. Forms/C.2118/12.

Army Form C. 2118.

Instructions regarding War Diaries and Intelligence Summaries are contained in F. S. Regs., Part II. and the Staff Manual respectively. Title Pages will be prepared in manuscript.

WAR DIARY
or
INTELLIGENCE SUMMARY

(Erase heading not required.)

Place	Date	Hour	Summary of Events and Information	Remarks and references to Appendices
RENINGHELST	Nov 6th		This difficulty is acute at proposed site of No 1 Latrine. Soakage pits must be used for urine at the other two latrines. Checked reports from all R.M.Os (weekly) & made abstract for information and necessary action of A.D.M.S.	
"	" 7th		Received report from Lce Cpl Stead at BOESCHEPE. Latrine accommodation appears to be sufficient for the present and may suffice on account of urgency of work elsewhere but Area Commandant has no sanitary squad the sanitation being evidently entirely regimental. (See letter 254) Correspondence. 1 Re additional accommodation at rear of 'G' Office replied to. 2 Latrine - Officers at 'A Mess' replied to. 3 Inspection of Estaminets OC Belgian Mission being dealt with. 4 Urinals for RENINGHELST dealt with through A.D.M.S - selected sites Inspectors' Reports of 6th Inst. Destructors urgently required in lines of 20th D.L.I. - ditto in lines of 11th R.W.S. & 11th R.W.K. (ALBERTA CAMP.) - ditto for transport lines of 11th R.W.K. and 18th K.R.R. A case of lousiness reported by Cpl Morley at 124 Bde M. Gun Coy. - being dealt with by C.O. 24th Brigade 112 How. Batty. Australian Div. Camp very bad - no sanitary arrangements & no sanitary man on duty. Latrine boxes are however being put in.	

2449 Wt. W14957/M90 750,000 1/16 J.B.C. & A. Forms/C.2118/12.

Instructions regarding War Diaries and Intelligence Summaries are contained in F. S. Regs., Part II. and the Staff Manual respectively. Title Pages will be prepared in manuscript.

WAR DIARY
or
INTELLIGENCE SUMMARY

(Erase heading not required.)

Army Form C. 2118.

Place	Date	Hour	Summary of Events and Information	Remarks and references to Appendices
RENINGHELST	Nov 7		123rd Bde. Signallers - Eastern Area H 34 a 9.5 drinking untreated water from lake. Awaiting further report. --- Complete report bad	
"	Nov 8th		I this day visited the REST CAMPS of ONTARIO ~~and~~ ALBERTA and QUEBEC. The condition of all of these camps is deplorable and one and all require immediate & urgent attention. The destruction of refuse and faeces necessitates a permanently constructed incinerator in each camp. I have seen the Ag ADMS re the sanitary condition of these camps & he tells me that the Area Commandant is taking the matter in hand. He was under the impression that San Sec 84 was building incinerators but this is not so and nothing official has come in about it. However I think that the Section ought to make a start ~~after~~ and get the material & erect one incinerator as an example - say at Ontario Camp. I went carefully into the question of sanitation for these camps & the following points require urgent attention (1) Drainage (2) Improvement of huts (stoves - ventilation) 3 Urinals 4 Latrines (duck-board approaches etc) 5 Ablution ~~benches~~ sheds 6 Improvements of surroundings of cookhouses 7 Incinerators 8, Drying rooms 9 Approaches to camps and duckboard paths are very bad. 10 will help to improve things. 10, Soakage pits 11 Grease traps.	

2449 Wt. W14957/M90 750,000 1/16 J.B.C. & A. Forms/C.2118/12.

Instructions regarding War Diaries and Intelligence Summaries are contained in F. S. Regs., Part II. and the Staff Manual respectively. Title Pages will be prepared in manuscript.

WAR DIARY
or
INTELLIGENCE SUMMARY
(Erase heading not required.)

Army Form C. 2118.

Place	Date	Hour	Summary of Events and Information	Remarks and references to Appendices
RENINGHELST	9 Nov		Finished inspection of Estaminets in RENINGHELST and sent return to ADMS Visited BOESCHEPE at request of Area Commandant & had a consultation as to the urgent sanitary requirements of the village. The following are noteworthy. Latrines - no public or military latrine - water supply (local) not investigated (now being done by L.Cpl. Stead) - Urinals absent - ablution sheds ditto - no sanitary squad - no P.B men - no implements for scavenging. In fact no means of attempting sanitary work Recommendations; Testing of wells and ~~ponds~~ pumps & indications put in as to potable etc 1 Two six seaters or one twelve seater fly proof latrine (pails) 2 Urinals as above 3 One properly constructed ablution shed 5 One good kitchen 6 One good incinerator - there is a very fair one at present which is quite good enough to carry on with There are a good number of small details billeted in this village but there is no supervision of quarters latrines cook houses etc. This is a matter which should be attended to by the Area Commandant and arrangements made with O.C 138 F.A for M.O of that unit stationed at BOESCHEPE to make a regular inspection of billets of troops stationed there. In connection with Corps Circular dealing specially with this area I am of the opinion that if the suggestions contained therein are put into effect X Corps N° 155/2 D.D.M.S., it will be the proper way to set about getting	

Instructions regarding War Diaries and Intelligence Summaries are contained in F. S. Regs., Part II. and the Staff Manual respectively. Title Pages will be prepared in manuscript.

WAR DIARY
or
INTELLIGENCE SUMMARY
(Erase heading not required.)

Army Form C. 2118.

Place	Date	Hour	Summary of Events and Information	Remarks and references to Appendices
RENINGHELST	Nov. 9th		the place in order. Till such time as this order is authorised, much may be done by attention to detail in connection with erecting sanitary conveniences	
"	Nov 10th		Various reports from different inspectors – dealt with all reports – slight improvement in various camps but the want of material for constructional work seems to be universal. The Inspector at OUDERDOM reported under chlorination of water at tanks under charge of 47th Division (20261) No need under the circumstances to report the water carts as they were properly chlorinated according to instructions at the tank I have on three different occasions endeavoured to find the area Commandant (RENINGHELST) with reference to condition of camps in the Divisional area but have failed to locate him. However I presume that in accordance with X Corps No 113/16 A. the Area Commandant will consult me should he require my assistance. The A. C arranged to see Camp Commandant and appointment with me at which we went fully into the whole question of camps in this Divisional Area and after consultation the following arrangement was come to. (1) That the Area Commandant will do everything in his power to secure (a) Immediate delivery of all requisite material for – (b) Fatigue parties to be detailed from units at rest (c) That the Pioneer Squad of this Battalion will as far as possible at the disposal of O.C San. Sec 84. for constructional purposes.	

2449 Wt. W14957/M90 750,000 1/16 J.B.C. & A. Forms/C.2118/12.

Instructions regarding War Diaries and Intelligence Summaries are contained in F. S. Regs., Part II. and the Staff Manual respectively. Title Pages will be prepared in manuscript.

WAR DIARY
or
INTELLIGENCE SUMMARY

(Erase heading not required.)

Army Form C. 2118.

Place	Date	Hour	Summary of Events and Information	Remarks and references to Appendices
RENINGHELST	Nov 10th		2. That the drainage of camps be the first matter attended to.	
			3. That the huts be made water proof and stoves installed in each.	
			4. That QM's Stores and cook-houses be so situated as to obviate vehicular traffic in the camps.	
			5. That ablution sheds be put in good sanitary state	
			6. That defective latrines be replaced by properly constructed ones	
			7. That urinals be erected	
			8. That soakage pits be made.	
			9. That a drying room be erected in each camp	
			10. That in order to assist & secure the proper carrying out of above, the O.C. Sanitary Section will detail a reliable N.C.O. from his Section to supervise the carrying out of above & that O.C. San. Sec. will be responsible for putting the camps in order on the above lines	
"	Nov 11th		It was agreed that acting on the above lines, ALBERTA CAMP should at once be taken in hand. Accordingly I arranged with the Adjutant 11th Queen's request, to send an N.C.O up at 2 pm to direct the work of a party of fatigue (40 men) in the drainage. When my N.C.O (Cpl. Morley) reported there, the fatigue party was unavailable as the C.O wished nothing to be done to the camps till the Brigd. Gen. had inspected it.	

Instructions regarding War Diaries and Intelligence Summaries are contained in F. S. Regs., Part II. and the Staff Manual respectively. Title Pages will be prepared in manuscript.

WAR DIARY
or
INTELLIGENCE SUMMARY
(Erase heading not required.)

Army Form C. 2118.

Place	Date	Hour	Summary of Events and Information	Remarks and references to Appendices
RENINGHELST	~~Nov 9th~~ Nov. 11th		Cpl Morley therefore reported back at this office. Under the circumstances it seems a waste of time to make out the estimate of material required for the necessary constructional work.	
"	Nov 12th		Nothing particular today arising from yesterdays reports. I had a visit from O.C. San. Sec. 4th Division with reference to my letter 261. He was very grateful I had taken steps to prevent the mistake in future. The M. O i/c 12 2nd Inf. Bde. called to see me. His camp however is not in my area. I visited D. R. S. ~~and~~ at HAZEBRUCK with D.A.D.M.S. in the afternoon. Permitted the men of 84th San Sec. to knock off work at 12.30pm in order to enable them to get washing etc done. They have done a very good weeks work. Staff Sgt Watkins & Cpl Lees-Smith were granted liberty to visit the trenches in the DICKEBUSCH sector	
"	Nov 13th		Today Capt Rutter asked me to make a report to him in connection with the work at ALBERTA CAMP which was not permitted to be started - reported accordingly. I saw A.P.M (acting) re cart for removing refuse which he had instructed the driver of not to keep standing in the street. He evidently did not realise for what purpose the cart was used. I have instructed the men to as far as possible avoid causing a block in the thoroughfare.	

2449 Wt. W14957/M90 750,000 1/16 J.B.C. & A. Forms/C.2118/12.

Instructions regarding War Diaries and Intelligence Summaries are contained in F. S. Regs., Part II. and the Staff Manual respectively. Title Pages will be prepared in manuscript.

WAR DIARY
or
INTELLIGENCE SUMMARY
(Erase heading not required.)

Army Form C. 2118.

Place	Date	Hour	Summary of Events and Information	Remarks and references to Appendices
RENINGHELST	Nov 13		The A.P.M. reported a nuisance arising from an incinerator situated in the camp of 2nd Army Bus Detachment RENINGHELST, owing to being kept dirty. I visited this camp but discovered no trace of nuisance the camp being apparently well kept in everyway. This afternoon I visited CHIPPEWA CAMP and found that drainage is needed, particularly the cleaning up of main drains along side the LA CLYTTE ROAD. This applies to almost all of the small camps situated on either side of this road. I also visited the M.D.S. of 139th Fd. Amb. and there were no complaints everything being in a satisfactory condition.	

2449 Wt. W14957/M90 750,000 1/16 J.B.C. & A. Forms/C.2118/12.

Instructions regarding War Diaries and Intelligence Summaries are contained in F. S. Regs., Part II. and the Staff Manual respectively. Title Pages will be prepared in manuscript.

WAR DIARY
or
~~INTELLIGENCE SUMMARY~~
(Erase heading not required.)

Army Form C. 2118.

Place	Date	Hour	Summary of Events and Information	Remarks and references to Appendices
			Continuation of War Diary by Of San Sec 84.	
RENINGHELST	Nov 16		I arranged with the occupants of ALBERTA camp for a fatigue party of 20 men for tomorrow morning to proceed with the draining of the camp & precincts, also for the construction of a permanent brick destructor & incinerator combined. The building of the destructor has been delayed thro the RE not supplying the materials. Until transport is kept out of ALBERTA camp it is useless to expect anything but mud. Waggons & limbers are driven right across the drains which are thus broken down as fast as they are dug. Company cookers must be kept out of the camp.	
			There are numbers of small fires lit "anywhere" in nearly every camp or bivouac. This ought to stop as it usually means that they are "centres of dirt". I am trying to put a stop to this indiscriminate placing of these fires & small cookhouses, they ought all to be located at one spot.	W.V.

2449 Wt. W14957/M90 750,000 1/16 J.B.C. & A. Forms/C.2118/12.

Instructions regarding War Diaries and Intelligence Summaries are contained in F. S. Regs., Part II. and the Staff Manual respectively. Title Pages will be prepared in manuscript.

WAR DIARY
or
~~INTELLIGENCE SUMMARY~~
(Erase heading not required.)

Army Form C. 2118.

Place	Date	Hour	Summary of Events and Information	Remarks and references to Appendices
REMINGHELST.	Nov 17.		I am receiving reports continually that watercarts of units in this Division do not carry the required details, alum & B.P. These are absolutely essential. In every case I am reporting cases where the above are found wanting to the M.O's concerned, thus giving them time to rectify matters, but where cases occur again after due warning I report to the A.D.M.S. & he deals with the matter.	
			One of my inspectors reported to me that the M.O. of a battalion told him that the camp which his battalion was now occupying, & which he handed over clean & tidy to another battalion, was left by this latter battalion in a dirty condition. Grease traps had been broken down, urine pits & hoppers dismantled, & refuse & excreta had been buried, & not properly covered over, in waterlogged ground. I told the M.O. to try & arrange some sort of system with the M.O. of the battalion taking over from him so as to prevent this state of affairs. If units would cooperate in the work more a great deal of labour would be saved. There is no attempt at this cooperation, & the result is that every time	

2149 Wt. W14957/M90 750,000 1/16 J.B.C. & A. Forms/C.2118/12.

Instructions regarding War Diaries and Intelligence Summaries are contained in F. S. Regs., Part II. and the Staff Manual respectively. Title Pages will be prepared in manuscript.

WAR DIARY
or
~~INTELLIGENCE SUMMARY~~
(Erase heading not required.)

Army Form C. 2118.

Place	Date	Hour	Summary of Events and Information	Remarks and references to Appendices
			a site is handed over the whole system of sanitation has to be started again, meaning extra work for the incoming unit.	
			I suggested to the area commandant with whom I visited a number of the camps that an effective manure incinerator ought to be built for the new horse standings which are being erected. At his request I furnished him with plans for the incinerator, which I drew up after consulting the RE's, who raised no objection to the amount of material which would be required. As the new horse standings are erected in pairs in many cases, i.e. for the transport of 2 units, I suggested one incinerator might be sufficient for 2 standings.	
			The wagon lines of our artillery batteries are in a very bad state, & in particular latrines of the covered in type with pails, & ablution sheds & drainage are required. I reported this to the area commandant, whose sanction is required before any new building can be erected.	H.V.

2449 Wt. W14957/M90 750,000 1/16 J.B.C. & A. Forms/C.2118/12.

Army Form C. 2118.

WAR DIARY
or
~~INTELLIGENCE SUMMARY~~
(Erase heading not required.)

Instructions regarding War Diaries and Intelligence Summaries are contained in F. S. Regs., Part II. and the Staff Manual respectively. Title Pages will be prepared in manuscript.

Place	Date	Hour	Summary of Events and Information	Remarks and references to Appendices
RENINGHELST.	Nov 18.		I made another application today for a fatigue party to work on the drainage &c of Alberta camp. This is slow work, & has been held up by the frost.	
			I again reported a water cart to the M.O. concerned owing to the fact that no details were on the cart, & the driver admitted he knew nothing of water duties or how to fill a cart. I must insist on proper attention being paid to water sterilization as the water in this area is very variable in its state of purity & requires constant attention. The water tanks @ the supply stations require cleaning. The whole quantity of water in them is not drawn off each day, & this remainder is very impure @ times. All the water should be drawn off every day to remove this source of contamination.	
			(The B.P. supplied by ADCOCKS which has been condemned by the 4th Army when this division was on the SOMME has been analysed again, & found to be quite as efficient as any other).	

2449 Wt. W14957/M90 750,000 1/16 J.B.C. & A. Forms/C.2118/12.

Instructions regarding War Diaries and Intelligence Summaries are contained in F. S. Regs., Part II. and the Staff Manual respectively. Title Pages will be prepared in manuscript.

WAR DIARY
or
~~INTELLIGENCE SUMMARY~~
(Erase heading not required.)

Army Form C. 2118.

Place	Date	Hour	Summary of Events and Information	Remarks and references to Appendices
			I note a gradual improvement in the sanitation of the area.	
			Units are realising that it is for their own good that this is being put before them, & are really trying to improve conditions.	
			It has been found that rats are causing a number of cases of Infective jaundice. Their part in spreading this is briefly as follows: The disease is caused by a spirochaete which inhabits the kidneys & urine of the rat. The spirochaete is left behind when the rat urinates. (Spirochaete Icterhemorrhagica in Japan).	
			The necessity for keeping all food under proper cover will be seen at once from this, as rats urinate everywhere.	F.J.

2449 Wt. W14957/M90 750,000 1/16 J.B.C. & A. Forms/C.2118/12.

Instructions regarding War Diaries and Intelligence Summaries are contained in F. S. Regs., Part II. and the Staff Manual respectively. Title Pages will be prepared in manuscript.

WAR DIARY

or

~~INTELLIGENCE SUMMARY~~

(Erase heading not required.)

Army Form C. 2118.

Place	Date	Hour	Summary of Events and Information	Remarks and references to Appendices
RENINGHELST	Nov 19.		I again has a report about a water cart without B.P. & dealt with it.	
			One of the Foden drivers attached to this section has not returned from leave altho' he left on Oct 28th. I have already notified the proper authorities.	
			The permanent fatigue party of 1 NCO & 10 men for this section, & furnished by the Brigade in reserve, did not arrive this morning for duty:– reported.	
			Work on ALBERTA was limited to 1/2 day.	H.V.
"	Nov 20.		Fatigue party from Brigade in reserve did not arrive for duty – reported	
			O/c San Sec 23rd Div made application for CLAYTON disinfector, which is Corps property, & is now in our possession. I replied that ~~the~~. I suggest application for it should be made thro' his A.D.M.S. & thus leave no	

2149 Wt. W14957/M90 750,000 1/16 J.B.C. & A. Forms/C.2118/12.

Instructions regarding War Diaries and Intelligence Summaries are contained in F. S. Regs., Part II. and the Staff Manual respectively. Title Pages will be prepared in manuscript.

WAR DIARY
or
~~INTELLIGENCE SUMMARY~~
(Erase heading not required.)

Army Form C. 2118.

Place	Date	Hour	Summary of Events and Information	Remarks and references to Appendices
			loophole for errors.	
			I had a circular asking for comments on value of the waterproof valises attached to army bicycles. I replied that it would be a pity to discontinue their issue.	
			I sent the area commandant estimates for 2 more brick incinerators for CHIPPEWA camp.	
			Note.	
			I have heard nothing more of my application sent to the A.D.M.S. @ the beginning of this month, for a party of 15 pioneers to be attached to this section in order that we might erect incinerators &c in each standing camp in this area. I did not intend to suggest that the San. Sec. should have a subsection for constructional work only but put in this application because the R.E. were [illegible] with work, & the only way by which these	

2149 Wt. W14957/M90 750,000 1/16 J.B.C. & A. Forms/C.2118/12.

Instructions regarding War Diaries and Intelligence Summaries are contained in F. S. Regs., Part II. and the Staff Manual respectively. Title Pages will be prepared in manuscript.

WAR DIARY
or
~~INTELLIGENCE SUMMARY~~
(Erase heading not required.)

Army Form C. 2118.

Place	Date	Hour	Summary of Events and Information	Remarks and references to Appendices
			structures could be erected, & camps put in order would be by allowing the San. Sec. to supervise a party of its own.)	
			The San. Sec. Lorry has been lent to a couple of units lately in order to cart bricks from YPRES.	
			I have arranged for parties to dig out drains in ONTARIO Camp & CHIPPEWA.	
			In practically all these camps drains exist, but they have been allowed to become choked. I do not intend to go into an elaborate system of drainage, but merely to open up existing drains. Drainage is R.E. work.	
			I was asked by the Corps Sanitary Officer (back area) to see what could be done @ the new trench warfare school (41st Div) at ABEELE, & promised to see to it. This site is a new camp & if it can be attended to in time, much could be done	

2149 Wt. W14957/M90 750,000 1/16 J.B.C. & A. Forms/C.2118/12.

Army Form C. 2118.

Instructions regarding War Diaries and Intelligence Summaries are contained in F. S. Regs., Part II. and the Staff Manual respectively. Title Pages will be prepared in manuscript.

WAR DIARY
or
~~INTELLIGENCE SUMMARY~~
(Erase heading not required.)

Place	Date	Hour	Summary of Events and Information	Remarks and references to Appendices
			to prevent it from falling into the state of the other standing camps.	
RENINGHELST.	Nov 21.		An inspector went over to the trench warfare school at ABEELE this morning.	
			I visited the camp this afternoon, & found that the principal needs are drains, & grease water & soapy water effluents to be treated. I saw the existing drains & suggested a simple means by which a large amount of the stagnant water could be drawn off.	
			One of the corps units has been using a water cart & drawing water from a supply tank for "photography". This will be stopped.	
			The supply tanks @ BOESCHEPE & near ABEELE were reported to be leaking. I reported this to the X Corps Water officer.	
			WATERTANKS at BRASSERIE nr DICKEBUSCH which were very dirty have been cleaned out, & water found good.	

Instructions regarding War Diaries and Intelligence Summaries are contained in F. S. Regs., Part II. and the Staff Manual respectively. Title Pages will be prepared in manuscript.

WAR DIARY
or
INTELLIGENCE SUMMARY
(Erase heading not required.)

Army Form C. 2118.

Place	Date	Hour	Summary of Events and Information	Remarks and references to Appendices
RENINGHELST	1st Nov 22		One of my inspectors was refused permission to inspect sanitation of batteries of a brigade of this Div. apparently the Battery Commander didn't know of D.R.O. 62 of 13/5/16 which gave members of this section authority to inspect any unit's sanitation in this area provided he had a pass.	
			I sent in a report to the A.D.M.S. about the cookhouses in general in this area, & the ~~[illegible]~~ dumping of small field kitchens anywhere. I suggested that X Corps orders as to rules to be observed in cookhouses & kitchens of messes should be issued to every M.O. & Company Commander.	
			Also I recommended that huts & billets should be cleaned out properly & systematically & that the interiors might be washed with whitewash.	
			A.A.&Q.M.G. of this Div asked for an estimate by villages, of number of carts necessary for mud collecting. I sent this	

2149 Wt. W14957/M90 750,000 1/16 J.B.C. & A. Forms/C.2118/12.

Instructions regarding War Diaries and Intelligence Summaries are contained in F. S. Regs., Part II. and the Staff Manual respectively. Title Pages will be prepared in manuscript.

WAR DIARY
or
~~INTELLIGENCE SUMMARY~~
(Erase heading not required.)

Army Form C. 2118.

Place	Date	Hour	Summary of Events and Information	Remarks and references to Appendices
			in, suggesting that it would be better [illegible] areas.	
			The drainage (& sanitation of) Trench Warfare School is nearly complete.	
			Drainage of other camps in this area held up owing to division reliefs.	
			Incinerator @ ALBERTA completed by this section.	
			Billet occupied by a Land Drainage Co in this div. adversely reported on by me. Very foul short trench latrines were in use: much refuse lying about, & no attempt made to clean up.	
			I saw area commandant & asked for more latrines seats from the R.E.	H.V.

2149 Wt. W14957/M90 750,000 1/16 J.B.C. & A. Forms/C.2118/12.

WAR DIARY
or
INTELLIGENCE SUMMARY
(Erase heading not required.)

Instructions regarding War Diaries and Intelligence Summaries are contained in F. S. Regs., Part II. and the Staff Manual respectively. Title Pages will be prepared in manuscript.

Place	Date	Hour	Summary of Events and Information	Remarks and references to Appendices
RENINGHELST	Nov 23.		I reported other watercarts to the M.O's concerned this morning for not carrying Bleaching Powder. A neglected billet of the Pioneers of this Div. was found in a very filthy condition & reported. One of my corporals was refused permission to inspect the sanitary arrangements of one of the artillery Brigades of this Div. I reported this, as DRO 64 of 13/5/16 authorised the personnel of this section to proceed anywhere on duty in this Divisional area provided they carried a pass. I applied for fatigue parties from several of the battalions in rest for the purpose of cleaning & draining their own camps under our supervision. In 2 cases I found that there were already permanent drainage parties told off for this purpose.	

2449 Wt. W14957/M90 750,000 1/16 J.B.C. & A. Forms/C.2118/12.

Instructions regarding War Diaries and Intelligence Summaries are contained in F. S. Regs., Part II. and the Staff Manual respectively. Title Pages will be prepared in manuscript.

WAR DIARY
or
~~INTELLIGENCE SUMMARY~~
(Erase heading not required.)

Army Form C. 2118.

Place	Date	Hour	Summary of Events and Information	Remarks and references to Appendices
			We finished the construction of a brick destructor & incinerator at ALBERTA camp this morning. This is now ready for use, & will entirely replace the clumsy sheet iron unsightly incinerator at present in use.	
			I find that some of the Horsepits in this area would be quite efficient if they could be repaired. One horsepit at CHIPPEWA only requires a new bottom. I propose trying to mend a few of these if possible.	
			I have great difficulty in obtaining material in sufficient amounts for erecting incinerators from the R.E. Indents are delayed for no apparently [reason] for when I have seen the C.R.E. myself days after the indents have gone in I find no notice has been taken of them.	
			Reports coming in show that a gradual improvement is being made in the condition of the artillery lines. In some cases however matters are still at a standstill as the artillery of the division is being reorganised, & nothing can be done till this reorganisation is complete.	

2449 Wt. W14957/M90 750,000 1/16 J.B.C. & A. Forms/C.2118/12.

Army Form C. 2118.

Instructions regarding War Diaries and Intelligence Summaries are contained in F. S. Regs., Part II. and the Staff Manual respectively. Title Pages will be prepared in manuscript.

WAR DIARY
or
~~INTELLIGENCE SUMMARY~~

(Erase heading not required.)

Place	Date	Hour	Summary of Events and Information	Remarks and references to Appendices
			a great amount of work is still necessary in the drainage of camps here. I find that in most camps there are quite a number of drains, but they need cleaning out.	
			The work at the Trench Warfare School (41st Div) at ABEELE is well in hand. Drains have been opened up well, & cleaned out. It was found necessary to open up a road in order to clean out one of the drains on which practically all the drainage of the living part of the camp depended. The ablution sheds & bath houses have been dealt with. Good latrines & urinals are being erected, & good cookhouses for the officers & men's quarters. I detailed a man from this section to attend to this work & see it completed.	H.V.
	Nov 24.		The box cover for the Clayton disinfector was sent to the D.D.M.S. X Corps today on instructions.	
			There is not much to report on today's work. I saw the C.R.E. [illegible] on the indents for materials for	

2149 Wt. W14957/M90 750,000 1/16 J.B.C. & A. Forms/C.2118/12.

Instructions regarding War Diaries and Intelligence Summaries are contained in F. S. Regs., Part II. and the Staff Manual respectively. Title Pages will be prepared in manuscript.

WAR DIARY
or
~~INTELLIGENCE SUMMARY~~
(Erase heading not required.)

Army Form C. 2118.

Place	Date	Hour	Summary of Events and Information	Remarks and references to Appendices
			incinerators. The Adj. R.E. gave me a note from the area commandant re the latrine accomodation required @ MURRUMBIDGEE. Latrines exist but are in need of repair, but more are required. There is a latrine @ the baths there but this is not attended to regularly: the staff @ the baths is too small & no sanitary man can be spared. I am ~~trying~~ to get the battalion in MURRUMBIDGEE to look after it.	H.V.
	Nov. 25.		We obtained materials for the 2 incinerators @ CHIPPEWA. As one of the Horsefalls can be easily repaired however I propose to erect one of the incinerators @ ONTARIO instead. The area commandant has sanctioned this. I sent in a report to the A.D.M.S. regarding the number of water carts which are not provided with the necessary details, alum & B. Powder. Altho I have been in communication with various M.O.s on this subject, this still goes on, & it is time some further action was taken on	

2149 Wt. W14957/M90 750,000 1/16 J.B.C. & A. Forms/C.2118/12.

Instructions regarding War Diaries and Intelligence Summaries are contained in F. S. Regs., Part II. and the Staff Manual respectively. Title Pages will be prepared in manuscript.

WAR DIARY

or

~~INTELLIGENCE~~ SUMMARY

(Erase heading not required.)

Army Form C. 2118.

Place	Date	Hour	Summary of Events and Information	Remarks and references to Appendices
			the matter.	
			The O/C of one of the R.E. Coys asked for a meeting with me @ MURRUMBIDGEE ~~re~~ the latrine accomodation. I arranged for 10.30 tomorrow morning.	
			—	
			I have been trying to get transport lines to clear their adjacent areas of tins, but it is difficult to fix responsibility. The same excuse is repeatedly made that "the rubbish was here when we came" & no attempt is made to remove it, tho' every unit declares that it is doing its utmost to clean up.	H.D.
			—	
	Nov 26		The O/C F Co. R.E. did not arrive @ MURRUMBIDGEE this morning altho I waited 1/2 an hour for him. I however sent him a list of suggestions for the latrine accomodation. Later he rang me up & we arranged for Tues aft @ 2.30 p.m.	
			A report from R.E. Med. Officer was sent to A.D.M.S. & subsequently to me that water ~~carts~~ from R.E. watercarts was often tested by him & found to be insufficiently chlorinated. On	

2449 Wt. W14957/M90 750,000 1/16 J.B.C. & A. Forms/C.2118/12.

Instructions regarding War Diaries and Intelligence Summaries are contained in F. S. Regs., Part II. and the Staff Manual respectively. Title Pages will be prepared in manuscript.

WAR DIARY
or
~~INTELLIGENCE SUMMARY~~
(Erase heading not required.)

Army Form C. 2118.

Place	Date	Hour	Summary of Events and Information	Remarks and references to Appendices
			investigation I found that the R.E. carts frequently drew water from tanks @ OUDERDOM which did not come under the control of this San Sec but that of the neighbouring Division. These tanks had been tested by us, & also water from carts which had filled there, & the water had been found to be insufficiently chlorinated.	
			I find in visiting the various camps that I can hardly ever find the M.O. & consequently anyone directly responsible for the sanitation. I could not see a single M.O. today altho I tried @ various places.	H.V.
RENINGHELST.	Nov 27.		Sent a specimen of Petit St Jean water to No 1 Mobile Laboratory today for examination. This water is reported to contain B. Coli in large quantities.	
			From detailed inspection of the artillery lines of this Div. I find the following points	
			1. A number of Deep trench latrines with open seats are still in use. It is a difficult & slow process obtaining	

2449 Wt. W14957/M90 750,000 1/16 J.B.C. & A. Forms/C.2118/12.

Army Form C. 2118.

Instructions regarding War Diaries and Intelligence Summaries are contained in F. S. Regs., Part II. and the Staff Manual respectively. Title Pages will be prepared in manuscript.

WAR DIARY

or

~~INTELLIGENCE SUMMARY~~

(Erase heading not required.)

Place	Date	Hour	Summary of Events and Information	Remarks and references to Appendices
			box seat latrines from the R.E., & pails from Ordnance.	
			2. Urinals. Night urine pails are not sufficiently [illegible]	
			3. Grease traps: very variable in efficiency - not emptied often enough, & the filtering medium is allowed to remain too long unchanged.	
			4. Incinerators: present in nearly every case, tho' efficiency is variable. Excreta is often burnt quite effectively with these open incinerators, & gives rise to no unpleasantness.	
			5. Manure: principally disposed of to the farmers. Dumped in a few cases, & allowed to be collected by the farmers at odd times.	
			6. Ablution sheds: practically non existent.	
			7. Drying sheds - none	
			8. Drainage of camps: bad, tho' much is being done, & much remains to be done.	P.V.

2449 Wt. W14957/M90 750,000 1/16 J.B.C. & A. Forms/C.2118/12.

Army Form C. 2118.

Instructions regarding War Diaries and Intelligence Summaries are contained in F. S. Regs., Part II. and the Staff Manual respectively. Title pages will be prepared in manuscript.

WAR DIARY

or

~~INTELLIGENCE SUMMARY.~~

(Erase heading not required.)

Place	Date	Hour	Summary of Events and Information	Remarks and references to Appendices
RENINGHELST	Nov 28.		In the constructional work I have undertaken, particularly with regard to incinerators, I have had no help at all from the R.E. Indents have been held up, & no making is forthcoming when the indents go there. I can get no men to help my men in the work. This work I have undertaken as it was essential, & to relieve the R.E. but it is not really part of the San. Sec's. work. If ~~the~~ a San. Sec is expected to do this sort of work a permanent party of men should be allotted to it when necessary.	
			No notice has been taken of my report to the A.D.M.S. about the bad state of cookhouses & kitchens.	
			There are too many detached sanitaries scattered about the camps: too many isolated & solitary badly built latrines & urinals. I am trying to get all these things centralised at one spot.	

2353 Wt. W2544/1454 700,000 5/15 D. D. & L. A.D.S.S. Forms/C 2118.

Army Form C. 2118.

WAR DIARY
or
~~INTELLIGENCE SUMMARY~~
(Erase heading not required.)

Instructions regarding War Diaries and Intelligence Summaries are contained in F. S. Regs., Part II. and the Staff Manual respectively. Title pages will be prepared in manuscript.

Place	Date	Hour	Summary of Events and Information	Remarks and references to Appendices
			Units will not pay attention to the draining of their camps, & tho I repeatedly ask for men for this purpose, what work they do is nullified by allowing transport to cross & churn up the drains which are made. I have had to give up this drainage work because carts & all sorts of transport are allowed to cross the new drains & plough up the camps.	
			The work on latrines @ MURRUMBIDGEE is still held up by the R.E.	
			One case of mumps occurred in the H.Q. of the Div. train. Disinfection of huts, & isolation of contacts who had not had the disease was carried out.	
			—	
			I was asked for, & sent in a report to the area commandant on	

2353 Wt. W2544/1454 700,000 5/15 D. D. & L. A.D.S.S. Forms/C 2118.

Instructions regarding War Diaries and Intelligence Summaries are contained in F. S. Regs., Part II. and the Staff Manual respectively. Title pages will be prepared in manuscript.

WAR DIARY
or
~~INTELLIGENCE SUMMARY.~~

(Erase heading not required.)

Army Form C. 2118.

Place	Date	Hour	Summary of Events and Information	Remarks and references to Appendices
			the number of Horsfall destructors in this Div. area. There are 4 workable ones; I suggested one for every camp & small town – about 12-15 in all. The Horsfall destructor would be much more largely used if a door for raking out were provided. At present it is a very difficult matter to clear it out, as this has to be done thro the top & is a lengthy process.	
			—	
			Some overlapping has occurred between this section & that of the neighbouring Divisional San. Sec. They are claiming some of our units. I have written to the O.C. San. Sec. concerned, as it has given rise to some confusion, & hope to rectify the matter soon.	
			—	
			The Foden Lorry M.T. A.S.C. Driver who was overdue from leave, returned this morning, & brought back ~~his~~ papers	

2353 Wt. W2544/1454 700,000 5/15 D. D. & L. A.D.S.S. Forms/C 2118.

Instructions regarding War Diaries and Intelligence Summaries are contained in F. S. Regs., Part II. and the Staff Manual respectively. Title pages will be prepared in manuscript.

WAR DIARY

or

~~INTELLIGENCE SUMMARY.~~

(Erase heading not required.)

Army Form C. 2118.

Place	Date	Hour	Summary of Events and Information	Remarks and references to Appendices
			showing that he had been detained in hospital in London, & discharged from them. This has been reported to the O/C 17th Supply column.	H.D.
			My report which I sent to the A.D.M.S on the 22nd re the insanitary state of camps has been published in a Special Div. order, & is as follows: "I made an extensive inspection of camps this morning in this area, & found that in only one case was the kitchen or cookhouse in a clean state. There appears to be no attention paid to the storage of food; old opened tins, scraps of food, bottles, dirty sacking are to be found everywhere. Large quantities of soldiers kit are hung up round the cookhouses which are very badly ventillated. In one case the cook told me that no accomodation in a hut	

Instructions regarding War Diaries and Intelligence Summaries are contained in F. S. Regs., Part II. and the Staff Manual respectively. Title pages will be prepared in manuscript.

WAR DIARY
or
~~INTELLIGENCE~~ SUMMARY.

(Erase heading not required.)

Army Form C. 2118.

Place	Date	Hour	Summary of Events and Information	Remarks and references to Appendices
			has been provided for him. Men sleep in kitchens. Huts generally require cleaning & provision for [illegible]."	
			The Divisional Commander directs that these several points are brought to notice of the units concerned, & receive immediate attention.	P.
RENINGHELST.	Nov 29.		I despatched Clayton disinfector to 23rd Div. at POPERINGHE this morning, & later received instructions to recall it & fit it up @ the baths here.	
			Work is proceeding on the incinerators @ Ontario & Chippewa camps.	
			As the Divisional artillery is reorganising & some of the batteries are moving it is impossible to make much	

Instructions regarding War Diaries and Intelligence Summaries are contained in F. S. Regs., Part II. and the Staff Manual respectively. Title pages will be prepared in manuscript.

WAR DIARY
or
INTELLIGENCE SUMMARY.
(Erase heading not required.)

Army Form C. 2118.

Place	Date	Hour	Summary of Events and Information	Remarks and references to Appendices
			headway with sanitation beyond what has already been recorded.	
			An order has been issued that old tins are to be carted to the R.E. yard @ OUDERDOM. There are numbers of insanitary mounds of tins in this area. The tins are to be utilised by the o/c hutting yard.	H.T.
			—	
RENINGHELST	Nov 20		I have not yet been able to meet the R.E. with regard to latrines @ MURRUMBIDGEE. This is due to them as they have failed to keep appointments I have made with them.	
			Apparently the area commandant has transferred the work of erecting buildings of latrines & sheds to me: This is likely to prove a more speedy process than before.	

2353 Wt. W2544/1454 700,000 5/15 D. D. & L. A.D.S.S. Forms/C. 2118.

Instructions regarding War Diaries and Intelligence Summaries are contained in F. S. Regs., Part II. and the Staff Manual respectively. Title pages will be prepared in manuscript.

WAR DIARY
or
~~INTELLIGENCE SUMMARY.~~
(Erase heading not required.)

Army Form C. 2118.

Place	Date	Hour	Summary of Events and Information	Remarks and references to Appendices
			Acting on A.D.M.S. instructions I applied to the O.C. of 140 F. Amb. for an ambulance in order to ~~take~~ me to the Field Stores @ CAESTRE. He was unwilling to lend me an ambulance, & I have had to apply elsewhere.	
			~~It~~ Altho' we have erected latrines @ DICKEBUSCH we cannot get pails for them. I thought it impossible for the San. Sec. to obtain a supply of the necessary materials for its work. It is now over three weeks since we erected these latrines & no pails have been available, nor have units using the latrines been able to draw pails. Oil drums have been used meanwhile.	
			—	
			This diary has to be despatched this afternoon.	[illegible initials]

2353 Wt. W2544/1454 700,000 5/15 D. D. & L. A.D.S.S. Forms/C 2118.

Dec 1916

41st Div.

145/1943

Vol 8

War Diary

Sanitary Section

84

B.E.F.

December 1916

Instructions regarding War Diaries and Intelligence Summaries are contained in F. S. Regs., Part II. and the Staff Manual respectively. Title pages will be prepared in manuscript.

WAR DIARY
or
~~INTELLIGENCE SUMMARY~~.
(Erase heading not required.)

Army Form C. 2118.

Place	Date	Hour	Summary of Events and Information	Remarks and references to Appendices
RENINGHELST	Dec 1.		Clayton Disinfector was sent to San. Sec 23rd Div. Dirty billet vacated by D.187 R.F.A. of this Div. was reported to me. I asked for it to be cleaned by its previous occupants. I am trying to insist that every watercart man & units in this Division chlorinates the water himself on refilling the carts. At present some of the water wardens do all the chlorinating & watercart men know nothing of water chlorination. This might lead to serious consequences if for any reason these water carts were compelled to refill away from the water tanks. I am giving orders to my water inspectors on this point; ie that every 41st Div. water cart must be chlorinated by the water cart men, & not by the water wardens.	AV.

2353 Wt. W2544/1454 700,000 5/15 D. D. & L. A.D.S.S. Forms/C 2118.

Instructions regarding War Diaries and Intelligence Summaries are contained in F. S. Regs., Part II. and the Staff Manual respectively. Title pages will be prepared in manuscript.

WAR DIARY
or
INTELLIGENCE SUMMARY.
(Erase heading not required.)

Army Form C. 2118.

Place	Date	Hour	Summary of Events and Information	Remarks and references to Appendices
RENINGHELST.	Dec 2.		I reported the presence of kit & bedding in a cookhouse to the M.O of the unit concerned. The men in the cookhouse told me that they had received no orders ~~contrary~~ to the effect that this was forbidden.	
			A party of men @ DICKEBUSCH Lake pumping station belonging to one of this Div. R.E. Field Coys, ~~needs~~ has no sanitary arrangements, & said they had no time to attend to sanitation. I reported this to their O.C. & M.O.	
			"Q" of this Div. told me that they had decided to erect a couple of urinals in RENINGHELST. This is quite unnecessary, as we have already erected the necessary urinal & latrine accomodation. It means that stricter discipline is necessary to prevent men from urinating	

Army Form C. 2118.

Instructions regarding War Diaries and Intelligence Summaries are contained in F. S. Regs., Part II. and the Staff Manual respectively. Title pages will be prepared in manuscript.

WAR DIARY
or
INTELLIGENCE SUMMARY.
(Erase heading not required.)

Place	Date	Hour	Summary of Events and Information	Remarks and references to Appendices
			anywhere.	H.V.
RENINGHELST.	Dec 3.		Work on the incinerator @ CHIPPEWA is hung up, as the bricks which we had placed there were stolen by one of the Regts in camp for the purpose of making small field kitchens. This was done on the order the D.A.A. & Q.M.G. altho' I am trying to get this abolished as ~~eve~~ field kitchens are placed anywhere in camps, & become centres of dirt & kitchen refuse. I must wait till the area commandant returns from leave as I can get no help from his deputy.	
			Reports from the inspectors of this section show that many units are without proper latrine accomodation ~~&~~ ablution benches. I am sending in a list of the requirements to the ADMS.	

2353 Wt. W2544/1454 700,000 5/15 D. D. & L. A.D.S.S. Forms/C. 2118.

Instructions regarding War Diaries and Intelligence Summaries are contained in F. S. Regs., Part II. and the Staff Manual respectively. Title pages will be prepared in manuscript.

WAR DIARY

or

~~INTELLIGENCE SUMMARY.~~

(Erase heading not required.)

Army Form C. 2118.

Place	Date	Hour	Summary of Events and Information	Remarks and references to Appendices
			The report I sent to the A.D.M.S. on 22/11/16, which was published in a special Div. order, has raised a storm of protest: Regiments denying that it applies to them. I was asked to state what camps I had visited & I sent in a second report giving details & mentioning units & camps. The way the first report was received goes to show that my report was correct.	
			I had a kit inspection of the section this morning.	W.V.
RENINGHELST	1st Dec 4.		I had to spend half the morning on a medical board for P.B. men & so was unable to go out till late.	
			Men were still found to be sleeping in cookhouses of several of the units. Reported. I am sending in to R.E. a simplified type of box latrine ~~for~~ the	

2353 Wt. W2544/1454 700,000 5/15 D. D. & L. A.D.S.S. Forms/C 2118.

Army Form C. 2118.

Instructions regarding War Diaries and Intelligence Summaries are contained in F. S. Regs., Part II. and the Staff Manual respectively. Title pages will be prepared in manuscript.

WAR DIARY

or

~~INTELLIGENCE SUMMARY.~~

(Erase heading not required.)

Place	Date	Hour	Summary of Events and Information	Remarks and references to Appendices
			hope that they can be turned out more quickly	H.V.
RENINGHELST.	6. Dec.		I visited 2 of the sets of water tanks in the 41st Div area as some trouble has arisen owing to complaints having been made that carts of this Div watering there had been found to be insufficiently chlorinated. Samples of water were taken from two different sets of tanks & were found O.K.	
			MICMAC camp is still very incomplete & much requires to be done with regard to the winter accomodation & latrine & ablution arrangements. I went very carefully over the camp of 19th Middlesex & the M.O. told me that he had not seen some of the latrines altho the Regt.	

Instructions regarding War Diaries and Intelligence Summaries are contained in F. S. Regs., Part II. and the Staff Manual respectively. Title pages will be prepared in manuscript.

WAR DIARY

or

~~INTELLIGENCE SUMMARY~~.

(Erase heading not required.)

Army Form C. 2118.

Place	Date	Hour	Summary of Events and Information	Remarks and references to Appendices
			has been in that camp for over six weeks.	
			I understand that M.O.s are being sent to HAZEBROUK for a 5 days course in sanitation.	
			We have used all material supplied to us by the R.E. for the latrines @ MURRUMBIDGEE, & are awaiting more.	
			I sent in a report to the A.D.M.S. that sanitary men of the 15th Hants had been sent out on working parties, which is against D.R.O.	
			Water cart of 122 M.G. Coy carrying no lime was reported to me & passed on by me to O.C. 122 M.G.C.	
			Motor lorry army marks in accordance with Army orders	

Instructions regarding War Diaries and Intelligence Summaries are contained in F. S. Regs., Part II. and the Staff Manual respectively. Title pages will be prepared in manuscript.

WAR DIARY
or
INTELLIGENCE SUMMARY.
(Erase heading not required.)

Army Form C. 2118.

Place	Date	Hour	Summary of Events and Information	Remarks and references to Appendices
			were readjusted today in accordance with prescribed ruling.	
			I applied for more material for latrines @ [illegible] Camp from R.E.	
			One of my NCOs. 2900 Cpl H.B. Lees-Smith reported as absentee having overstayed his leave.	
			I am endeavouring to obtain latrines myself from the R.E. & to supply them to units requiring them without interfering with work in the Div. winter accommodation scheme.	H.V.

2353 Wt. W2544/1454 700,000 5/15 D. D. & L. A.D.S.S. Forms/C 2118.

Army Form C. 2118.

WAR DIARY
or
~~INTELLIGENCE SUMMARY~~
(Erase heading not required.)

Instructions regarding War Diaries and Intelligence Summaries are contained in F. S. Regs., Part II. and the Staff Manual respectively. Title pages will be prepared in manuscript.

Place	Date	Hour	Summary of Events and Information	Remarks and references to Appendices
RENINGHELST.	Dec 7.		I saw the area commandant this eve with regard to the extremely slowness of the winter accomodation scheme now being carried out by the ~~area comm~~ R.E's. I complained that I could not get the necessary materials for my work; the latrine accomodation & washing accomodation ~~too~~ has not been seen to, & that existing now is quite insufficient.	
			One of the incinerators this section built has had the top broken to pieces by one of the units, thro' carelessness, & another one has the top badly damaged.	
			I visited Murrumbidgee, Chippewa, Quebec & Alberta & Ontario this afternoon, & found that more care appears to be taken	

2353 Wt. W2544/1454 700,000 5/15 D. D. & L. A.D.S.S. Forms/C 2118.

Army Form C. 2118.

Instructions regarding War Diaries and Intelligence Summaries are contained in F. S. Regs., Part II. and the Staff Manual respectively. Title pages will be prepared in manuscript.

WAR DIARY
or
INTELLIGENCE SUMMARY.
(Erase heading not required.)

Place	Date	Hour	Summary of Events and Information	Remarks and references to Appendices
			with cookhouses & storage of food &c, tho' a great deal requires to be done yet. I will make another inspection extending over the same area precisely, with a view to seeing whether anything has been done to improve matters after my 2nd report on 8/12/16.	

Instructions regarding War Diaries and Intelligence Summaries are contained in F. S. Regs., Part II. and the Staff Manual respectively. Title pages will be prepared in manuscript.

WAR DIARY

or

~~INTELLIGENCE SUMMARY~~.

(Erase heading not required.)

Army Form C. 2118.

Place	Date	Hour	Summary of Events and Information	Remarks and references to Appendices
RENINGHELST.	Dec 7.		I can still report that R.E.s are not proceeding with latrines @ MURRUMBIDGEE Camp. I can get no reply to my correspondence. These latrines are in a very bad state.	
			Gregory Corporals has not returned from leave, & has been reported as "absentee".	
			I applied to R.E. for more latrines, as we can obtain them more quickly than units, & then pass them on.	R.V.
"	8.		The closed in incinerators that we have built @ Ontario & Alberta camps have been badly knocked about thro' careless use by units. I cannot get all I want from R.E. to build these incinerators satisfactorily. Men in charge of incinerators	

2353 Wt. W2544/1454 700,000 5/15 D. D. & L. A.D.S.S. Forms/C. 2118.

Instructions regarding War Diaries and Intelligence Summaries are contained in F. S. Regs., Part II, and the Staff Manual respectively. Title pages will be prepared in manuscript.

WAR DIARY
or
~~INTELLIGENCE SUMMARY.~~
(Erase heading not required.)

Army Form C. 2118.

Place	Date	Hour	Summary of Events and Information	Remarks and references to Appendices
			pack them absolutely full of rubbish & leave them burn overnight. The result is, that a solid red hot mass is blazing away half the night, & no incinerator will stand this amount of heat. @ least no brick one. I have told the A.D.M.S. that I will not ask for any more closed in incinerators in this area, & will only have open ones built.	
			Two water carts of Div. R.F.A. reported to me as not carrying B. Powder: reported.	
			The 'absentee' Corporal has had leave extended to Dec. 31st.	
			Area commandant asked me to state roughly the amount of latrine accomodation still req'd in this	

2353 Wt. W2544/1454 700,000 5/15 D. D. & L. A.D.S.S. Forms/C. 2118.

Army Form C. 2118.

WAR DIARY
or
~~INTELLIGENCE SUMMARY.~~
(Erase heading not required.)

Instructions regarding War Diaries and Intelligence Summaries are contained in F. S. Regs., Part II. and the Staff Manual respectively. Title pages will be prepared in manuscript.

Place	Date	Hour	Summary of Events and Information	Remarks and references to Appendices
			area: I did this. I also sent him some plans for showing how to reduce the amount of wood used in making the box seat latrines. Units should have greater facilities for obtaining latrine pails.	W.
			~~[illegible]~~	
RENINGHELST	10.		Water in Water cart of "B" 189 of this Div reported to me as not having been sufficiently chlorinated. Reported to M.O.	
			(Two of the men in this section are being taken to form part of the Div. Troup for Xmas entertainment, & this handicaps our work still further.)	
			Nothing further is being done by us with regard to	

Instructions regarding War Diaries and Intelligence Summaries are contained in F. S. Regs., Part II. and the Staff Manual respectively. Title pages will be prepared in manuscript.

WAR DIARY

or

~~INTELLIGENCE SUMMARY.~~

(Erase heading not required.)

Army Form C. 2118.

Place	Date	Hour	Summary of Events and Information	Remarks and references to Appendices
			the draining of camps here, particularly Alberta & Ontario on which I had been working. This is R.E. land drainage work and not San. Sec.	
			I still maintain that the work of a San. Sec. is advisory only. We have ~~had to~~ done other work in order to help the overworked units. Building incinerators is not San. Sec. work tho' if we hadn't done this nothing would have been done at all. In future I shall insist on having working parties from the R.E. or pioneers for constructional work.	H.
	11.		The Belgian artillery watercarts which refill at water stations in this area do not carry the necessary lime. I have reported this. I have also drawn the attention of the area Commandant	

2353 Wt. W2544/1454 700,000 5/15 D. D. & L. A.D.S.S. Forms/C. 2118.

Army Form C. 2118.

Instructions regarding War Diaries and Intelligence Summaries are contained in F. S. Regs., Part II. and the Staff Manual respectively. Title pages will be prepared in manuscript.

WAR DIARY
or
~~INTELLIGENCE SUMMARY.~~

(Erase heading not required.)

Place	Date	Hour	Summary of Events and Information	Remarks and references to Appendices
			to the state of Murrumbidgee camp latrines, & the delay of the R.E. in dealing with the erection of same.	
			I also reported to him that those incinerators we had erected were broken thro' careless use. We agreed to try & erect "fool proof" open brick incinerators instead of the covered in type.	
			Water carts of 19th Mx. again reported as not carrying necessary lime & details.	
			I received an order to test the water in Dickebusch daily for presence of metallic poisons as some hostile shells had fallen in the lake which supplies the drinking water for a very large area.	H.V.

2353 Wt. W2544/1454 700,000 5/15 D. D. & L. A.D.S.S. Forms/C. 2118.

Instructions regarding War Diaries and Intelligence Summaries are contained in F. S. Regs., Part II. and the Staff Manual respectively. Title pages will be prepared in manuscript.

WAR DIARY

or

~~INTELLIGENCE SUMMARY.~~

(Erase heading not required.)

Army Form C. 2118.

Place	Date	Hour	Summary of Events and Information	Remarks and references to Appendices
Reninghelst.	Dec 12.		Sample of water from Dickebusch Lake tested for metallic poisons gave negative results.	
			Barrel of cement supply tins for constructional work & supplied tins by R.E. found to be useless on opening the barrel.	M.
	Dec 13.		A.D.M.S. inspected San. Sec. this aft. & found everything satisfactory: huts & billets & camp ground were acknowledged to be clean & tidy & men steady on parade & well turned out. Gas drill - good knowledge generally.	
			No other work was done today owing to this inspection.	M.

2353 Wt. W2544/1454 700,000 5/15 D. D. & L. A.D.S.S. Forms/C 2118.

Instructions regarding War Diaries and Intelligence Summaries are contained in F. S. Regs., Part II. and the Staff Manual respectively. Title pages will be prepared in manuscript.

WAR DIARY

or

~~INTELLIGENCE SUMMARY.~~

(Erase heading not required.)

Army Form C. 2118.

Place	Date	Hour	Summary of Events and Information	Remarks and references to Appendices
	Dec. 13.		Water cart of 41st A.S.C. is not accompanied by regular waterman i reported. The waterman knows nothing about water duties.	
			Also carts of "B" 189 as above.	
			I asked for particulars re the grouping of 41st Div. artillery in order to be able to fix responsibility for sanitation &c on definite M.Os. The artillery M.Os take charge of group artillery & do not remain responsible for their own brigades.	
			Samples of water drawn from Dickebusch Lake tested for metallic poisons gave negative results. This water was drawn from the point where the water is drawn to the pumping station.	H.V.

2353 Wt. W2544/1454 700,000 5/15 D. D. & L. A.D.S.S. Forms/C. 2118.

Instructions regarding War Diaries and Intelligence Summaries are contained in F. S. Regs., Part II. and the Staff Manual respectively. Title pages will be prepared in manuscript.

Army Form C. 2118.

WAR DIARY
or
~~INTELLIGENCE SUMMARY.~~
(Erase heading not required.)

Place	Date	Hour	Summary of Events and Information	Remarks and references to Appendices
RENINGHELST.	Dec 14.		The N.C.O. on leave – extended to Dec 31. has been transferred to Class W. T.F. Reserve. & is struck off the strength of this section.	
			I went round CHIPPEWA camp this morning & found quantities of kit still in cookhouse, & also quantities of tea leaves thrown about the camp. This I reported to the M.O's of the battalions there.	
			Brick incinerator finished @ CHIPPEWA. This is an open one, tho' I started it as a closed one. I changed this because units cannot look after the closed ones & pull them to pieces tho' careless usage.	
			Found kit & men sleeping in cookhouses of 122 Brig. H.Q.,	

2353 Wt. W2544/1454 700,000 5/15 D. D. & L. A.D.S.S. Forms/C. 2118.

Army Form C. 2118.

Instructions regarding War Diaries and Intelligence Summaries are contained in F. S. Regs., Part II. and the Staff Manual respectively. Title pages will be prepared in manuscript.

WAR DIARY
or
~~INTELLIGENCE SUMMARY.~~
(Erase heading not required.)

Place	Date	Hour	Summary of Events and Information	Remarks and references to Appendices
			also 122 ~~[illegible]~~ Machine Gun Coy. This reported to Staff Capt & O.C. concerned.	
			Latrines are still required for 122 & 123 M.G. Coys, & no attempt appears to have been made to order these. I have communicated c the Ofcs, with a view to expediting matters.	
			Sample of water taken from Dickebusch Lake & tested for metallic poisons gave negative results.	
			I am ordering quantities of latrines from the R.E. & supplying them myself direct to Units, as units cannot get them from the R.Es. Ontario camp is still requiring latrines altho the R.E. have had these in hand for six weeks. [illegible]	

2353 Wt. W2544/1454 700,000 5/15 D. D. & L. A.D.S.S. Forms/C. 2118.

Instructions regarding War Diaries and Intelligence Summaries are contained in F. S. Regs., Part II. and the Staff Manual respectively. Title pages will be prepared in manuscript.

WAR DIARY
or
~~INTELLIGENCE SUMMARY~~.

(Erase heading not required.)

Army Form C. 2118.

Place	Date	Hour	Summary of Events and Information	Remarks and references to Appendices
RENINGHELST.	Dec 15.		Watercart of No 2 Coy Div. train found to contain insufficiently chlorinated water. Reported to M.O.	
			Watercart of No 41 R.F.C. carrying no B.P. reported to me & passed on.	
			Watercart of "B" 189 reported in a leaky condition — passed to O.C. concerned: also bombardier i/c of cart is taken off for other duties.	
			Billet of 187 R.F.A. reported to M.O. as in a dirty condition.	
			Watercart of B 189 reported to me as carrying unchlorinated water reported to O.C.	
			Nothing has been done by R.E. to the latrines @ Murrumbidgee. Reported to area commandant.	
			Watercart of 23rd Middlesex reported to me as carrying no B.P. Passed to M.O.	H.V.
			I again asked the area commandant to hurry on the engineers in their work on Murrumbidgee camp.	

A5834 Wt. W4973/M687 750,000 8/16 D. D. & L. Ltd. Forms/C.2118/13

Instructions regarding War Diaries and Intelligence Summaries are contained in F. S. Regs., Part II. and the Staff Manual respectively. Title pages will be prepared in manuscript.

WAR DIARY
or
~~INTELLIGENCE SUMMARY.~~
(Erase heading not required.)

Army Form C. 2118.

Place	Date	Hour	Summary of Events and Information	Remarks and references to Appendices
			Nothing has been done to the latrines @ Ontario Camp altho the matter has been in the R.E's hands for over six weeks.	
			I have asked for large quantities of latrine seats from R.E.	H.V.
	16		Samples of water taken from Dickebusch Lake & tested for metallic poisons gave negative results.	H.V.
	1		One of my inspectors reported very filthy latrines, badly fouled @ "C" 187. R.F.A. The o/c said he & his men have no time to attend to sanitation, so we could report him which we did.	
			Water @ cookhouse of 41st D.A.C. found unchlorinated: reported.	
			Water cart of 41st Div A.S.C. found to contain unchlorinated water: reported.	
			The artillery waggon lines of this Div. are still in a	

A5834 Wt. W4973/M687 750,000 8/16 D. D. & L. Ltd. Forms/C.2118/13

WAR DIARY
or
~~INTELLIGENCE SUMMARY.~~
(Erase heading not required.)

Army Form C. 2118.

Instructions regarding War Diaries and Intelligence Summaries are contained in F. S. Regs., Part II. and the Staff Manual respectively. Title pages will be prepared in manuscript.

Place	Date	Hour	Summary of Events and Information	Remarks and references to Appendices
			deplorable condition: this is partly due to the fact that they have been reorganising the artillery, & no unit of the artillery would do anything as there was the uncertainty of moving. It is hoped that this method of dealing with sanitary condition will cease to be displayed in any unit. It is the duty of every unit to better the existing sanitary conditions whether they occupy a billet for one night or one month.	R.V.
	17		I have seen the R.E. about more incinerators & the work @ [illegible], & hope to get on with these now. I have arranged to go round [illegible] with the R.E. on Monday morning & explain all that is wanting. I had a bad report about one of our battery lines: the artillery always say they are too busy to attend to sanitation.	

A5834 Wt. W4973/M687 750,000 8/16 D. D. & L. Ltd. Forms/C.2118/13.

Instructions regarding War Diaries and Intelligence Summaries are contained in F. S. Regs., Part II. and the Staff Manual respectively. Title pages will be prepared in manuscript.

WAR DIARY
or
~~INTELLIGENCE SUMMARY.~~
(Erase heading not required.)

Army Form C. 2118.

Place	Date	Hour	Summary of Events and Information	Remarks and references to Appendices
	17		I suggested to the adj Div trench warfare school that he should try & obtain a supply of wood &c in order to make food cupboards &c. This camp is a very good one & it would be a pity if it were allowed to run to ruin thro' slackness. I have approached the camp commandant with a view to having the large amount of tins which have been accumulated round the incinerators @ Reninghelst taken away. Some days ago he told me that he could use these tins for roads & paths @ his stables, but as yet nothing has been done.	W.V.
RENINGHELST	Dec 18		I went round Murrumbidgee camp to day with [illegible] & told them exactly what was wanted. I was told that it was difficult to obtain material. ~~[illegible]~~ I offered the assistance of some of my section & would provide a couple of sappers as the work would be done more quickly by us.	

A5834 Wt. W4973/M687 750,000 8/16 D. D. & L. Ltd. Forms/C.2118/13

Instructions regarding War Diaries and Intelligence Summaries are contained in F. S. Regs., Part II. and the Staff Manual respectively. Title pages will be prepared in manuscript.

WAR DIARY
or
~~INTELLIGENCE SUMMARY.~~
(Erase heading not required.)

Army Form C. 2118.

Place	Date	Hour	Summary of Events and Information	Remarks and references to Appendices
			I also gave him my plans for ~~an~~ incinerators @ the various Camps.	
			Div. H.Q. watercart has been under repairs for a fortnight & it was found that water which had not been chlorinated had been used. This water supply was tested & was found to require chlorination: this reported to the M.O. of Div. HQ.	
			The fortnightly report on the whole Div. area which I have made up for my own use shows a great improvement in the sanitary condition of the area.	
			The R.E. have made some improvements in the box seat latrines which I suggested. A tin baffle is being put in the front part of the aperture to deflect urine in to the buckets & so prevent fouling of the front of the box. I also suggested using less timber in the construction of the seats but they do not seem to have done	

A5834 Wt. W4973/M687 750,000 8/16 D. D. & L. Ltd. Forms/C.2118/13

Instructions regarding War Diaries and Intelligence Summaries are contained in F. S. Regs., Part II. and the Staff Manual respectively. Title pages will be prepared in manuscript.

WAR DIARY
or
~~INTELLIGENCE SUMMARY.~~
(Erase heading not required.)

Army Form C. 2118.

Place	Date	Hour	Summary of Events and Information	Remarks and references to Appendices
			anything in regard to this.	HV.
	19.		I have had some difficulty in persuading one of the battalion commanders that his cookhouses have bit lined all round their walls. However as the orders come from Corps ~~there is nothing more to be said.~~ He also says that the R.M.O. is only a secondary person & has no authority to enforce sanitation & is merely a technical adviser. That may or may not be but the O/c San Sec. is directly under the A.D.M.S. ~~who~~ & so is the R.M.O. Any question of sanitation therefore is dealt with by the 3 people mentioned. If O/c's battalions wish to take an interest in sanitation so much the better – they should in fact – but the fact remains that the O/c San Sec. deals direct with the R.M.O.	
			I asked Area Commandant to let me know exactly	

A5834 Wt. W4973/M687 750,000 8/16 D. D. & L. Ltd. Forms/C.2118/13.

Instructions regarding War Diaries and Intelligence Summaries are contained in F. S. Regs., Part II. and the Staff Manual respectively. Title pages will be prepared in manuscript.

WAR DIARY
or
~~INTELLIGENCE SUMMARY.~~
(Erase heading not required.)

Army Form C. 2118.

Place	Date	Hour	Summary of Events and Information	Remarks and references to Appendices
			how much of Quebec camp was to be left for habitation as the latrines are v bad & require attention by the R.E. I have obtained a supply of box seat latrines from the R.E. & am now seeing to the fitting out of these units myself as the R.E. are too slow. I have now a supply of latrines for RIDGEWOOD camp, & these will be taken there as soon as I can get the R.M.O. to arrange for transport. — More attention should be paid to keeping huts in a good state of repair. They are very badly ventillated in most cases. It would be very easy to fit a couple of windows in the roofs of huts, one or 2 on each side for instance so that they could be raised from the inside & the hut ventillated daily. Many of the huts are pitch dark inside. The Nissen huts might easily be improved with this slight addition.	H.V.

A5834 Wt. W4973/M687 750,000 8/16 D. D. & L. Ltd. Forms/C.2118/13

Army Form C. 2118.

Instructions regarding War Diaries and Intelligence Summaries are contained in F. S. Regs., Part II. and the Staff Manual respectively. Title pages will be prepared in manuscript.

WAR DIARY
or
~~INTELLIGENCE~~ SUMMARY.
(Erase heading not required.)

Place	Date	Hour	Summary of Events and Information	Remarks and references to Appendices
RENINGHELST	Dec 30		I sent in a report to the A.P.M. certifying that no motor cycles had been found by me in the Sections quarters. I sent to the area commandant a report stating that proper ablution sheds & benches were still wanted in many of the camps. I also asked that the R.E. might be approached with a view to dealing with this. — Public urinals erected by "Q" alongside the church @ Reninghelst about three weeks ago are still incomplete & have been badly fouled. I applied to R.E. for more latrine seats. I have the requisite no. now for the battalion @ RIDGWOOD & have approached the adjutant of the battalion there with a view to having them transported	

A5834 Wt. W4973/M687 750,000 8/16 D. D. & L. Ltd. Forms/C.2118/13.

Instructions regarding War Diaries and Intelligence Summaries are contained in F. S. Regs., Part II. and the Staff Manual respectively. Title pages will be prepared in manuscript.

WAR DIARY

or

~~INTELLIGENCE SUMMARY.~~

(Erase heading not required.)

Army Form C. 2118.

Place	Date	Hour	Summary of Events and Information	Remarks and references to Appendices
			to Ridgwood by the Regimental transport as we have no transport for the purpose. —	
			The watercart of "B" 189 R.F.A. continues to be unsatisfactory in spite of what I have said to the M.O. I reported this to the A.D.M.S. giving all particulars of previous correspondence. —	
			We have been fitting small tin baffles in the box seat latrines supplied by the R.E., ~~so~~ & in the box seats as made by the R.E. the front of the seat is easily fouled by urine.	
			These baffles will be supplied to every seat in future, & are being fixed to those already in use. —	R.V.

A5834 Wt. W4973/M687 750,000 8/16 D. D. & L. Ltd. Forms/C.2118/13.

Army Form C. 2118.

WAR DIARY

or

~~INTELLIGENCE SUMMARY.~~

(Erase heading not required.)

Instructions regarding War Diaries and Intelligence Summaries are contained in F. S. Regs., Part II. and the Staff Manual respectively. Title pages will be prepared in manuscript.

Place	Date	Hour	Summary of Events and Information	Remarks and references to Appendices
RENINGHELST.	Dec 21.		R.E. failed to start on latrines @ Murrumbidgee as they ~~proposed~~ promised. Bricks for incinerator @ CHIPPEWA were left there. — Som men of 23rd Middlesex were taken off sanitary work for other duties. Reported. — In view of the fact that it is impossible to leave any R.E. material unguarded, I advised the adjutant of battalion @ CHIPPEWA that material was to be placed there for our use. Watercart of 23rd Mx. reported to me as not having the correct no. of details present @ time of refilling: Passed on for action ~~& report~~. also watercart of 2nd Tunneling Co: reported. — The incinerators @ Ontario & Alberta which we built are now in a very bad way owing to bad usage.	

Instructions regarding War Diaries and Intelligence Summaries are contained in F. S. Regs., Part II. and the Staff Manual respectively. Title pages will be prepared in manuscript.

WAR DIARY
or
~~INTELLIGENCE SUMMARY.~~
(Erase heading not required.)

Army Form C. 2118.

Place	Date	Hour	Summary of Events and Information	Remarks and references to Appendices
			have advised the area commandant to have them reconstructed as open ones. It is impossible to keep any structures to be anything but foolproof owing to the ignorance & lack of discipline among troops.	H.V.
Renin[illegible]	22 Dec		Sample of water taken from tank filled from a water cart of the 4th D.A.C. showed insufficient chlorination: Reported.	
			I sent the area commandant particulars of material Reqd. to complete the public urinal erected by order of "Q" & not completed	
			I also reported to area commandant that iron doors for incinerator to be erected @ CHIPPEWA had been removed altho the unit in occupation had been asked to guard material placed there for us.	H.V.

A5834 Wt. W4973/M687 750,000 8/16 D. D. & L. Ltd. Forms/C.2118/13.

Instructions regarding War Diaries and Intelligence Summaries are contained in F. S. Regs., Part II. and the Staff Manual respectively. Title pages will be prepared in manuscript.

WAR DIARY
or
~~INTELLIGENCE SUMMARY.~~
(Erase heading not required.)

Army Form C. 2118.

Place	Date	Hour	Summary of Events and Information	Remarks and references to Appendices
Reninghelst	Dec 23.		Water sample from 124 M.G.C. tested & found insufficiently chlorinated – reported to O/C.	
			Indents going thro' from R.E. for necessary material to convert the existing brick destructors which we built @ ALBERTA & Ontario into open incinerators. Nothing however can be done for the next 2 days.	
			A good many of the small units have now been supplied with box seat latrines (since the 14th of this month). ~~This~~ We shall continue to supply them as this is much the quicker way.	
			The R.E. are fitting up Ontario Camp with box seat latrines (after 7 weeks delay).	
			We are getting [illegible] fixed up gradually – with the help of one R.E. sapper.	R.V.

A5834 Wt. W4973/M687 750,000 8/16 D. D. & L. Ltd. Forms/C.2118/13

Instructions regarding War Diaries and Intelligence Summaries are contained in F. S. Regs., Part II. and the Staff Manual respectively. Title pages will be prepared in manuscript.

WAR DIARY
or
~~INTELLIGENCE~~ SUMMARY.

(Erase heading not required.)

Army Form C. 2118.

Place	Date	Hour	Summary of Events and Information	Remarks and references to Appendices
Remy Siding	Dec 26.		Work on latrines @ [illegible] is held up again owing to the disappearance of some of the material which the R.E. placed there. I reported this to area commandant.	
			It was reported to me that San. Squad men from one of the Regts in this Div were taken off San. Duties & put on to other work. I am investigating this, & have reported it for confirmation.	
			Work on brick incinerators which are being built by R.E. for [illegible] as @ the battalion camps is held up owing to the [illegible] changing over.	
			I have given orders that all water wardens or tanks & water cart men of units within this area are to make this Div [illegible] the water in the carts themselves. The water wardens are [illegible] know how to do it. [illegible] that these water cart men [illegible] are very useful but they should [illegible] water wardens [illegible] for chlorination of all water carts. They [illegible] responsible [illegible]	

A5834 Wt. W4973/M687 750,000 8/16 D. D. & L. Ltd. Forms/C.2118/13.

Instructions regarding War Diaries and Intelligence Summaries are contained in F. S. Regs., Part II. and the Staff Manual respectively. Title pages will be prepared in manuscript.

WAR DIARY
or
INTELLIGENCE SUMMARY.
(Erase heading not required.)

Army Form C. 2118.

Place	Date	Hour	Summary of Events and Information	Remarks and references to Appendices
			should make the watercartmen do their own chlorination & report any inefficiency or inability to do this on the part of the watercartmen. When a div gets on the move water discipline goes to the wall if the water duty men have not had practice themselves.	
			Ridgwood Camp continues to be unsatisfactory. We have supplied them with the proper fly proof seat latrines. The whole camp needs proper draining, & the billets are badly ventilated dug outs.	[initials]

A5834 Wt. W4973/M687 750,000 8/16 D. D. & L. Ltd. Forms/C.2118/13.

Instructions regarding War Diaries and Intelligence Summaries are contained in F. S. Regs., Part II. and the Staff Manual respectively. Title pages will be prepared in manuscript.

WAR DIARY
or
INTELLIGENCE SUMMARY.
(Erase heading not required.)

Army Form C. 2118.

Place	Date	Hour	Summary of Events and Information	Remarks and references to Appendices
Reninghelst	Dec 27.		Regimental San Squad men, reported to me as having been taken off San. work & put on to other work.	
			—	
			Work at [illegible] &c (on Sanitary constructional work) is held up for 2 days owing to R.E. F. Coys changing over.	
			The R.E.'s have not yet finished the filter tanks for baths & laundry @ Reninghelst, on which they have been working since the beginning of November.	
			—	
			We are still supplying latrines direct to units, as the R.E. do not seem to be able to supply units, or to supply us.	
			We have converted the brick covered in destructor which we built @ Alberta camp into an open brick one.	

A5834 Wt. W4973/M687 750,000 8/16 D. D. & L. Ltd. Forms/C.2118/13

Instructions regarding War Diaries and Intelligence Summaries are contained in F. S. Regs., Part II. and the Staff Manual respectively. Title pages will be prepared in manuscript.

WAR DIARY
or
~~INTELLIGENCE SUMMARY.~~
(Erase heading not required.)

Army Form C. 2118.

Place	Date	Hour	Summary of Events and Information	Remarks and references to Appendices
Remy Siding	Dec 28.		We converted the brick destructor @ Ontario into an open one. This reconstruction has been necessitated because units did not know how to use the destructors. "Foolproof" structures are essential. It is quite possible to burn excreta on these open incinerators. I wrote to the area commandant asking him to hurry on the R.E.s in their work of building other ~~[illegible]~~ brick incinerators in the big camps. There is a good deal of overlapping with the San. Sec. of the Div. on our left, who persist in visiting units in our area, altho I have pointed this out to them. They have been issuing orders contrary to those in force in our area. There ought to be ~~more~~ cooperation between San. Secs, at any rate those in the same corps.	[illegible]

Instructions regarding War Diaries and Intelligence Summaries are contained in F. S. Regs., Part II. and the Staff Manual respectively. Title pages will be prepared in manuscript.

WAR DIARY
or
~~INTELLIGENCE SUMMARY.~~
(Erase heading not required.)

Army Form C. 2118.

Place	Date	Hour	Summary of Events and Information	Remarks and references to Appendices
Reninghelst	Dec 29.		More material which the R.E. placed @ [illegible] for the latrines has been removed & is not traceable. I reported this to the area commandant.	
			There is too much dumping of manure: units do not attempt to burn it, & save themselves by dumping manure on the farmers, & in many cases this is causing a nuisance.	
			I asked the M.O. 9 B'R.G. [?] if he could provide a more efficient incinerator for this unit.	
			The Brigade H.Q. do not appear to take any trouble over their sanitation, & altho' my inspectors report to them each time they visit the camp on the defects, no attention is paid to them. I have approached the Staff Capt. on a [illegible] B.T. [?]	

A5834 Wt. W4973/M687 750,000 8/16 D. D. & L. Ltd. Forms/C.2118/13

Army Form C. 2118.

WAR DIARY
or
~~INTELLIGENCE SUMMARY.~~
(Erase heading not required.)

Instructions regarding War Diaries and Intelligence Summaries are contained in F. S. Regs., Part II. and the Staff Manual respectively. Title pages will be prepared in manuscript.

Place	Date	Hour	Summary of Events and Information	Remarks and references to Appendices
Reninghelst	Dec 30		More material has been taken from Murrumbidgee Camp. The latrines have been stripped of wood, & they are now in the original bad state. I reported this to the area commandant. At the present time the R.E. are finding great difficulty in supplying sufficient material, & it is impossible to do any work if this sort of thing goes on. We cannot put a guard over everything.	
			—	
			The Y.M.C.A. hut @ Dickebusch is using old tins &c instead of mugs or cups. These tins are not properly washed after use each time, but reissued dirty with tea &c. I drew the attention of the manager to this, & advised the complete washing of each tin after use in boiling water.	R.D.
			—	

A5834 Wt. W4973/M687 750,000 8/16 D. D. & L. Ltd. Forms/C.2118/13

WAR DIARY

or

~~INTELLIGENCE SUMMARY.~~

(Erase heading not required.)

Army Form C. 2118.

Instructions regarding War Diaries and Intelligence Summaries are contained in F. S. Regs., Part II. and the Staff Manual respectively. Title pages will be prepared in manuscript.

Place	Date	Hour	Summary of Events and Information	Remarks and references to Appendices
Reninghelst	Dec 31.		The water Cart of “B” 1 9 is still in a very unsatisfactory condition; leaking pipes, pumps out of order, no B.P. on the cart; no cloths for the Clamper are carried on the cart. I reported this to the A.D.M.S. The fortnightly report which I have made out shows a good deal of improvement in the units. Most of them have the proper latrines; excreta is burned in the majority of cases; cookhouses are a bit better; incinerators are dealing better with the refuse. More attention should be paid to food storage & protection from rats, who could be starved out. A crusade is to be made against rats shortly by every unit.	R.V.

A5834 Wt. W4973/M687 750,000 8/16 D. D. & L. Ltd. Forms/C.2118/13

Jan. 1917

41st Div.

140/1947

Vol 9

84 San Section

War Diary

January 1917

Sanitary Section 84.

W. Vickers
Capt.

Instructions regarding War Diaries and Intelligence Summaries are contained in F. S. Regs., Part II. and the Staff Manual respectively. Title pages will be prepared in manuscript.

WAR DIARY
or
~~INTELLIGENCE~~ SUMMARY.

(Erase heading not required.)

Army Form C. 2118.

Place	Date	Hour	Summary of Events and Information	Remarks and references to Appendices
RENINGHELST.	January 1. 1917.		Severe disciplinary action should be taken against men who "commit a nuisance" in the roads & billets. I have reported several instances of this to the APM. lately, & sent in A.F. B252, (Charge sheets) made out against the men.	
			"B" 189th RFA asked for assistance in obtaining material & building an incinerator at their waggon lines. I have applied to R.E. for materials for them, & for the 19th Middlesex (Pioneers), who also applied to me for help in this respect.	
			No fatigue party was furnished to me today from the Brigade in reserve as men were "excused all fatigues".	
			Work on Murrumbidgee camp latrines ~~has~~ has stopped, all the material having been stolen: in one case a latrine shed has been pulled down completely &	

A5834 Wt. W4973/M687 750,000 8/16 D. D. & L. Ltd. Forms/C.2118/13.

Instructions regarding War Diaries and Intelligence Summaries are contained in F. S. Regs., Part II. and the Staff Manual respectively. Title pages will be prepared in manuscript.

WAR DIARY
or
INTELLIGENCE SUMMARY.
(Erase heading not required.)

Army Form C. 2118.

Place	Date	Hour	Summary of Events and Information	Remarks and references to Appendices
			every bit of material removed.	
			—	
			R.E. have finished an open brick incinerator at Chippewa camp, & have started on another one at Murrumbidgee camp – from plans supplied by us.	
			—	
			I have had to take in one of the District men & make him clerk in the office, & I make this note for the following reason. This section is only 25 men strong, of these 25, 2 are performing nightly on the string band, commonly called the "Generals band", 2 others are performing daily in the Div. pierrot troup. All the morning is spent in rehearsing, & the men come back late @ night, & are unfit for duty the following morning. It is all very well to amuse the troops, but work should not be allowed to suffer. The band & pierrot troup will be performing daily for weeks to come.	[initials]

Army Form C. 2118.

Instructions regarding War Diaries and Intelligence Summaries are contained in F. S. Regs., Part II. and the Staff Manual respectively. Title pages will be prepared in manuscript.

WAR DIARY
or
~~INTELLIGENCE~~ SUMMARY.

(Erase heading not required.)

Place	Date	Hour	Summary of Events and Information	Remarks and references to Appendices
RENINGHELST.	January 2nd		It was reported to me that the Sanitary Squad men of the 15th Hants. of this Div. were taken off Sanitary work & put on other fatigues: I have asked for a report on this from the M.O.	
			D.R.O. orders all huts to be tarred in this area.	
			I visited Mummelbiggee Camp this aft. The battalion there was moving out into the trenches. The camp was left in a filthy condition, & I sent in a report to the A.D.M.S. about it. Pools of urine were everywhere, tea leaves, scraps of food, dead rats, soapy water were thrown broadcast, also scraps of paper. The latrines were filthy.	
			I reported the water cart of 6th Drag. Guards X Corps to their M.O. for not having details present when the car filled	

A5834 Wt. W4973/M687 750,000 8/16 D. D. & L. Ltd. Forms/C.2118/13.

Instructions regarding War Diaries and Intelligence Summaries are contained in F. S. Regs., Part II. and the Staff Manual respectively. Title pages will be prepared in manuscript.

WAR DIARY

or

~~INTELLIGENCE SUMMARY.~~

(Erase heading not required.)

Army Form C. 2118.

Place	Date	Hour	Summary of Events and Information	Remarks and references to Appendices
RENINGHELST.	Jan 3.		I have again applied to the area commandant for material for Mammeligee Latrines. I told him that the work must be done, & that if the R.E. supplied the material & 2 sappers we would see that the work was done. I told him exactly what was required.	
			I have had several applications for the A.F. B122 of the 2 Foden M.T. A.S.C. Drivers who are attached to this section. The conduct sheets of these men have never been supplied to me. Their names are Ptes Bryant & Lawrence, & they came to me from II. Corps in August 1916.	
			The necessary latrines have been obtained for the Brasserie, & I have applied to the Battalion there for transport to convey these latrine seats there.	
			A new school of Sanitation is being started @ BOESCHEPE	

A5834 Wt. W4973/M687 750,000 8/16 D. D. & L. Ltd. Forms/C.2118/13

Instructions regarding War Diaries and Intelligence Summaries are contained in F. S. Regs., Part II. and the Staff Manual respectively. Title pages will be prepared in manuscript.

WAR DIARY
or
~~INTELLIGENCE SUMMARY.~~
(Erase heading not required.)

Army Form C. 2118.

Place	Date	Hour	Summary of Events and Information	Remarks and references to Appendices
			by the X corps. I have sent one N.C.O. from this section to assist in the School. This N.C.O. will also help in supervising the sanitation of BOESCHEPE, & I am called in the other N.C.O. of this section stationed there, as I cannot spare 2 men away from the section.	
			—	
			I am redistributing the personnel of this section in the area, the same numbers in the subareas will be retained in nearly every case.	
RENINGHELST.	Jan. 4		—	H.V.
			I am having some small models of various sanitary contrivances made for demonstration purposes & to be used @ the X corps school of sanitation BOESCHEPE. I am also having some large scale drawings made for the same purposes.	
			—	
			The Report advanced centre of our Div. Hqs. which is outside this Divisional area is in an insanitary state. By arrangement & the O/C San. Sec. on our left, I will	

Army Form C. 2118.

Instructions regarding War Diaries and Intelligence Summaries are contained in F. S. Regs., Part II. and the Staff Manual respectively. Title pages will be prepared in manuscript.

WAR DIARY
or
~~INTELLIGENCE SUMMARY.~~
(Erase heading not required.)

Place	Date	Hour	Summary of Events and Information	Remarks and references to Appendices
			see that this is attended to, altho' it is in his area.	
			—	
			The latrine accomodation at Ontario Camp is nearly complete now, & only the seats are required.	
			—	
			Nothing has been done yet with regard to the latrines at [illegible].	
			—	
			2 Corps units are reported to me as having no proper details to attend to water carts. This will be investigated.	
			—	
			The rest billets of the 122 & 123 Brigade H.Q.s (shared alternately) which have been adversely reported on from time to time, are showing a gradual improvement after persistent 'nagging'!	H.V.

A5834 Wt. W4973/M687 750,000 8/16 D. D. & L. Ltd. Forms/C.2118/13

Instructions regarding War Diaries and Intelligence Summaries are contained in F. S. Regs., Part II. and the Staff Manual respectively. Title pages will be prepared in manuscript.

WAR DIARY

or

~~INTELLIGENCE SUMMARY.~~

(Erase heading not required.)

Army Form C. 2118.

Place	Date	Hour	Summary of Events and Information	Remarks and references to Appendices
RENINGHELST	Jan 5.		Commandant X corps School of Sanitation asked me for bricks, lime, tar, for the school, but I have not been able to supply them as R.E. wont supply me.	
			—	
			Water cart of X corps reinforcement camp refilled @ Abeele tanks, no details were sent with the cart: reported. Same with water cart of 6th Drag. guards X corps: this I also reported.	
			—	
			I have been in communication with the R.E. again re mmm bridges latrines, with a view to fixing them up definitely. They have once more promised to supply me with men & materials	
			—	
			It was reported to me that san. squad men of another of the battalions in this division were taken off sanitary work & put on to other fatigues. D.R.O. of this division forbids this & I am investigating this.	W.V.

A5834 Wt. W4973/M687 750,000 8/16 D. D. & L. Ltd. Forms/C.2118/13

Instructions regarding War Diaries and Intelligence Summaries are contained in F. S. Regs., Part II. and the Staff Manual respectively. Title pages will be prepared in manuscript.

WAR DIARY

or

~~INTELLIGENCE SUMMARY.~~

(Erase heading not required.)

Army Form C. 2118.

Place	Date	Hour	Summary of Events and Information	Remarks and references to Appendices
RENINGHELST.	Jan 6.		We have completed the latrine accomodation @ Ontario Camp with the help of the R.E.s. It has taken the R.E. since the beginning of November to supply this accomodation for a battalion!	
			—	
			We supplied the brasserie c latrines seats, & also the 41st Div Sigs Adv. centre today.	
			—	
			The R.E. have been putting in a filter & settling tank for the soapy effluent from the baths & laundry here. After 2 months work the plant is faulty for the soapy water is filtering in thro' the sides of the 14" brick wall settling tank they have built. Soapy water is also escaping all round the walls of this pit from other tanks. The plant is useless as it stands.	R.V.

A5834 Wt. W4973/M687 750,000 8/16 D. D. & L. Ltd. Forms/C.2118/13

Instructions regarding War Diaries and Intelligence Summaries are contained in F. S. Regs., Part II. and the Staff Manual respectively. Title pages will be prepared in manuscript.

WAR DIARY
or
~~INTELLIGENCE SUMMARY.~~
(Erase heading not required.)

Army Form C. 2118.

Place	Date	Hour	Summary of Events and Information	Remarks and references to Appendices
RENINGHELST.	Jan 7.		I reported to M.O. Concerned, a watercart of X Corps reinforcement camp for not sending water details with the cart when it was sent to refill.	
			I also reported the same to M.O. 3rd Spec. Batt R.E. concerning his watercart.	
			The offence "committing a nuisance" is still very common, & I am continually reporting men for the offence. It should be very heavily punished.	
			The following promotions were made in this section: they were necessitated in order to complete to establishment, one of the corporals being struck off strength of this section thro having been transferred to Class W T.F. reserve – War Office authority dated 1/1/17. (1) L'Cpl F.H. Morley 3098 to be act. corporal without pay vice Corpl Lees Smith H.B. 3900 transferred to T.F. reserve. (2) Pte G. Allsop 2930 to be act. L'Cpl with pay, vice Cpl F.H. Morley promoted. Both to date 2/1/1917	H.V.

A5834 Wt. W4973/M687 750,000 8/16 D. D. & L. Ltd. Forms/C.2118/13

Instructions regarding War Diaries and Intelligence Summaries are contained in F. S. Regs., Part II. and the Staff Manual respectively. Title pages will be prepared in manuscript.

WAR DIARY
or
~~INTELLIGENCE SUMMARY.~~
(Erase heading not required.)

Army Form C. 2118.

Place	Date	Hour	Summary of Events and Information	Remarks and references to Appendices
Field Reninghelst	Jan 8.		I went to the Corps School of Sanitation BOESCHEPE this afternoon, & gave 2 demonstrations there (1) Water bottles, water tanks & water carts. Their care & management. (2) Practical demonstration on construction of urinals & latrines. I also took over with me for the use of the School, a number of models of various sanitary contrivances which I had had made. I append to this months diary a syllabus of the course of instruction @ this School.	A. 1. attached to this months diary.
			Correspondence was passed to me from Camp Commandant re. a wheeled road sweeper which was to be used on the streets in Reninghelst. If this is in good condition it ought to simplify the work of street cleaning considerably.	

A5834 Wt. W4973/M687 750,000 8/16 D. D. & L. Ltd. Forms/C.2118/13.

Instructions regarding War Diaries and Intelligence Summaries are contained in F. S. Regs., Part II. and the Staff Manual respectively. Title pages will be prepared in manuscript.

WAR DIARY
or
~~INTELLIGENCE SUMMARY.~~

(Erase heading not required.)

Army Form C. 2118.

Place	Date	Hour	Summary of Events and Information	Remarks and references to Appendices
			2 will be run by the Camp Commandant, who is responsible for ~~the~~ the sanitation of Div. H.Q. altho' he seems to be under the impression that the San Sec is responsible. After all these months it is not yet properly known that the San. Sec. is not a fatigue party & that units must do their own sanitary work; if they don't they must expect the San. Sec. to demand reasons for negligence; & when this is done O/C's battalions get nasty & accuse us of spying.	R.V.

A5834 Wt. W4973/M687 750,000 8/16 D. D. & L. Ltd. Forms/C.2118/13

Army Form C. 2118.

Instructions regarding War Diaries and Intelligence Summaries are contained in F. S. Regs., Part II. and the Staff Manual respectively. Title pages will be prepared in manuscript.

WAR DIARY
or
~~INTELLIGENCE~~ SUMMARY.

(Erase heading not required.)

Place	Date	Hour	Summary of Events and Information	Remarks and references to Appendices
Reninghelst	Jan 9.		I reported the insufficient latrine accommodation @ CHIPPEWA Camp to the A.D.M.S. I asked if the R.E. could not be asked to provide more accommodation. After 2 months employed in constructing these latrines @ CHIPPEWA, they have only provided 2 for the battalion – ~~seat~~ 12 seats for NCOs & men.	
			The G.O.C. II Army was inspecting this area today.	
			I asked the A.D.M.S. if he could supply a horse & driver from the Field Ambulance here for the road sweeper.	
			The incinerator for H.Q. & Reninghelst which was demolished by an accident yesterday aft. I have applied to R.E. for material for a new destructor, & propose to build one like those we erected @ Ontario & Alberta, as we will be able to keep it under supervision, & we have a man who will look after it carefully. This will be completed [illegible]	

A5834 Wt. W4973/M687 750,000 8/16 D. D. & L. Ltd. Forms/C.2118/13

Army Form C. 2118.

Instructions regarding War Diaries and Intelligence Summaries are contained in F. S. Regs., Part II. and the Staff Manual respectively. Title pages will be prepared in manuscript.

WAR DIARY
or
~~INTELLIGENCE SUMMARY.~~

(Erase heading not required.)

Place	Date	Hour	Summary of Events and Information	Remarks and references to Appendices
Reninghelst	Jan 10.		I reported to the Commandant X Corps School of Sanitation the uncared for & delapidated state of the 3 water carts which were supplied to the School by the 138th F. Amb & 6 Dragoons for demonstration on Monday. I suggested that some action should be taken with regard to the cart of 6 Dragoons in particular, as I have already complained of the bad state in which this cart was kept.	
			—	
			A sample of water was taken from Dickebusch Lake & tested for metallic poisons as enemy shells had fallen in the lake – water was taken from point where it is drawn into the feed pipe of the pumping station. The result was negative.	
			—	
			I asked R.E. for 50 yds Duckboarding for the San. Sec camp.	

A5834 Wt. W4973/M687 750,000 8/16 D. D. & L. Ltd. Forms/C.2118/13

Instructions regarding War Diaries and Intelligence Summaries are contained in F. S. Regs., Part II. and the Staff Manual respectively. Title pages will be prepared in manuscript.

WAR DIARY
or
~~INTELLIGENCE SUMMARY.~~

(Erase heading not required.)

Army Form C. 2118.

Place	Date	Hour	Summary of Events and Information	Remarks and references to Appendices
Reningbelst	Jan 10.		Road sweeper was @ work today. It requires a new brush.	
			We have obtained necessary materials with difficulty, from R.E. for an incinerator of the closed type - destructor, made of bricks - for Div. H.Q. Appended is a drawing of this destructor, which I have found as near perfection as possible when worked ~~properly~~ by an intelligent man.	A.2.
			The open incinerators which we ~~have~~ asked the R.E. built at the camps are quite efficient. They were not built as large as we asked however; the R.E. appearing to leave off when they wish.	
			There ought to be more of these brick incinerators, but I cannot get them built by the R.E. Human excreta is disposed of efficiently in the open incinerators if mixed with rubbish.	[illegible initials]

1577 Wt. W10791/1773 500,000 1/15 D. D. & L. A.D.S.S./Forms/C. 2118.

Instructions regarding War Diaries and Intelligence Summaries are contained in F. S. Regs., Part II. and the Staff Manual respectively. Title pages will be prepared in manuscript.

WAR DIARY

or

~~INTELLIGENCE SUMMARY~~.

(Erase heading not required.)

Army Form C. 2118.

Place	Date	Hour	Summary of Events and Information	Remarks and references to Appendices
Reninghelst	Jan 11.		A well near Scottish Wood near Dickebusch Lake was inspected today & the water tested. The water was found to require more than 7 scoops of B.P. per 110 gals, & therefore was condemned.	
			I also inspected the following camps, as they were those chiefly concerned in the report I sent in on camps some time ago. Ontario, Alberta, Chippewa, Murrumbidgee. They were in a much more sanitary state, Murrumbidgee in particular having been cleaned up. This camp however is in need of proper sheds or huts for cookhouses, a drying room, & proper ablution sheds & benches. The latter are receiving attention & I have reported the want of cookhouses & drying room to the area commandant.	
			Ontario has at last been fitted up c latrines & the old disused	

1577 Wt. W10791/1773 500,000 1/15 D. D. & L. A.D.S.S./Forms/C. 2118.

Instructions regarding War Diaries and Intelligence Summaries are contained in F. S. Regs., Part II. and the Staff Manual respectively. Title pages will be prepared in manuscript.

WAR DIARY

or

~~INTELLIGENCE SUMMARY~~.

(*Erase heading not required.*)

Army Form C. 2118.

Place	Date	Hour	Summary of Events and Information	Remarks and references to Appendices
			latrine shed I have asked to be pulled down as the ground inside had been badly fouled & used as a latrine altho there were no latrine buckets or seats in it.	
			I also saw the sanitary arrangements of 123 Brigade H.Q. which are not good.	
			There is still a good deal of kit &c to be seen in cookhouses & sleeping in cookhouses; I am trying to enforce X Corps orders on this matter.	
			More cupboards & meatsafes are wanted generally.	
			Watercart of "C" 187 reported to me as out of order. I sent for a report on this.	
			Also watercart of 41st D.A.C. similarly treated.	

Instructions regarding War Diaries and Intelligence Summaries are contained in F. S. Regs., Part II. and the Staff Manual respectively. Title pages will be prepared in manuscript.

WAR DIARY
or
~~INTELLIGENCE SUMMARY~~.
(Erase heading not required.)

Army Form C. 2118.

Place	Date	Hour	Summary of Events and Information	Remarks and references to Appendices
			I have made the permanent N.C.O.s on the strength of this section acting sergeants without pay with the exception of the L/Cpl. who is an acting corporal without pay. The district [?] men are unpaid L/Cpls. This I find is the best method. It draws a distinction between the N.C.O.s on the establishment & the men, which is necessary.	H.V. [?]
Field.	Jan 12.		Watercart of "C" 187 R.F.A. was reported by me as having 1 Pump missing: no cloths for clarifier: no tin box for clarifying cloths.	
			Watercart of 41st D.A.C. was reported by me as having one pump requiring cleaning & oiling.	
			I reported the insufficient Latrine accomodation at Kenora & Victoria camps to the area commandant, & he	

1577 Wt. W10791/1773 500,000 1/15 D. D. & L. A.D.S.S./Forms/C. 2118.

Instructions regarding War Diaries and Intelligence Summaries are contained in F. S. Regs., Part II. and the Staff Manual respectively. Title pages will be prepared in manuscript.

WAR DIARY

or

~~INTELLIGENCE SUMMARY~~.

(Erase heading not required.)

Army Form C. 2118.

Place	Date	Hour	Summary of Events and Information	Remarks and references to Appendices
			suggested that as they were Corps camps we should not ~~to~~ attend to them ~~unless~~ the matter were urgent. —	
			Carts of N. Irish Horse, X Corps troops, & 3rd Spec Batt^n R.E. were reported by me as sending watercarts to fill @ tanks without accompanying details.	
			Samples of water taken from Dickebusch Lake near the pumping station, & tested for metallic poisons gave negative results on 2 separate examinations. —	
			(Reported to A.P.M. that 4 sparking plugs had been taken out of the box of spare parts belonging to the lorry of this section). —	
			There is one point with regard to the state of battalion camps	

1577 Wt. W10791/1773 500,000 1/15 D. D. & L. A.D.S.S./Forms/C. 2118.

Instructions regarding War Diaries and Intelligence Summaries are contained in F. S. Regs., Part II. and the Staff Manual respectively. Title pages will be prepared in manuscript.

WAR DIARY

or

~~INTELLIGENCE SUMMARY~~.

(Erase heading not required.)

Army Form C. 2118.

Place	Date	Hour	Summary of Events and Information	Remarks and references to Appendices
			to which I wish to draw attention, is this. I have often noticed that a battalions lines may be in a very clean condition during their stay. The unit relieving ~~them~~ will report that the lines were left in a dirty & insanitary condition. I know that cleaning up parties are left behind to see that the place is left tidy. It is largely the incoming "oddments" who are responsible for this untidy state of affairs. A more thorough routine of "handing over" & inspection by a responsible officer or N.C.O. of the incoming & outgoing units should be instituted, & this applies to every branch of the army.	W.V.
Field.	Jan 13.		In reply to a "secret" letter asking for the site of this units dump in the event of a forward move, I gave ~~the~~ the site as G 34 d 2.7. Sheet 28 N.W.	

1577 Wt. W10791/1773 500,000 1/15 D. D. & L. A.D.S.S./Forms/C. 2118.

Instructions regarding War Diaries and Intelligence Summaries are contained in F. S. Regs., Part II. and the Staff Manual respectively. Title pages will be prepared in manuscript.

WAR DIARY

or

~~INTELLIGENCE SUMMARY.~~

(Erase heading not required.)

Army Form C. 2118.

Place	Date	Hour	Summary of Events and Information	Remarks and references to Appendices
			I applied for 2 pairs of lumbermen's boots for the use of "cook & general fatigue men" of this section, in reply to X Corps R.O. 197.	
			Samples of water taken from Dickebusch Lake near the pumping station, & tested for metallic poisons gave negative results on 2 separate examinations.	R.
Field.	Jan 14		I again reported the water cart of K. Irish Horse as not having the necessary details present at the time of filling.	
			I reported water cart of "D" 90 R.F.A. for: not carrying Bleaching powder: no cloths for clarifier.	

Instructions regarding War Diaries and Intelligence Summaries are contained in F. S. Regs., Part II. and the Staff Manual respectively. Title pages will be prepared in manuscript.

WAR DIARY

or

~~INTELLIGENCE SUMMARY.~~

(Erase heading not required.)

Army Form C. 2118.

Place	Date	Hour	Summary of Events and Information	Remarks and references to Appendices
			The usual fortnightly report on the sanitation of this area's troops which have made up. Shows the following: (1) nearly every unit is taking more care in keeping food from rats & in proper safes & covered boxes.	
			(2) More ablution sheds have been built, & filters made for dealing with the soapy water: more are still required	
			(3). Proper sanitary latrines are still required for many units. These are being made as quickly as the R.E. can supply material. The R.E. seem to place every obstacle in the way of providing material for sanitary purposes.	
			(4) Incineration of excreta is more efficiently carried out. In many cases this is done in open incinerators.	
			(5) It is becoming increasingly difficult to	

1577 Wt. W10791/1773 500,000 1/15 D. D. & L. A.D.S.S./Forms/C. 2118.

Instructions regarding War Diaries and Intelligence Summaries are contained in F. S. Regs., Part II. and the Staff Manual respectively. Title pages will be prepared in manuscript.

WAR DIARY
or
~~INTELLIGENCE SUMMARY~~.
(Erase heading not required.)

Army Form C. 2118.

Place	Date	Hour	Summary of Events and Information	Remarks and references to Appendices
			make incinerators of tins & oil drums, as these have nearly all to be returned to railhead.	
			This section is being called on to do an increasing number of small "jobs" for the X Corps School of Sanitation BOESCHEPE.	
			One man of this section has been evacuated to a "C.C.S." & is accordingly struck off the strength of this unit from 13/1/17	H.V.
Field	Jan 15.		I reported watercart of 2nd Canadian Tunnelling Co R.E. for having a pump out of order.	
			Manure is being allowed to collect @ H.Q. transport lines of	

1577 Wt. W10791/1773 500,000 1/15 D. D. & L. A.D.S.S./Forms/C. 2118.

Instructions regarding War Diaries and Intelligence Summaries are contained in F. S. Regs., Part II. and the Staff Manual respectively. Title pages will be prepared in manuscript.

WAR DIARY
or
~~INTELLIGENCE SUMMARY~~.
(Erase heading not required.)

Army Form C. 2118.

Place	Date	Hour	Summary of Events and Information	Remarks and references to Appendices
			122 Inf. Brigade of this Div. I have asked for its removal.	
			Public latrine in RENINGHELST was moved today to a new position, & converted into a fly proof seat & pail latrine	
			I spent the afternoon lecturing at the X Corps School of Sanitation BOESCHEPE.	W.
Field.	Jan 16.		Watercart of D190 again reported in bad condition.	
			Watercart of 2nd Can Tunnelling Co. R.E. reported as having one of the pumps out of order.	
			Public Latrine & Urinal in RENINGHELST is being	

1577 Wt. W10791/1773 500,000 1/15 D. D. & L. A.D.S.S./Forms/C. 2118.

Instructions regarding War Diaries and Intelligence Summaries are contained in F. S. Regs., Part II. and the Staff Manual respectively. Title pages will be prepared in manuscript.

WAR DIARY

or

~~INTELLIGENCE SUMMARY.~~

(Erase heading not required.)

Army Form C. 2118.

Place	Date	Hour	Summary of Events and Information	Remarks and references to Appendices
			moved to a new site adjoining the present one. The old site was found to be nothing but foul ground. The old long trench was filled in. All the foul ground has been screened off & marked "foul ground". I have asked the R.E. to construct a large urinal trough & sign board.	W.V.
Field	Jan 16.		The disposal of the soapy water effluent from the baths & laundry ~~to~~ in RENINGHELST is still very unsatisfactory. In fact it is worse than it ever was. The R.E. have been working for the past 2 months on pits to be used as settling tanks. Owing to faulty work these are no use, & I have suggested to the A.D.M.S. that the R.E. be asked to make a channel which will lead the effluent direct to the stream without passing thro the tanks. This procedure is allowed	

1577 Wt. W10791/1773 500,000 1/15 D. D. & L. A.D.S.S./Forms/C. 2118.

Instructions regarding War Diaries and Intelligence Summaries are contained in F. S. Regs., Part II. and the Staff Manual respectively. Title pages will be prepared in manuscript.

WAR DIARY

or

~~INTELLIGENCE SUMMARY.~~

(Erase heading not required.)

Army Form C. 2118.

Place	Date	Hour	Summary of Events and Information	Remarks and references to Appendices
			by II Army order - Urbany when the streams are running full. It will also allows all the existing pits to be emptied, repaired & thoroughly cleaned out.	
			Several of the cellars of houses in RENINGHELST & other places are flooded with what appears to be urine. In one case here a large pit previously existed & was used by the Civilians for their own hop industry. One Division using the premises made use of this pit as a urine pit & it is now a filthy insanitary cesspool, necessitating clearing out. The Colonial troops are responsible for many insanitary indiscretions of this nature.	
			I applied to R.E. for pump to clear out a pit & cellar for the Amb. Dressing Station here.	

Instructions regarding War Diaries and Intelligence Summaries are contained in F. S. Regs., Part II. and the Staff Manual respectively. Title pages will be prepared in manuscript.

WAR DIARY
or
~~INTELLIGENCE SUMMARY.~~
(Erase heading not required.)

Army Form C. 2118.

Place	Date	Hour	Summary of Events and Information	Remarks and references to Appendices
			a water cart of 20th D.L.I. reported not in proper working order.	T.V.
Field	Jan 17.		Water tank 37 - 16th Div. area, was reported to me as requiring cleansing:- passed to proper channels.	
			I received orders from D.A.G. 3rd Echelon today, letter ~~No~~ C.R. No 31625/84/A. of 12/1/17, to the effect that Sergt J.W. Hoflin, 2147, of ~~this~~ section was of German parentage. I was instructed to send him forthwith to O/C Reinforcements, ROUEN. from where he was to proceed to England to report to O/C 31st Battn. Middlesex Regt. with a view to his transfer to that battalion. I gave him the necessary orders to leave POPERINGHE by the usual train next day. i.e. 18/1/17.	
			Water ~~-~~ cart of "A". 187 R.F.A. reported as being out of order.	

1577 Wt. W10791/1773 500,000 1/15 D. D. & L. A.D.S.S./Forms/C. 2118

Instructions regarding War Diaries and Intelligence Summaries are contained in F. S. Regs., Part II. and the Staff Manual respectively. Title pages will be prepared in manuscript.

WAR DIARY
or
~~INTELLIGENCE SUMMARY~~.
(Erase heading not required.)

Army Form C. 2118.

Place	Date	Hour	Summary of Events and Information	Remarks and references to Appendices
			Water in Cart of "D" 189 reported as insufficiently chlorinated. Cart also reported not complete & in working order.	
			Water cart of 41st A.S.C. also reported not complete & in working order.	
			also reported water cart of 18th K.R.R. for a similar reason.	
			also reported water cart of 12th E. Surreys.	H.V.
Field.	Jan 18.		I visited a control post 29, near ABEELE this afternoon to investigate a "cess pit" which was causing a nuisance. I found the "pit" was not a cess pit, but was a "trap"	

2353 Wt. W2544/1454 700,000 5/15 D. D. & L. A.D.S.S./Forms/C. 2118.

Army Form C. 2118.

Instructions regarding War Diaries and Intelligence Summaries are contained in F. S. Regs., Part II. and the Staff Manual respectively. Title pages will be prepared in manuscript.

WAR DIARY
or
~~INTELLIGENCE SUMMARY.~~
(Erase heading not required.)

Place	Date	Hour	Summary of Events and Information	Remarks and references to Appendices
			in the culvert which was stopped up. It lay half in Belgium & half in France & the French authorities would not allow the road to be opened up. I passed my report on this on to the A.D.M.S. & also to X Corps, as the "pit" is out of our area.	
			I again saw the R.E. @ [illegible] with a view to fixing up the latrines there. They promised to see to these, & also to erect new cookhouses or sheds as the existing ones were reported insanitary sometime ago. They are also erecting ablution sheds & washhouses for the camp.	A.V.
Field	Jan 19.		Stable refuse from Div. H.Q. stables is being dumped in the main street & left to lie as unsightly insanitary heaps for the greater part of the day. I have asked for this	

Instructions regarding War Diaries and Intelligence Summaries are contained in F. S. Regs., Part II. and the Staff Manual respectively. Title pages will be prepared in manuscript.

WAR DIARY
or
INTELLIGENCE SUMMARY.
(Erase heading not required.)

Army Form C. 2118.

Place	Date	Hour	Summary of Events and Information	Remarks and references to Appendices
			to be rectified.	
			Receipt was acknowledged to A.D.M.S. of "secret" communication referring to disposal of surplus stores of this unit in the event of a forward move. A report is to be sent to "Q" in due course regarding orders for disposal of same & custody, with a view to subsequent removal to railhead depot. See later.	
			Refuse cart used by us for collection of refuse from Div. H.Q. was stolen during the night from our "dump" reported to A.P.M.	
	Jan 20		Water cart 41st D.A.C. reported not in working order.	
			More latrines of the approved type are required in	

2353 Wt. W2544/1454 700,000 5/15 D. D. & L. A.D.S.S./Forms/C. 2118.

Army Form C. 2118.

Instructions regarding War Diaries and Intelligence Summaries are contained in F. S. Regs., Part II. and the Staff Manual respectively. Title pages will be prepared in manuscript.

WAR DIARY
or
~~INTELLIGENCE SUMMARY.~~
(Erase heading not required.)

Place	Date	Hour	Summary of Events and Information	Remarks and references to Appendices
			this area: R.E. dont supply them rapidly enough.	
			My visits to camps today showed that manure is not burnt properly & is allowed to accumulate	
			I myself tried the experiment of putting a few pieces of burning refuse from an incinerator in a heap of wet manure. The manure has been burning continuously now for 48 hours without any attention.	
			I found in one camp a cylinder of expanded metal on a base of bricks & sheet iron & all the camp refuse & excreta from 200 men & horses was disposed of daily in this. It shows that it is not necessary to have elaborate incinerators if the sanitary men know how to work	

Army Form C. 2118.

WAR DIARY

or

~~INTELLIGENCE SUMMARY.~~

(Erase heading not required.)

Instructions regarding War Diaries and Intelligence Summaries are contained in F. S. Regs., Part II. and the Staff Manual respectively. Title pages will be prepared in manuscript.

Place	Date	Hour	Summary of Events and Information	Remarks and references to Appendices
			an incinerator. In 2 other camps I found 2 brick incinerators piled to the top & alone with ~~wet~~ refuse which would not burn: if it did burn the result would be a red hot mass which would ~~burst~~ the sides of any incinerator.	R.
Field	Jan 21.		Report mentioned on 19/1/17, was sent in today.	
			Very strict "fire" orders have been issued by me for observance in the quarters & camps of this section:	
			More plans & drawings were got ready for X Corps School of Sanitⁿ at BOESCHEPE.	

2353 Wt. W2544/1454 700,000 5/15 D. D. & L. A.D.S.S./Forms/C. 2118.

Army Form C. 2118.

Instructions regarding War Diaries and Intelligence Summaries are contained in F. S. Regs., Part II. and the Staff Manual respectively. Title pages will be prepared in manuscript.

WAR DIARY
or
~~INTELLIGENCE SUMMARY.~~
(Erase heading not required.)

Place	Date	Hour	Summary of Events and Information	Remarks and references to Appendices
Field	Jan 22.		I reported further instances of water carts of 1st Irish Horse filling @ water tanks without carrying necessary details to H.D.M.S. & so to Corps; altho' this case was similarly reported some time ago, no action had been taken.	
			I spent the aft. lecturing @ X Corps School of Sanitation @ BOESCHEPE.	
			The R.E. have completed the new outlet for soapy water effluent from baths here, vide note on Jan 16th: the effluent now runs direct into the stream ~~running~~ alongside the baths & laundry in RENING-HELST.	
			Nothing has yet been done to providing better latrines @ MURRUMBIDGEE.	

2353 Wt. W2544/1454 700,000 5/15 D. D. & L. A.D.S.S./Forms/C. 2118.

Instructions regarding War Diaries and Intelligence Summaries are contained in F. S. Regs., Part II. and the Staff Manual respectively. Title pages will be prepared in manuscript.

WAR DIARY
or
~~INTELLIGENCE SUMMARY.~~

(Erase heading not required.)

Army Form C. 2118.

Place	Date	Hour	Summary of Events and Information	Remarks and references to Appendices
			Incinerators have been provided @ CHIPPEWA, but they are not properly used & a most insanitary heap of rubbish is accumulating there.	
			A new prisoners of war cage is being erected on the road to La Clyte, & the latrines have been fouled already tho' being left incomplete:	
			Manure is not being properly disposed of, & large heaps are being accumulated near camps & waggon lines. The present system of waiting for the farmers to collect it is inadequate.	
			We still receive complaints & reports from the inspectors of this section about insufficient latrine accommodation among units. This also applies to ~~sheds~~ & places	

2353 Wt. W2544/1454 700,000 5/15 D. D. & L. A.D.S.S./Forms/C. 2118.

Army Form C. 2118.

Instructions regarding War Diaries and Intelligence Summaries are contained in F. S. Regs., Part II. and the Staff Manual respectively. Title pages will be prepared in manuscript.

WAR DIARY

or

~~INTELLIGENCE SUMMARY.~~

(Erase heading not required.)

Place	Date	Hour	Summary of Events and Information	Remarks and references to Appendices
			for washing.	
			The cellar of ambulance dressing station in RENINGHELST was pumped out today, but filled up again @ once. I think that the only thing to be done in these cases is to spray the water thickly with paraffin & to close up the cellars & leave the water undisturbed.	
			I have had to obtain civilian labour to repair the cart used for rubbish collection in RENINGHELST as it had broken down, & it was the only vehicle available for the purpose.	N.

Instructions regarding War Diaries and Intelligence Summaries are contained in F. S. Regs., Part II. and the Staff Manual respectively. Title pages will be prepared in manuscript.

WAR DIARY

or

~~INTELLIGENCE SUMMARY.~~

(Erase heading not required.)

Army Form C. 2118.

Place	Date	Hour	Summary of Events and Information	Remarks and references to Appendices
Field.	Jan 23.		I sent in a report to the A.D.M.S. on the generally uncared for state of watercarts in this div. The complaints were mainly due to the fact that owing to the existing methods of filling carts from watertanks @ stationary points, the pumps, pipings, clampers were totally neglected & rarely if ever overhauled. The correct spare parts & containers were not kept clean & free from rust & dirt.	
			I reported watercart of 124 M.G.C. for carrying unchlorinated water; & also for not carrying efficient B.P.!	
			I asked the R.E. for help in the public latrines & urinals here.	K.D.

Army Form C. 2118.

Instructions regarding War Diaries and Intelligence Summaries are contained in F. S. Regs., Part II. and the Staff Manual respectively. Title pages will be prepared in manuscript.

WAR DIARY

or

~~INTELLIGENCE SUMMARY~~.

(Erase heading not required.)

Place	Date	Hour	Summary of Events and Information	Remarks and references to Appendices
Field.	Jan 24		This Section is now 3 below strength – one man going to England for a commission today. Two others have left recently, one being sick & the other recalled to England by D.A.G.: G.H.Q.	
			I asked for a new urine trough for Public urinal here in RENINGHELST from R.E. thro' area commandant.	
			I also asked area commandant about a brick incinerator for MICMAC camp. R.E. replied that there were no bricks or material available.	
			I asked for material to extend the Public Latrines in RENINGHELST, as the orig. was not considered large enough.	
			I sent in to A.D.M.S. a further report on the question of	

2353 Wt. W2544/1454 700,000 5/15 D. D. & L. A.D.S.S./Forms/C. 2118.

Instructions regarding War Diaries and Intelligence Summaries are contained in F. S. Regs., Part II. and the Staff Manual respectively. Title pages will be prepared in manuscript.

WAR DIARY
or
~~INTELLIGENCE SUMMARY.~~
(Erase heading not required.)

Army Form C. 2118.

Place	Date	Hour	Summary of Events and Information	Remarks and references to Appendices
			dealing with the soapy effluent from Baths here. I suggested "short circuiting" the present foul sedimentation pit & allowing the effluent to run in to the stream direct as they did @ the laundry: see previous note for Jan 16 & Jan 22nd.	
			Samples of water taken from watercarts of 10 Queens of this div. Tests showed insufficient chlorination. Reported.	R.V.
Field	Jan 25.		Samples of water taken from pumping station at Dickebusch Lake & tested for metallic poisons gave negative results. (Test necessitated thro' hostile shells falling in lake).	
			Other work as normal.	R.V.

2353 Wt. W2544/1454 700,000 5/15 D. D. & L. A.D.S.S./Forms/C. 2118.

Instructions regarding War Diaries and Intelligence Summaries are contained in F. S. Regs., Part II. and the Staff Manual respectively. Title pages will be prepared in manuscript.

WAR DIARY

or

~~INTELLIGENCE SUMMARY.~~

(*Erase heading not required.*)

Army Form C. 2118.

Place	Date	Hour	Summary of Events and Information	Remarks and references to Appendices
Field	Jan 26.		Sample of water taken from Dickebusch Lake & tested for metallic poisons gave negative results.	
			2 offered to fix in the "short circuit" for baths soap [illegible] if R.E. would supply us with material. No reply was received.	R.V.
			Watercart of X corps Cyclists was inspected today & found to have the oblong tin kettle missing. Reported.	
			Also watercart of 123 M.G. Coy of this Div: following points noted: Wooden stores box missing. Oblong tin kettle missing. Woodwork of frame of cart broken. This was also reported.	R.V.

2353 Wt. W2544/1454 700,000 5/15 D. D. & L. A.D.S.S./Forms/C. 2118.

Instructions regarding War Diaries and Intelligence Summaries are contained in F. S. Regs., Part II. and the Staff Manual respectively. Title pages will be prepared in manuscript.

WAR DIARY
or
~~INTELLIGENCE SUMMARY.~~
(Erase heading not required.)

Army Form C. 2118.

Place	Date	Hour	Summary of Events and Information	Remarks and references to Appendices
Field	Jan 28		Sample of water taken from Pumping Station Dickebusch Lake, & tested for metallic poisons gave negative results.	
			Absence of details from watercart of 34th Batty. R.F.A. att'd this div. reported.	
			Water in cart of 9th Mx. found unchlorinated: also absence of water tester box & notes. Reported.	
			Water cart of 41st A.S.C. found filling without details today: also water found unchlorinated. Reported.	
			I have had a "record book" made of work done by this section which shows the actual constructional work & supervision done by this section since coming	

2353 Wt. W2544/1454 700,000 5/15 D. D. & L. A.D.S.S./Forms/C. 2118.

Instructions regarding War Diaries and Intelligence Summaries are contained in F. S. Regs., Part II. and the Staff Manual respectively. Title pages will be prepared in manuscript.

WAR DIARY

or

~~INTELLIGENCE SUMMARY~~.

(Erase heading not required.)

Army Form C. 2118.

Place	Date	Hour	Summary of Events and Information	Remarks and references to Appendices
			into this area 3 months ago.	
			I attended a conference of O.Cs. San Sec. in this army @ HAZEBROOK this aft. The subjects for discussion ~~was~~ were the proposed "standardisation" of work which fell to a San Sec. & the proposed scheme for making San Secs. Army troops. Nothing definite could be settled as no agenda had been offered, & the D.A.D.M.S. 2nd Army could give us no definite points to go upon. Without these it was impossible to say what the best working scheme would be.	A.K.

Instructions regarding War Diaries and Intelligence Summaries are contained in F. S. Regs., Part II. and the Staff Manual respectively. Title pages will be prepared in manuscript.

WAR DIARY
or
~~INTELLIGENCE SUMMARY.~~
(Erase heading not required.)

Army Form C. 2118.

Place	Date	Hour	Summary of Events and Information	Remarks and references to Appendices
Field.	Jan 29.		The usual fortnightly return which I have drawn up shows continued improvement, tho' increasing shortness in the amount of assistance given us by R.E.	
			I reported dumping of manure from HQ stables of this Division along the roadside to A.D.M.S. as my previous suggestions to Camp Commandant had been ignored.	
			I spent the afternoon lecturing at BOESCHEPE to the X Corps School of Sanitn.	
			I have been told that the R.E. have decided to alter the plant for disposal of the soapy effluent from the baths here.	
			San. work operation normal.	[initials]

2353 Wt. W2544/1454 700,000 5/15 D. D. & L. A.D.S.S./Forms/C. 2118.

Army Form C. 2118.

WAR DIARY
or
~~INTELLIGENCE SUMMARY.~~
(Erase heading not required.)

Instructions regarding War Diaries and Intelligence Summaries are contained in F. S. Regs., Part II. and the Staff Manual respectively. Title pages will be prepared in manuscript.

Place	Date	Hour	Summary of Events and Information	Remarks and references to Appendices
Field.	Jan 30.		Another conference of O/c's San Secs II Army is to be held @ HAZEBROOK on 31/1/17 @ 3.30 P.M.	
			I found several instances in the camps today of wanton destruction of box seat latrines.	
			No further progress has been made by the R.E. on the latrines @ Mummlidgee camp. They have completed 2 ablution sheds however.	
			The ablution shed @ Ontario is still in the unfinished state in which the R.E. left it over 3 weeks ago.	
			As a result of report which was sent to A.D.M.S. on the neglected state of watercarts in this Div. the A.D.M.S. has asked me to arrange for a series	

2353 Wt. W2544/1454 700,000 5/15 D. D. & L. A.D.S.S./Forms/C. 2118.

Instructions regarding War Diaries and Intelligence Summaries are contained in F. S. Regs., Part II. and the Staff Manual respectively. Title pages will be prepared in manuscript.

WAR DIARY

or

~~INTELLIGENCE SUMMARY.~~

(Erase heading not required.)

Army Form C. 2118.

Place	Date	Hour	Summary of Events and Information	Remarks and references to Appendices
			of demonstrations to the watercart men in this division. These will be arranged.	H.V.
Fees	Jan 31.		Diary to Becourt this morning.	H.V.

2353 Wt. W2544/1454 700,000 5/15 D. D. & L. A.D.S.S./Forms/C. 2118.

X^th^ Corps School of Sanitation.

SYLLABUS OF COURSE OF INSTRUCTION.

A. 1.

Date	Time	Subject	Lecturer.
MONDAY	9.0am	Introductory lecture on General principles of preventing disease.	Commandant.
"	10.30am	Air and Ventilation. Insects and Disease with special reference to Flies	Capt: Galpin.
"	1.30pm	Practical instruction in Water testing. Class will be instructed in Sections	Sanitary Instructors. (Capt Gosse).
"	2.20pm	Water Carts, Water bottles and Water tanks. Their care and management	Capt Vickers O.C.84.San Sec.
"	3.30pm	Practical demonstration on construction of Urinals and latrines	Capt Vickers.
TUESDAY	9.0am	Foods and Food storage, and the principles of cooking	Commandant.
	10.30am	Lecture on Rats in Trenches and destruction.	Capt Gosse
	1.30pm to 5.0pm	Practical demonstration on cookhouses, camp baths and latrines. Visiting various selected camps	Commandant.
WEDNESDAY	9.0am to 12 noon	Practical work dealing with construction of incinerators latrines trench, and urine pits	Commandant.
	1.30pm	Lecture on personal Hygiene and the prevention of Trench foot, Scabies and Lice.	Capt Gosse.
	2.45pm.	Practical work in the construction of improvised meat safes and food stores.	Sanitary Instructors (Capt Gosse).
THURSDAY	9.0a,	Lecture on Infectious and contageous disease	Commandant
	10.0am to 12 noon	Lecture on disposal of excreta and refuse, and demonstration of working of destructors	Capt: Hessent.
	2pm to 4pm	Water and Water supplies with practical demonstration of sources and supplies	Capt Hessent
FRIDAY	9.0am tp 12 noon	Lecture on Camp construction and visit to camps	Commandant.
	2.0pm	Lecture on disinfectants, their use and abuse. Demonstrations will be given of various methods of disinfecting	Capt Gosse

SATURDAY.	9.0am	Lecture on Sanitary arrangements in Trenches	Capt Galpin O.C.19.San Sec.
	10.30am	Demonstration on Trench Latrines and Urinals	Capt Galpin.
	11.45am	Final Lecture	Commandant.
	2.0pm	Class dismissed.	

=-=

Classes for constructional work will be held each evening from 7 to 8 pm by the Sanitary Instructors. This work will embrace the making of improvised meatsafes, stores for food, urine funnels etc.

Samples and models of various contrivances used in Camp Sanitation will also be exhibited and the working explained

Length of course ONE WEEK.

Classes join SUNDAY afternoon and the 'buses that bring the incoming class to the school take the outgoing class back to their Divisions.

Albert E. Knight

4th JANUARY 1916

Captain R.A.M.C.
COMMANDANT.

~~A.D.M.S., 41st Div~~
No. M./2.B.

Officer Commanding,
~~Field Ambulance~~.
84th Sanitary Section.

Forwarded for information.

[signature]
Major,

6th January 1917

for A.D.M.S., 41st Division.

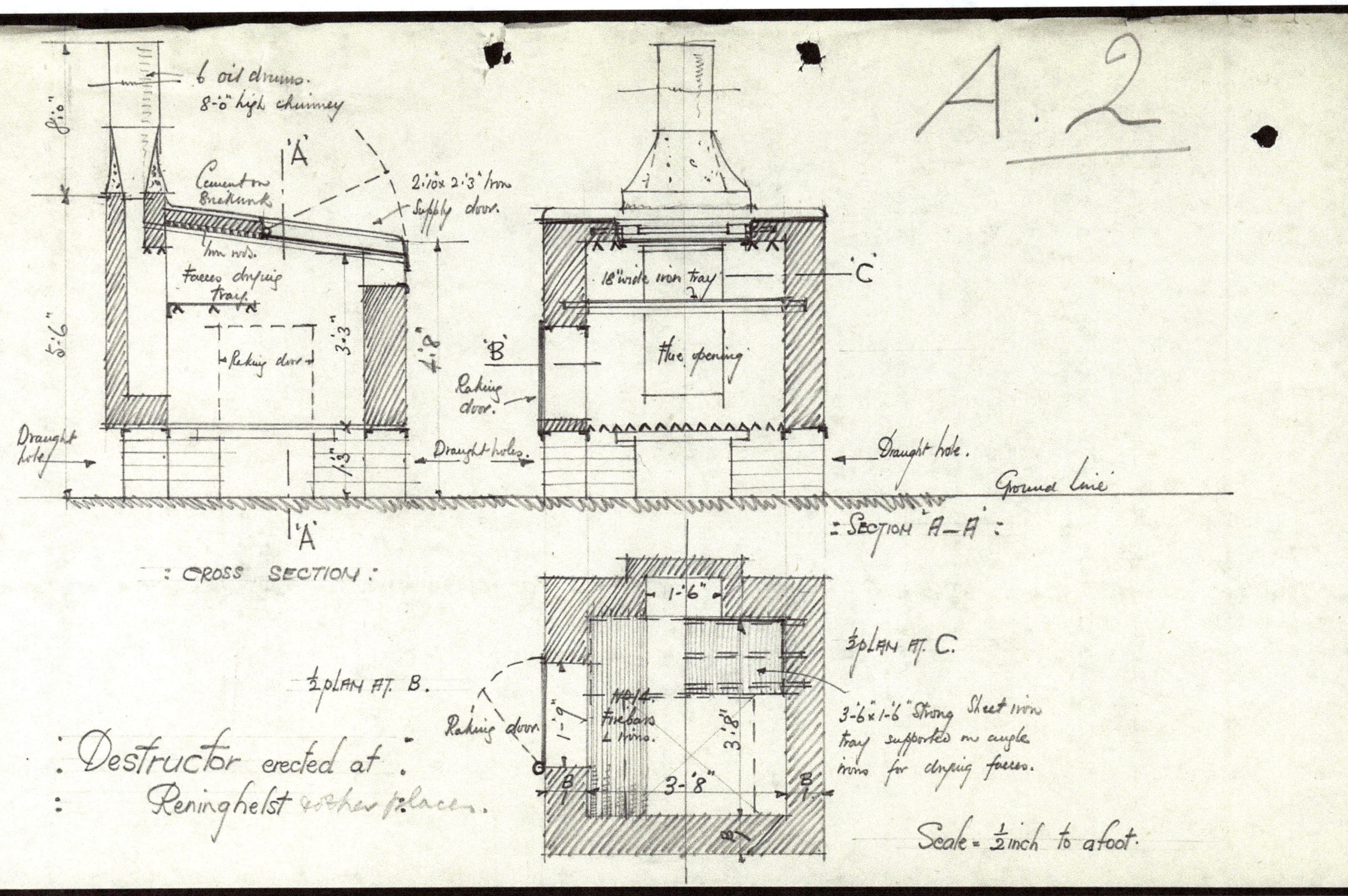
A.2
6 oil drums.
8-0" high chimney
Cement on Brickwork
2'10" x 2'3" iron supply door.
Iron rods.
Faeces drying tray.
Raking door
3'3"
4'8"
5'6"
8'0"
1'3"
Draught hole
Draught holes.
'A'
'B'
Raking door.
18" wide iron tray
C
Flue opening
Draught hole.
Ground Line
: CROSS SECTION :
: SECTION A–A :
1-6"
½ PLAN AT. C.
½ PLAN AT. B.
Raking door.
1-9"
Firebars L irons.
3'8"
3-8"
B
3'6" x 1'6" Strong Sheet iron tray supported on angle irons for drying faeces.
: Destructor erected at :
: Reninghelst & other places.
Scale = ½ inch to a foot.

Feb. 1917.

Confidential

140/2087.

Vol 10

War Diary

84TH Sanitary Section

From:- Feby 1. 1917

To:- Feby 28 1917

Confidential.

War Diary

of

Sanitary Section 84

from Feb 1. 1917. to Feb 28. 1917

Volume. X

Instructions regarding War Diaries and Intelligence Summaries are contained in F. S. Regs., Part II. and the Staff Manual respectively. Title pages will be prepared in manuscript.

WAR DIARY

or

~~INTELLIGENCE~~ SUMMARY.

(Erase heading not required.)

Army Form C. 2118.

Place	Date	Hour	Summary of Events and Information	Remarks and references to Appendices
RENINGHELST.	Feb. 1.		War Diary was sent to A.D.M.S. last evening (for January). Duplicates of War Diary for Oct. Nov. & Dec. were sent to T.F. Records London for custody. Commandant X Corps School of Sanitn. asked me for some lime for the school. Conference of O/Cs San. Secs. II Army @ Hazebrouck yesterday was called in order to tell them about the forthcoming campaign against rats. It has been arranged that returns of rats killed &c should be sent to San. Section by M.Os. of units. Stretcher bearers were to be provided with traps, each regiment having a different kind of trap. Nothing more was said about the proposed changes of making San. Secs. Army troops.	K.V.

2353 Wt. W2544/1454 700,000 5/15 D. D. & L. A.D.S.S./Forms/C. 2118.

WAR DIARY
or
~~INTELLIGENCE SUMMARY.~~
(*Erase heading not required.*)

Army Form C. 2118.

Instructions regarding War Diaries and Intelligence Summaries are contained in F. S. Regs., Part II. and the Staff Manual respectively. Title pages will be prepared in manuscript.

Place	Date	Hour	Summary of Events and Information	Remarks and references to Appendices
Field	Feb 2.		Jasper RE for more latrine seats, also material to [illegible] one of the existing public latrines. Latrines but no other material was supplied. We are having to salve what we can use that. This shows how impossible it is to "standardise" the work of a San. Sec. Sanitary ~~sectance~~ structures in the field must necessarily be ~~to~~ to a very large extent of an improvised type. If they then fulfill the conditions required "are clean & effective," it must be admitted that they are what is required. From my fortnightly reports find that only 2 small units have not got the prescribed latrines now. All the others of this Div. & att. troops have been supplied by ~~this~~ this section. At one of the camps, altho the latrines are [minimum of fee]	

2353 Wt. W2544/1454 700,000 5/15 D. D. & L. A.D.S.S./Forms/C. 2118.

Army Form C. 2118.

Instructions regarding War Diaries and Intelligence Summaries are contained in F. S. Regs., Part II. and the Staff Manual respectively. Title pages will be prepared in manuscript.

WAR DIARY

or

~~INTELLIGENCE SUMMARY.~~

(Erase heading not required.)

Place	Date	Hour	Summary of Events and Information	Remarks and references to Appendices
			not finished yet, there are the approved ~~seats~~, but no covering structures.	
Field.	Feb. 3.		I was ordered by A.D.M.S. to write for copy of S.S. 135 Instructions for the training of Divisions for offensive actions.	H.V.
			Watercart of A 187 Bt. F.A. reported by me as out of order.	
			R.E. have supplied wooden trough, as asked for dealing with the effluent from the baths here. This will be fixed by us @ once.	
			The scheme which I suggested to A.D.M.S. for demonstrating the watercart to water men in this	

2353 Wt. W2544/1454 700,000 5/15 D. D. & L. A.D.S.S./Forms/C. 2118.

Instructions regarding War Diaries and Intelligence Summaries are contained in F. S. Regs., Part II. and the Staff Manual respectively. Title pages will be prepared in manuscript.

WAR DIARY

or

~~INTELLIGENCE SUMMARY.~~

(Erase heading not required.)

Army Form C. 2118.

Place	Date	Hour	Summary of Events and Information	Remarks and references to Appendices
			Divisional area has been put bye, until the frost breaks, by the A. A&Q.M.G.	W.
Fiess.	Feb. 4.		Trough for effluent @ Baths fixed by this Section today. It was necessary to break down a good deal of the existing structures which were useless. It seems a great waste of time & labour & material for the R.E. to erect any structures dealing with sanitation with consulting the Sanitary Officer from time to time while building is going on. I have found that if I have asked the R.E. to make anything they adapt the plans to such an extent that very little benefit results from their work.	W.

Instructions regarding War Diaries and Intelligence Summaries are contained in F. S. Regs., Part II. and the Staff Manual respectively. Title pages will be prepared in manuscript.

WAR DIARY
or
~~INTELLIGENCE SUMMARY.~~
(Erase heading not required.)

Army Form C. 2118.

Place	Date	Hour	Summary of Events and Information	Remarks and references to Appendices
Field.	Feb 5.		I asked the area commandant for permission to have 2 Horsfall destructors repaired by R.E. & together with a 3rd have them removed to the ambulances. I am of opinion that Horsfalls are not efficient for dealing with ~~camp~~ refuse if there are quantities of tins in the rubbish. To be useful for this purpose a sufficiently large "raking out door" should be provided. I asked O/c D.R.S. to use & utilise one of these Horsfalls. I sent to the A.D.M.S. a report on the proper state of water carts & tanks @ water stations. Watermen, cooks &c are drawing water from any wells pumps which have not all been tested. I suggested that to simplify matters, samples of water should be sent direct to this office where they would	

A5834 Wt. W4973/M687 750,000 8/16 D. D. & L. Ltd. Forms/C.2118/13.

Instructions regarding War Diaries and Intelligence Summaries are contained in F. S. Regs., Part II. and the Staff Manual respectively. Title pages will be prepared in manuscript.

WAR DIARY
or
~~INTELLIGENCE SUMMARY.~~
(Erase heading not required.)

Army Form C. 2118.

Place	Date	Hour	Summary of Events and Information	Remarks and references to Appendices
			be tested forthwith & returned without delay.	
			Sample of water taken from Dickebusch Lake @ the pumping station & tested for metallic poisons gave negative results.	
		11 p.m.	41st D.R.S. have agreed to take unused Horsfall from Hanon Camp.	
			I have offered one of the Horsfalls from Chippewa to one of the other ambulances in this area. They will notify if it can be worked & repaired.	H.V.
			I spent the afternoon lecturing @ X Corps School of Sanitation BOESCHEPE.	

A5834 Wt. W4973/M687 750,000 8/16 D. D. & L. Ltd. Forms/C.2118/13

Army Form C. 2118.

WAR DIARY

or

~~INTELLIGENCE SUMMARY.~~

(Erase heading not required.)

Instructions regarding War Diaries and Intelligence Summaries are contained in F. S. Regs., Part II. and the Staff Manual respectively. Title pages will be prepared in manuscript.

Place	Date	Hour	Summary of Events and Information	Remarks and references to Appendices
Field.	Feb 6.		Sample of water taken from nr. pumping station Dickebusch Lake & tested for metallic poisons gave negative results.	
			One of the Horsfall destructors which I promised to one of the ambulances fell to pieces as soon as it was moved. It will not be possible to repair it.	
			Sanitary work normal.	RV.

A5834 Wt. W4973/M687 750,000 8/16 D. D. & L. Ltd. Forms/C.2118/13.

Instructions regarding War Diaries and Intelligence Summaries are contained in F. S. Regs., Part II. and the Staff Manual respectively. Title pages will be prepared in manuscript.

WAR DIARY

or

~~INTELLIGENCE SUMMARY~~

(Erase heading not required.)

Army Form C. 2118.

Place	Date	Hour	Summary of Events and Information	Remarks and references to Appendices
Field.	Feb. 7.		Two reinforcements joined this section today. Both men are sanitary inspectors. The section is still one rank below strength.	
			New public latrine erected in RENINGHELST. This was necessitated by the erection of the new Soldiers Club in RENINGHELST. In erecting this club, the R.E. have again given no thought as to the disposal of refuse, ablution & sullage water. I propose to take this matter in hand & have suitable structures erected to deal with conditions arising.	
			It is getting increasingly difficult to obtain material from the R.E.	
			Water cart of X Corps reinforcement camp reported	

2353 Wt. W2544/1454 700,000 5/15 D. D. & L. A.D.S.S. Forms/C. 2118.

Instructions regarding War Diaries and Intelligence Summaries are contained in F. S. Regs., Part II. and the Staff Manual respectively. Title pages will be prepared in manuscript.

WAR DIARY
or
~~INTELLIGENCE SUMMARY.~~
(Erase heading not required.)

Army Form C. 2118.

Place	Date	Hour	Summary of Events and Information	Remarks and references to Appendices
			by me as not carrying necessary details on filling. Attention is particularly necessary in the case of filling watercarts now as all the waterstations are frozen & unworkable, & water has to be drawn from any convenient source	H.V.
Field.	Feb 8.		Nominal roll of M.T. A.S.C. personnel in this unit asked for by O.C. A.S.C. section, A.G.'s office base. This was sent to him.	
			Three samples of water from front line sent to me by one of the M.O.s for testing. Two samples required 1 scoop B.P. per 110 gals & the third 2 scoops. These results were wired to the M.O.s.	
			It was found advisable not to remove the Horsfall	

Army Form C. 2118.

WAR DIARY
or
~~INTELLIGENCE~~ SUMMARY.
(Erase heading not required.)

Instructions regarding War Diaries and Intelligence Summaries are contained in F. S. Regs., Part II. and the Staff Manual respectively. Title pages will be prepared in manuscript.

Place	Date	Hour	Summary of Events and Information	Remarks and references to Appendices
			from Chippewa Camp as I intended. It was however repaired with pieces from a broken Horsfall, & is now in perfect working condition.	
			There are now only 2 water tank stations working in this area owing to the frost: they are (1) tank 13 at Dickebusch (2) tank 1 @ L 33 b 3.9 nr BOESCHEPE. The water is being taken from the feed pipe & not from the tanks. Most of the water carts are frozen & unusable, & farm-house pump supplies are being used.	
			It is impossible to dig fresh pits for soakage &c owing to the frozen state of the ground.	
			I have obtained some material from R.E. for latrines for new soldiers	

2353 Wt. W2544/1454 700,000 5/15 D. D. & L. A.D.S.S. Forms/C 2118.

Instructions regarding War Diaries and Intelligence Summaries are contained in F. S. Regs., Part II. and the Staff Manual respectively. Title pages will be prepared in manuscript.

WAR DIARY
or
~~INTELLIGENCE SUMMARY.~~
(Erase heading not required.)

Army Form C. 2118.

Place	Date	Hour	Summary of Events and Information	Remarks and references to Appendices
			club: this extra [illegible] is rendered necessary because of the employment of civilian women in the canteen.	W.P.
Field	Feb 9.		I again asked area commandant if the R.E. could not be asked to improve the latrine accommodation @ [illegible] Camp. Altho' I have seen no less than 4 R.E. officers about the matter & written & seen the area commandant about it repeatedly nothing can be done. This section is doing all it can but cannot do much if material is not forthcoming.	
			Watercart of 2nd Can. Tun. Co. attached to this Div. found to contain unchlorinated water: Reported.	

Instructions regarding War Diaries and Intelligence Summaries are contained in F. S. Regs., Part II. and the Staff Manual respectively. Title pages will be prepared in manuscript.

WAR DIARY

or

~~INTELLIGENCE SUMMARY.~~

(Erase heading not required.)

Army Form C. 2118.

Place	Date	Hour	Summary of Events and Information	Remarks and references to Appendices
			The A.D.M.S. has asked me to prepare brief plans & summaries of work & accommodation &c in this area so as to be able to hand over the district at a moment's notice. These are being done at once.	
			Report on the use & efficiency of water sterilising tablets has been called for by A.D.M.S. I am carrying out a series of tests & will report on them in due course.	
			Plans for an incinerator with a boiler for heating water were sent home by A.D.M.S. It is proposed to erect this type of incinerator at the 41st D.R.S. if materials forthcoming.	W.

Instructions regarding War Diaries and Intelligence Summaries are contained in F. S. Regs., Part II. and the Staff Manual respectively. Title pages will be prepared in manuscript.

WAR DIARY

or

~~INTELLIGENCE SUMMARY~~.

(Erase heading not required.)

Army Form C. 2118.

Place	Date	Hour	Summary of Events and Information	Remarks and references to Appendices
Field	Feb. 10.		I tried a series of tests with the water sterilising tablets today & tried to compare their efficiency with B. P. The only conclusion I could come to was that they were slightly less efficient than B. P. I suggested that a stock of 50 bottles of these tablets that is approx. 2 tablets per man should be kept in the Q.M.'s stores of each battalion. Other stocks could be varied according to the strength & character of the unit.	

2353 Wt. W2544/1454 700,000 5/15 D. D. & L. A.D.S.S./Forms/C. 2118.

Instructions regarding War Diaries and Intelligence Summaries are contained in F. S. Regs., Part II. and the Staff Manual respectively. Title pages will be prepared in manuscript.

WAR DIARY

or

~~INTELLIGENCE SUMMARY.~~

(Erase heading not required.)

Army Form C. 2118.

Place	Date	Hour	Summary of Events and Information	Remarks and references to Appendices
Field	Feb 11.		I sent to A.D.M.S. a report on the bad state in which Chippewa camp was handed over by the last occupants. The incinerator was in a broken condition was filled & over flowing with excreta. The camp too was not left clean. The M.O. of the battalion in occupation confirmes this. My own opinion is that altho' the previous party may have left a "clearing up" squad behind, it was withdrawn before the work was completed. This is the state of things which exists & when complaints are made the reply is, "a clearing up party was left behind."	
			I also reported to A.D.M.S. that owing to the rough usage they had suffered, they would soon be unfit for use. This section built 3 covered in brick destructors. Owing to	

2353 Wt. W2544/1454 700,000 5/15 D. D. & L. A.D.S.S. Forms/C. 2118.

Instructions regarding War Diaries and Intelligence Summaries are contained in F. S. Regs., Part II. and the Staff Manual respectively. Title pages will be prepared in manuscript.

WAR DIARY

or

~~INTELLIGENCE SUMMARY.~~

(Erase heading not required.)

Army Form C. 2118.

Place	Date	Hour	Summary of Events and Information	Remarks and references to Appendices
			improper use, we converted them into open incinerators, & the R.E. built another one. All these have had such rough usage that the top layers have been taken away, & in 2 cases they are a foot lower than their original height. (There are other brick incinerators but they have not been so badly used.)	
			I sent copies of X Corps rules to be observed in cookhouses to the transport officers of 124 Brigade & to O.C. 21 K.R.R.C. (?) as cookhouses are not being properly cared for.	
			Two huts in Murrumbidgee camp were sprayed & whitewashed by us this morning, as cases of "Spotted fever" had occurred in them.	
			I asked R.E. for material for erecting latrines to 58 [illegible]	

Army Form C. 2118.

WAR DIARY
or
~~INTELLIGENCE SUMMARY.~~
(Erase heading not required.)

Instructions regarding War Diaries and Intelligence Summaries are contained in F. S. Regs., Part II. and the Staff Manual respectively. Title pages will be prepared in manuscript.

Place	Date	Hour	Summary of Events and Information	Remarks and references to Appendices
			for a battery of heavy guns which has moved into this area.	
			I sent in suggestions for a permanent grease trap & system for dealing with kitchen refuse @ the new Soldiers Club in Reninghelst. I suggested that we should be supplied with material & build the structures ourselves.	
			I reported to A.P.M. 2 men for committing a nuisance in the street in Reninghelst this evening.	T.V.

Instructions regarding War Diaries and Intelligence Summaries are contained in F. S. Regs., Part II. and the Staff Manual respectively. Title pages will be prepared in manuscript.

WAR DIARY

or

~~INTELLIGENCE SUMMARY.~~

(Erase heading not required.)

Army Form C. 2118.

Place	Date	Hour	Summary of Events and Information	Remarks and references to Appendices
Field	Feb 12.		I again sent in requirements for Murmuhyll latrines to R.E. & asked that material might be delivered to us to erect the latrines & repair as far as necessary. We have been instructed to draw this material & proceed with the work	
			I asked the Commandant X Corps School of Sanitn whether water duty men of this Division could not attend the school to be instructed in water duties this would be the simplest way of having the men instructed.	
			Spent the afternoon lecturing @ X Corps School of Sanitation at BOESCHEPE.	
			(Apart from the unclean condition of the collections	

Army Form C. 2118.

WAR DIARY

or

~~INTELLIGENCE SUMMARY.~~

(Erase heading not required.)

Instructions regarding War Diaries and Intelligence Summaries are contained in F. S. Regs., Part II. and the Staff Manual respectively. Title pages will be prepared in manuscript.

Place	Date	Hour	Summary of Events and Information	Remarks and references to Appendices
			of old tins at incinerator dumps, I think these tins ought not to be wasted but sent down to the base for melting & then shipped to England for use there. (It is a significant fact that large quantities of these tins from town destructors in England were shipped to Germany before the war).	N.

Army Form C. 2118.

Instructions regarding War Diaries and Intelligence Summaries are contained in F. S. Regs., Part II. and the Staff Manual respectively. Title pages will be prepared in manuscript.

WAR DIARY
or
~~INTELLIGENCE SUMMARY~~.

(Erase heading not required.)

Place	Date	Hour	Summary of Events and Information	Remarks and references to Appendices
Field	Feb 13.		One reinforcement reported his arrival for this section today, & is accordingly taken on the strength of this section, which is now numerically @ full strength.	
			More latrines asked for from the R.E.	
			Constructional work is still held up by frozen condition of ground, & also of lack of material.	
			X Corps School of Sanitation visited this area today for instructional purposes.	
			Demonstrations for watercartmen of this Div. will be arranged as soon as the frost breaks.	
			Watertanks @ most water stations are still frozen, & in	

2353 Wt. W2544/1454 700,000 5/15 D. D. & L. A.D.S.S. Forms/C 2118.

Army Form C. 2118.

Instructions regarding War Diaries and Intelligence Summaries are contained in F. S. Regs., Part II. and the Staff Manual respectively. Title pages will be prepared in manuscript.

WAR DIARY

or

~~INTELLIGENCE SUMMARY.~~

(Erase heading not required.)

Place	Date	Hour	Summary of Events and Information	Remarks and references to Appendices
			some cases the water mains have broken	
			A.D.M.S circular memorandum states that each Field Ambulance will keep a stock of 10000 water sterilising tablets as a reserve.	A.V.

2353 Wt. W2544/1454 700,000 5/15 D. D. & L. A.D.S.S. Forms/C. 2118.

Army Form C. 2118.

Instructions regarding War Diaries and Intelligence Summaries are contained in F. S. Regs., Part II. and the Staff Manual respectively. Title pages will be prepared in manuscript.

WAR DIARY

or

~~INTELLIGENCE SUMMARY.~~

(Erase heading not required.)

Place	Date	Hour	Summary of Events and Information	Remarks and references to Appendices
Field	Feb 14.		I applied to Area Commandant for lamps to light up the Public Latrines & Urinals in RENINGHELST at night time. Also, owing to the shortage of paraffin a special supply of paraffin would be necessary.	
			I applied to R.E. for oiled linen to make luminous night signs for the public latrines in the neighbourhood.	
			Also applied for more latrine seats from R.E. Now that the rest billets are nearly all supplied with proper sanitary latrines, we are turning our attention to ~~real~~ constructional work. A latrine was erected at the BRASSERIE today for the RAP.	
			I sent to A.D.M.S. suggestions as to date for water-	

Army Form C. 2118.

WAR DIARY
or
~~INTELLIGENCE SUMMARY.~~

(Erase heading not required.)

Instructions regarding War Diaries and Intelligence Summaries are contained in F. S. Regs., Part II. and the Staff Manual respectively. Title pages will be prepared in manuscript.

Place	Date	Hour	Summary of Events and Information	Remarks and references to Appendices
			carts – Owing to further frost, these will I think again have to be held over.	
			I went ~~over~~ Mummlikee camp this afternoon with the D.A.D.M.S. of this Division. He was able to see for himself the existing conditions. I have reported the bad condition of this camp to A.D.M.S. & area commandant numberless times as will be seen from previous notes in this Diary, & no notice has been taken. Apart from the deficiency in the latrine accomodation, cookhouses, drying room, washing stands the huts for men are very unhealthy. I drew the attention of area commandant to this last point in November last. The huts are badly ventillated, & earth has been piled up round the sides so that in practically every case the floor of the huts is below the ground	

WAR DIARY
or
~~INTELLIGENCE SUMMARY.~~
(Erase heading not required.)

Army Form C. 2118.

Place	Date	Hour	Summary of Events and Information	Remarks and references to Appendices
			level outside. There is not very much overcrowding in the huts.	
			I propose sending a certain amount of material to Mummlidgee tomorrow, & to try & rectify as much as is possible under the circumstances. I had to obtain a G.S. waggon from the Div. train as the lorry of this section is still under repairs.	
			We are making numbers of long trough urinals for the standing camps, as the existing "hopper" type are not found satisfactory. The material for these has been salved, & nothing obtained from R.E.	H.V.

2353 Wt. W2544/1454 700,000 5/15 D. D. & L. A.D.S.S./Forms/C. 2118.

Army Form C. 2118.

WAR DIARY
or
~~INTELLIGENCE~~ SUMMARY.
(Erase heading not required.)

Instructions regarding War Diaries and Intelligence Summaries are contained in F. S. Regs., Part II. and the Staff Manual respectively. Title pages will be prepared in manuscript.

Place	Date	Hour	Summary of Events and Information	Remarks and references to Appendices
Field.	Feb 15.		I again asked R.E. for a brick incinerator to be built at MICMAC camp. It is urgently needed there for the transport of the 123rd. Inf. Brigade. I asked Camp Commandant for the loan of D.H.Q. watercart for a series of watercart demonstrations which I propose to give to every unit in this Division. I propose giving two demonstrations to each of the 3 sections into which I have divided the Div. troops. The 1st. Demonstration will be on the care & treatment of watercart. the 2nd. a summary of the 1st. & the demonstration of the Horrock's test. It has been arranged to start these demonstrations on Feb 20. at the camp of this section in RENINGHELST. With the material we obtained from R.E., this section has	

2353 Wt. W2544/1454 700,000 5/15 D. D. & L. A.D.S.S. Forms/C 2118.

Army Form C. 2118.

Instructions regarding War Diaries and Intelligence Summaries are contained in F. S. Regs., Part II. and the Staff Manual respectively. Title pages will be prepared in manuscript.

WAR DIARY

or

~~INTELLIGENCE SUMMARY.~~

(Erase heading not required.)

Place	Date	Hour	Summary of Events and Information	Remarks and references to Appendices
			nearly completed the latrine steps in Mammalipee. The seats have been broken up by battalions for firewood, & will take time to replace.	
			We have salved a considerable amount of C.S. iron & timber for uprights	
			Ordinary San. work normal.	[illegible]

2353 Wt. W2544/1454 700,000 5/15 D. D. & L. A.D.S.S. Forms/C 2118.

Instructions regarding War Diaries and Intelligence Summaries are contained in F. S. Regs., Part II. and the Staff Manual respectively. Title pages will be prepared in manuscript.

WAR DIARY

or

~~INTELLIGENCE SUMMARY.~~

(Erase heading not required.)

Army Form C. 2118.

Place	Date	Hour	Summary of Events and Information	Remarks and references to Appendices
Field	Feb 16.		Owing to shortage of paraffin we are unable to keep lights burning at night to show up the public latrines & urinals. I asked A.S.C. for a regular supply.	
			The fireclay bricks & some odd pieces of iron which we salved from old broken Horsfalls in this area are being used to repair another one.	
			I again asked Camp Commandant to have the brush of road sweeper repaired.	
			We are making a new kind of luminous sign for night use, & are experimenting on it.	
			I have asked Camp Commandant if he could provide dungaree	

2353 Wt. W2544/1454 700,000 5/15 D. D. & L. A.D.S.S. Forms/C. 2118.

Instructions regarding War Diaries and Intelligence Summaries are contained in F. S. Regs., Part II. and the Staff Manual respectively. Title pages will be prepared in manuscript.

WAR DIARY

or

~~INTELLIGENCE SUMMARY~~

(Erase heading not required.)

Army Form C. 2118.

Place	Date	Hour	Summary of Events and Information	Remarks and references to Appendices
			suits for the cooks in H.Q. messes.	N.V.
Field.	Feb 17.		Watercarts of Div H.Q. found to be very incomplete & in very bad working order. I reported this.	
			Note: I reported to G.S.O. in the fact that I had overheard very indiscreet conduct between officers in the Field Cashier's office this morning, & within the hearing of civilians.	
			San. work as usual. We are experiencing still greater difficulty in getting material from the R.E.	

Army Form C. 2118.

Instructions regarding War Diaries and Intelligence Summaries are contained in F. S. Regs., Part II. and the Staff Manual respectively. Title pages will be prepared in manuscript.

WAR DIARY
or
INTELLIGENCE SUMMARY.
(Erase heading not required.)

Place	Date	Hour	Summary of Events and Information	Remarks and references to Appendices
Field	Feb 18.		Sampled water taken from water storage tubs @ the Y.M.C.A. in RENINGHELST today showed no signs of chlorination. These tubs are filled by one of the Div. water-carts; reported. I also had to report to the M.O. of 12 East Surreys, that the Reg. watercarts were not being used & that water was drawn from a well near their transport lines instead. This water was of very doubtful character, & not fit for drinking, requiring more than 3 scoops of B.P. I had to spend the afternoon preparing demonstrations on watercarts which were to be given to all the Div watercarts. I have arranged the demonstrations as follows:— I have divided up the Div. units into 3 detachments namely 1st. 123rd & 24 Brigades – 20th & 21st Feb. @ 2 P.M.	

Instructions regarding War Diaries and Intelligence Summaries are contained in F. S. Regs., Part II. and the Staff Manual respectively. Title pages will be prepared in manuscript.

WAR DIARY

or

~~INTELLIGENCE SUMMARY~~.

(Erase heading not required.)

Army Form C. 2118.

Place	Date	Hour	Summary of Events and Information	Remarks and references to Appendices
			2nd. ~~Inf Brig~~ R. Artillery on Feb. 22 & 23. @ 2 P.M. 3rd. 122 Inf. Brigade, R.E. A.S.C. Div. H.Q. on day following their next relief from trenches. The scheme is briefly: Two demonstrations to each detachment. The 1st demonstration being on the care & treatment of a water cart & the method of filling a cart using the pump & clarifiers, &c. The 2nd demonstration being a summary of the 1st followed by a demonstration of the Horrock's test. I have had notes on these demonstrations, together with a list of the spare parts of a water cart typed for distribution among the personnel attending the demonstrations.	[illegible]

Instructions regarding War Diaries and Intelligence Summaries are contained in F. S. Regs., Part II. and the Staff Manual respectively. Title pages will be prepared in manuscript.

WAR DIARY

or

~~INTELLIGENCE SUMMARY.~~

(Erase heading not required.)

Army Form C. 2118.

Place	Date	Hour	Summary of Events and Information	Remarks and references to Appendices
Field.	Feb 19.		I spent the afternoon lecturing @ X Corps School of Sanitation BOESCHEPE.	
			I asked R.E. for a supply of fireclay for repairing a Horsfall destructor @ the Dressing Station in RENINGHELST. They are unable to obtain any.	
			I asked O/C Belgian mission if it could be arranged that all cases of infectious diseases occurring amongst civilians should be notified to us so as to enable us to take precautions against the spread of infection amongst troops. This will be done.	
			I asked that pump @ Ablution shed @ ALBERTA camp could be repaired as troops cannot obtain enough water for washing.	

2353 Wt. W2544/1454 700,000 5/15 D. D. & L. A.D.S.S. Forms/C 2118.

Instructions regarding War Diaries and Intelligence Summaries are contained in F. S. Regs., Part II. and the Staff Manual respectively. Title pages will be prepared in manuscript.

WAR DIARY
or
~~INTELLIGENCE SUMMARY.~~
(Erase heading not required.)

Army Form C. 2118.

Place	Date	Hour	Summary of Events and Information	Remarks and references to Appendices
			I again had to ask Camp Commandant to have the manure @ H.Q. stables kept in sacks inside the stables till it was collected & so remove the nuisance it causes by being dumped in the main street.	
			Also asked Camp Commandant to remove the unsightly heaps of manure from outside H.Q. horselines; these heaps have been collected & dumped along the roadside & are a nuisance & insanitary collection.	H.V.
Field.	Feb 20.		Asked R.E. for duckboarding for "soldiers' Club" latrines.	
			A reinforcement reported his arrival today, & is taken on the strength of this section, which is now one man overstrength. He comes from 2nd Lon San Co. RAMC.	

Instructions regarding War Diaries and Intelligence Summaries are contained in F. S. Regs., Part II. and the Staff Manual respectively. Title pages will be prepared in manuscript.

WAR DIARY

or

~~INTELLIGENCE SUMMARY.~~

(Erase heading not required.)

Army Form C. 2118.

Place	Date	Hour	Summary of Events and Information	Remarks and references to Appendices
			I spent the whole of this morning inspecting the washing arrangements in private houses for soldiers washing, & also a great part of the afternoon.	
			First demonstration given to 123rd & 124 Brigades water duty men this afternoon. Two battalions of 124 Brigade failed to send water duty men.	AV
Field.	Feb 21.		I spent the morning inspecting washing places again, & sending my report to the A.D.M.S. The arrangements are generally clean; in practically every case the living rooms ~~[illegible]~~ & kitchens are used as drying rooms. I do not favour this arrangement & reported to this effect.	
			2nd Demonstration given to 123rd & 124 Brigades water	

2353 Wt. W2544/1454 700,000 5/15 D. D. & L. A.D.S.S. Forms/C 2118.

Instructions regarding War Diaries and Intelligence Summaries are contained in F. S. Regs., Part II. and the Staff Manual respectively. Title pages will be prepared in manuscript.

WAR DIARY
or
~~INTELLIGENCE SUMMARY.~~
(Erase heading not required.)

Army Form C. 2118.

Place	Date	Hour	Summary of Events and Information	Remarks and references to Appendices
			duty men. The same 2 battalions as reported yesterday failed to send men. I sent a full report on the attendance to the A.D.M.S.	
			I sent the A.P.M. a copy of rules to be observed with regard to washing of drinking vessels in canteens, cafés & estaminets & asked that copies might be handed round & posted in a conspicuous place in every canteen, café, estaminet &c.	
			I asked S.S.O. of this Div. if it would be possible to supply us with formaldehyde for disinfecting. Cresol is not very satisfactory for spraying huts & billets after infectious cases have occurred.	
			Hut in Chippewa camp sprayed by us after case of measles.	V.V.

A5834 Wt. W4973/M687 750,000 8/16 D. D. & L. Ltd. Forms/C.2118/13

Instructions regarding War Diaries and Intelligence Summaries are contained in F. S. Regs., Part II. and the Staff Manual respectively. Title pages will be prepared in manuscript.

WAR DIARY

or

~~INTELLIGENCE SUMMARY.~~

(Erase heading not required.)

Army Form C. 2118.

Place	Date	Hour	Summary of Events and Information	Remarks and references to Appendices
Field	Feb 22.		I gave 1st of the 2 watercart demonstrations to water duty men of the R.A. of this div today. Only one dozen men were sent by R.A. & some of these were not water duty men.	
			—	
			I am alloting one inspector of this section to the work of inspecting all estaminets, canteens & cafes, (laundries) in the area. Another inspector I am putting on to food inspection in all cookhouses, messes, &c. This high sick rate must be brought down, tho as far as I can see the sickness is not due to insanitary conditions.	
			In one battalion found that very doubtful well water was being used while the battalion was in rest, while the watercarts were not being used at all. This matter I reported to the M.O. concerned. This batt. is showing a v. high sick rate.	D.V.

A5834 Wt. W4973/M687 750,000 8/16 D. D. & L. Ltd. Forms/C.2118/13

Instructions regarding War Diaries and Intelligence Summaries are contained in F. S. Regs., Part II. and the Staff Manual respectively. Title pages will be prepared in manuscript.

WAR DIARY
or
~~INTELLIGENCE SUMMARY.~~
(Erase heading not required.)

Army Form C. 2118.

3

Place	Date	Hour	Summary of Events and Information	Remarks and references to Appendices
Field.	Feb 23.		I had to report to area commandant on the insanitary condition of surroundings of ALBERTA camp & its cookhouses. The ground is used as a dumping ground for all sorts of scraps of rubbish, & greasy water is thrown broadcast.	
			I asked area commandant for permission to pull down an old unused hut @ one of the camps in order to obtain timber &c.	
			I also reported the foul state of Div. Salv. Co. premises.	
			I would like to comment on the method of building accomodation ~~provided~~ practised by the R.E. In ~~nearly~~ every case I have seen where buildings and huts & camps are being constructed by R.E. no allowance or provision is made for drainage &c in the sites. I thought the the 1st thing to be seen to - it is in civilian life. The R.E. have built a new soldier's club in Reninghelst, & this	

A5834 Wt. W4973/M687 750,000 8/16 D. D. & L. Ltd. Forms/C.2118/13

Army Form C. 2118.

3

WAR DIARY

or

~~INTELLIGENCE SUMMARY.~~

(Erase heading not required.)

Instructions regarding War Diaries and Intelligence Summaries are contained in F. S. Regs., Part II. and the Staff Manual respectively. Title pages will be prepared in manuscript.

Place	Date	Hour	Summary of Events and Information	Remarks and references to Appendices
			to be used largely as a dining room. No allowance was made for dealing with kitchen waste water, & tho' I approached them very early in the work, nothing has yet been done, & it's proposed to open the club today. It is always as an "after thought" that the R.E. will attend to sanitation.	H.V.

A5834 Wt. W4973/M687 750,000 8/16 D. D. & L. Ltd. Forms/C.2118/13

Instructions regarding War Diaries and Intelligence Summaries are contained in F. S. Regs., Part II. and the Staff Manual respectively. Title pages will be prepared in manuscript.

WAR DIARY
or
INTELLIGENCE SUMMARY.
(Erase heading not required.)

Army Form C. 2118.

Place	Date	Hour	Summary of Events and Information	Remarks and references to Appendices
Field	26 24.		I reported the insanitary condition of the surroundings of a civilian slaughter house today to A.P.M. Billets belonging of an N.C.O. who died of tuberculosis were disinfected thoroughly on orders from D.D.M.S. X Corps.	[illegible]
"	25		I sent in a report to the D.A.D.M.S. today on the subject of the unaccountable large percentage of sick in the division. My report was briefly to the effect that I had come to the conclusion that the high percentage of sickness in the division was due not to actually insanitary conditions but to the fact that there was overcrowding in the huts in rest billets. The average air capacity of the huts is about 2500 cu ft. 20–25 even 30 men are crowded into each hut. In addition there is no ventilation	

A5834 Wt. W4973/M687 750,000 8/16 D. D. & L. Ltd. Forms/C.2118/13.

Instructions regarding War Diaries and Intelligence Summaries are contained in F. S. Regs., Part II. and the Staff Manual respectively. Title pages will be prepared in manuscript.

WAR DIARY
or
INTELLIGENCE SUMMARY.
(Erase heading not required.)

Army Form C. 2118.

Place	Date	Hour	Summary of Events and Information	Remarks and references to Appendices
			& the huts too warm & very unhealthy. Fewer men ought to be allotted to each hut, & each hut ought to be provided with proper ventilation. I made these suggestions to the area commandant some months ago - after we came into this area, but nothing has been done yet.	
			Lamp from public urinal ~~stolen~~ night reported by me.	
			Fortnightly report from District was handed in to me. Continued slight improvement shewn. I find it is practically impossible to keep pace with the moves of the artillery: they move every other day, or change their titles, & it is impossible to fix any responsibility for sanitation.	[initials]

A5834 Wt. W4973/M687 750,000 8/16 D. D. & L. Ltd. Forms/C.2118/13

Instructions regarding War Diaries and Intelligence Summaries are contained in F. S. Regs., Part II. and the Staff Manual respectively. Title pages will be prepared in manuscript.

WAR DIARY
or
INTELLIGENCE SUMMARY.
(Erase heading not required.)

Army Form C. 2118.

Place	Date	Hour	Summary of Events and Information	Remarks and references to Appendices
Field.	26. Feb		I spent the whole afternoon lecturing @ X Corps School of sanitation ROZESCHEPE. M.O. i/c 1st E. Surrey Regt. reported to me that he was unable to supply battalion with enough sterilised water as one of the battalion watercarts had been taken away to supply a reinforcement camp since Feb 19th. In addition the remaining cart was called upon to supply the Y.M.C.A. hut from time to time. The result was that men were using doubtful water from untested sources. I sent on this report to the D.D.M.S.	H.V.

A5834 Wt. W4973/M687 750,000 8/16 D. D. & L. Ltd. Forms/C.2118/13.

Instructions regarding War Diaries and Intelligence Summaries are contained in F. S. Regs., Part II. and the Staff Manual respectively. Title pages will be prepared in manuscript.

WAR DIARY
or
~~INTELLIGENCE SUMMARY.~~
(Erase heading not required.)

Army Form C. 2118.

Place	Date	Hour	Summary of Events and Information	Remarks and references to Appendices
Field	Feb 27	1st	Demonstration on water cart given to water men of 123 Inf Brigade, Div. H.Q., A.S.C., R.E. of this division.	
			A.P.M. has furnished me with copies of rules for washing drinking vessels in all estaminets, cafés, Canteens &c. These will be posted up in due course. The rules are:	
			(1) A vessel with an adequate supply of clean water, changed frequently, & a suitable cloth will be provided. The glass or mug will be thoroughly cleansed & then momentarily dipped in a vessel containing water kept continuously on the boil	
			or (2) After careful washing in clean water the drinking vessel will be placed in a solution of Pot. Permang. of [illegible]	

A5834 Wt. W4373/M687 750,000 8/16 D. D. & L. Ltd. Forms/C.2118/13

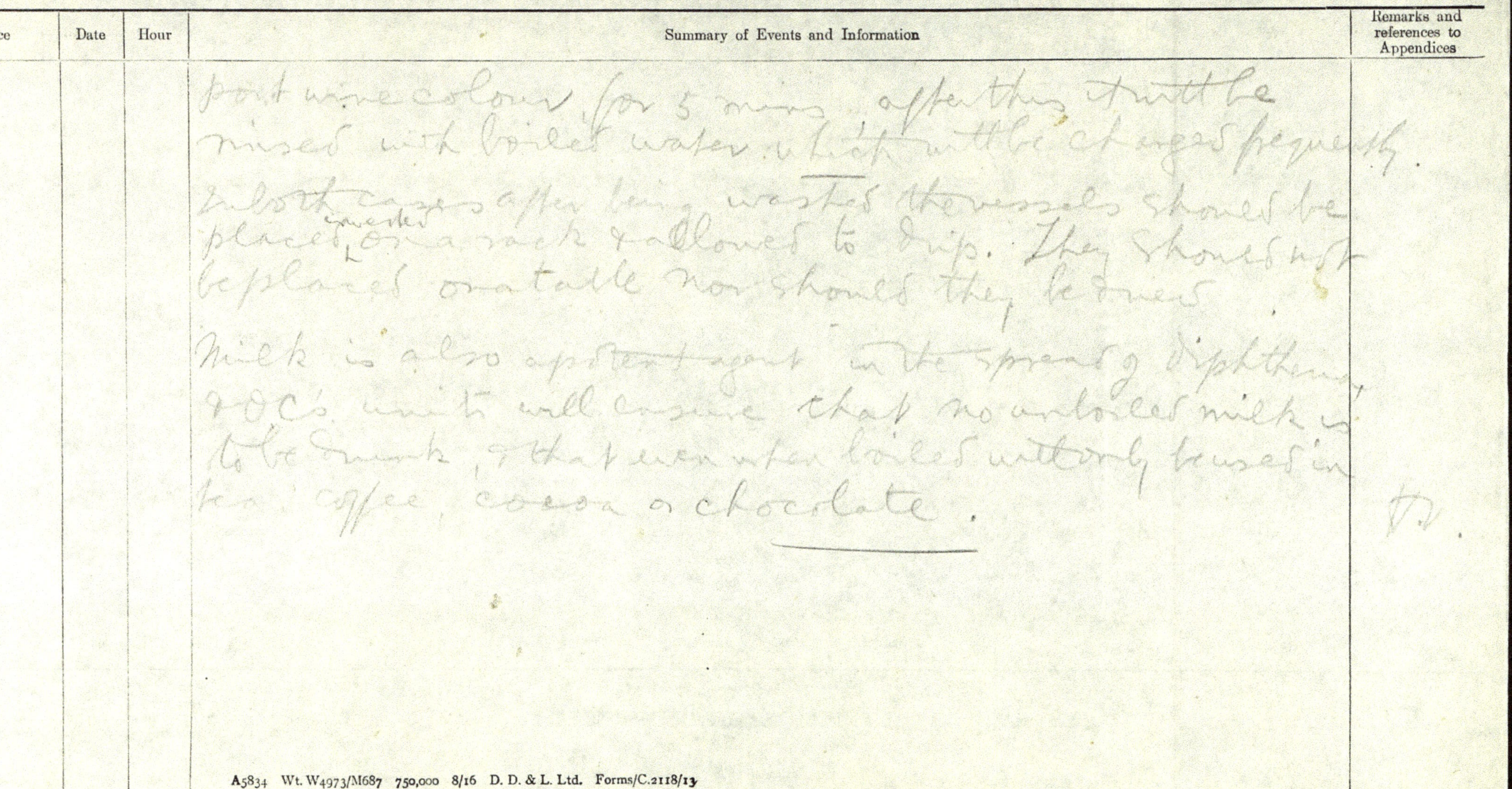

Instructions regarding War Diaries and Intelligence Summaries are contained in F. S. Regs., Part II. and the Staff Manual respectively. Title pages will be prepared in manuscript.

WAR DIARY

or

~~INTELLIGENCE SUMMARY.~~

(Erase heading not required.)

Army Form C. 2118.

Place	Date	Hour	Summary of Events and Information	Remarks and references to Appendices
			port wine colour for 5 mins after this it will be rinsed with boiled water which will be changed frequently.	
			In both cases after being washed the vessels should be placed inverted on a rack & allowed to drip. They should not be placed on a table nor should they be dried.	
			Milk is also a potent agent in the spread of diphtheria & OC's units will ensure that no unboiled milk is to be drunk, & that even when boiled it will only be used in tea, coffee, cocoa or chocolate.	

A5834 Wt. W4973/M687 750,000 8/16 D. D. & L. Ltd. Forms/C.2118/13

Instructions regarding War Diaries and Intelligence Summaries are contained in F. S. Regs., Part II. and the Staff Manual respectively. Title pages will be prepared in manuscript.

WAR DIARY
or
~~INTELLIGENCE~~ SUMMARY.

(Erase heading not required.)

Army Form C. 2118.

Place	Date	Hour	Summary of Events and Information	Remarks and references to Appendices
Field	Feb 28.		2nd Demonstration of water cart & Horrocks box with the [illegible] mentioned in notes on 27/1/17. today. Systematic inspection of private laundries & estaminets &c started: this will ensure that each place is visited at least once a week. also systematic inspection of food in regimental cookers, officers messes &c. The system of cleaning knives & forks @ the new Soldiers' club at RENINGHELST leaves a great deal to be desired; they are merely wiped c a cloth & not thoroughly washed. The report sent to A.D.M.S. on the amount of accommodation in the rest camps has been forwarded by him to [illegible].	H. V.

Mar. 1917.

Confidential

140/2043. Vol XI

War Diary

84th Sanitary Section

From 1st March 1917

To 31st March 1917

Instructions regarding War Diaries and Intelligence Summaries are contained in F. S. Regs., Part II. and the Staff Manual respectively. Title pages will be prepared in manuscript.

Army Form C. 2118

WAR DIARY
or
~~INTELLIGENCE SUMMARY.~~ 84th SANITARY SECTION

(Erase heading not required.)

Place	Date	Hour	Summary of Events and Information	Remarks and references to Appendices
Field.	March 1.		War Diary for month of February was sent in to A.D.M.S. yesterday afternoon. —	
			Jasked X Corps water officer if the various water points in this area could soon be placed in working order again after the late frost.	
			Water in cart of "C" 190 found unchlorinated: reported by me. —	
			Water cart of 41st Div. R.E. found to have water taps broken & water was being drawn from it thro' the opening in top of tank. Reported by me.	
			123 Inf. Brigade still have no permanent Sanitary fatigue man, & the sanitation is therefore done spasmodically. This is receiving attention by me.	

A5834 Wt. W4973/M687 750,000 8/16 D. D. & L. Ltd. Forms/C.2118/13

Instructions regarding War Diaries and Intelligence Summaries are contained in F. S. Regs., Part II. and the Staff Manual respectively. Title pages will be prepared in manuscript.

WAR DIARY
or
~~INTELLIGENCE SUMMARY.~~
(Erase heading not required.)

Army Form C. 2118.

Place	Date	Hour	Summary of Events and Information	Remarks and references to Appendices
			Motor lorry of this section still away @ workshops.	
			—	
			We fixed up the Clayton disinfector @ the baths in Reninghelst: O/C Baths is trying to work this in addition to the Foden-thresh disinfector.	
			—	
			I made a careful inspection of all arrangements @ the ~~new~~ Soldier's club here, of the kitchen, disposal of waste water, storage of food &c, & found it most unsatisfactory. Altho' this soldier's club is run by officers on the Div Staff, very little knowledge of the elements of cleanliness is shewn.	
			I propose not only seeing those responsible for the catering department, but seeing to the actual carrying out of sanitary disposal of waste water; ventilation of the building & kitchen; storage of food in rat proof receptacles myself. The kitchen is already in a very dirty state, & the ground around the grease trap & rubbish tin is already	

A5834 Wt. W4973/M687 750,000 8/16 D. D. & L. Ltd. Forms/C.2118/13

Instructions regarding War Diaries and Intelligence Summaries are contained in F. S. Regs., Part II. and the Staff Manual respectively. Title pages will be prepared in manuscript.

WAR DIARY
or
~~INTELLIGENCE SUMMARY.~~
(Erase heading not required.)

Army Form C. 2118.

Place	Date	Hour	Summary of Events and Information	Remarks and references to Appendices
			badly fouled c food scraps & tea leaves.	
			Other San. work normal.	
			Attention has been directed to the bad hygienic conditions of the rest camps lately owing to the increasing sick returns. These conditions I have tried to alter from the time we came to this area, & tho' I have reported them & discussed them from time to time with various heads of departments, nothing was done to ventilate huts, & increase the amount of accomodation. The drainage of camps too was given up as unnecessary work, but it is seen now that I was right in asking that it should be seen to. Once, the Brigadier went so far as to ask the area commandant what business I had to do with drainage of camps. Other O.Cs refused to give me working parties to supervise the drainage of their rest camps.	H.V.

A5834 Wt. W4973/M687 750,000 8/16 D. D. & L. Ltd. Forms/C.2118/13

Instructions regarding War Diaries and Intelligence Summaries are contained in F. S. Regs., Part II. and the Staff Manual respectively. Title pages will be prepared in manuscript.

WAR DIARY
or
~~INTELLIGENCE SUMMARY.~~
(Erase heading not required.)

Army Form C. 2118.

Place	Date	Hour	Summary of Events and Information	Remarks and references to Appendices
Field.	March 2.		I asked X Corps Water Officer whether the repair of water mains & Water Stations in this area, necessitated by the late frost, could not be expedited, as the water was being obtained pure only with great difficulty. A negative reply was given.	
	March 3.		I asked Brigade Major 123 Brigade if a permanent sanitary man could be "told off" for Brigade H.Q. as the state of affairs is very bad, both in the rest & advanced billets.	
			I sent to A.D.M.S., & subsequently to Area Commandant sketches of "louvring" for insertion into the roofs of huts in the rest billets in this area: also of a simple form of opening skylight for the same purpose. This would greatly increase the ventilation in huts.	A.V.

A5834 Wt. W4973/M687 750,000 8/16 D. D. & L. Ltd. Forms/C.2118/13

Army Form C. 2118.

Instructions regarding War Diaries and Intelligence Summaries are contained in F. S. Regs., Part II. and the Staff Manual respectively. Title pages will be prepared in manuscript.

WAR DIARY
or
INTELLIGENCE SUMMARY.

(Erase heading not required.)

Place	Date	Hour	Summary of Events and Information	Remarks and references to Appendices
Field.	Mar 4.		The 23rd Inf Regt of this Div. are making no attempt to burn excreta: they apparently ~~[illegible]~~ are determined to use every means for disobeying orders on this subject.	
			Sanitary Copy returned from supply Col. workshops 2/3/17, having been under repairs.	
			I saw the manager of the new Soldiers' club in connec. of the disposal of scraps, sullage water, & keeping the kitchen clean.	
			I usually allow the men of this section ½ day off on Sundays.	[illegible]

A5834 Wt. W4973/M687 750,000 8/16 D. D. & L. Ltd. Forms/C.2118/13

Instructions regarding War Diaries and Intelligence Summaries are contained in F. S. Regs., Part II. and the Staff Manual respectively. Title pages will be prepared in manuscript.

WAR DIARY
or
~~INTELLIGENCE SUMMARY.~~
(Erase heading not required.)

Army Form C. 2118.

Place	Date	Hour	Summary of Events and Information	Remarks and references to Appendices
Field.	Mar 5.		I spent aft. lecturing @ X Corps School of Sanitation BOESCHEPE. Motor lorry returned to San. Sec. to day from workshops! San. work normal. I asked X Corps water officer if the repair of the various water stations in this area could be expedited: the pipes were either still frozen or burst as a result of the late heavy frost. He replied that it depended on the weather, but it was hoped to open the stations again in about a week or 10 days.	H.V.

A5834 Wt. W4973/M687 750,000 8/16 D. D. & L. Ltd. Forms/C.2118/13

Instructions regarding War Diaries and Intelligence Summaries are contained in F. S. Regs., Part II. and the Staff Manual respectively. Title Pages will be prepared in manuscript.

WAR DIARY
or
~~INTELLIGENCE SUMMARY~~
(Erase heading not required.)

Army Form C. 2118.

Place	Date	Hour	Summary of Events and Information	Remarks and references to Appendices
Field.	Nov 7.		I asked R.E. for more latrine seats. There is a great general scarcity of timber now, & it is doubtful if any more box seat latrines will be constructed. Other methods of making flyproof latrines must be devised.	
			R.E. offered me some iron tops for incinerators. This just shows the useless work that R.E's. undertake. I have asked over & over again for proper brick incinerators in adequate numbers for camps in this area & have been refused. Now they offer me some iron tops in order to clear their workshops.	W.V.

2449 Wt. W14957/M90 750,000 1/16 J.B.C. & A. Forms/C.2118/12.

Army Form C. 2118.

Instructions regarding War Diaries and Intelligence Summaries are contained in F. S. Regs., Part II. and the Staff Manual respectively. Title Pages will be prepared in manuscript.

WAR DIARY

or

~~INTELLIGENCE SUMMARY~~

(Erase heading not required.)

Place	Date	Hour	Summary of Events and Information	Remarks and references to Appendices
Field	Mar. 8.		I have again reported the neglected & delapidated condition of the bricks incinerators @ CHIPPEWA camp: it is becoming increasingly difficult to dispose of excreta by burning, & yet the units occupying this camp make no attempt to keep their incinerators in repair.	
			I asked R.E. to supply me with an ablution bench which is unclaimed in their yard.–	
			I spent the afternoon lecturing at Corps School of Sanitation BOESCHEPE.	
			I asked area commandant to sanction purchase of padlocks & chains in order to tie down securely the camps which are used in the Public latrines at night time, as they are constantly being stolen.	[illegible]

2449 Wt. W14957/M90 750,000 1/16 J.B.C. & A. Forms/C.2118/12.

Instructions regarding War Diaries and Intelligence Summaries are contained in F. S. Regs., Part II. and the Staff Manual respectively. Title Pages will be prepared in manuscript.

WAR DIARY

or

~~INTELLIGENCE SUMMARY~~

(Erase heading not required.)

Army Form C. 2118.

Place	Date	Hour	Summary of Events and Information	Remarks and references to Appendices
Field.	May 9.		I received reports that certain water carts of this Division were not conforming to rules for water carts & were in addition using water stations outside this area. Action will be taken. I sent A.D.M.S. a report, as called for on the water supply of this Division. Went to 2nd Army Medical Society meeting in BAILLEUL this aft. hoping to hear some views on sanitation in modern warfare, but heard instead the much discussed subject of duties of a San. Sec.	H.V.

2449 Wt. W14957/M90 750,000 1/16 J.B.C. & A. Forms/C.2118/12.

Army Form C. 2118.

Instructions regarding War Diaries and Intelligence Summaries are contained in F. S. Regs., Part II. and the Staff Manual respectively. Title Pages will be prepared in manuscript.

WAR DIARY
or
~~INTELLIGENCE SUMMARY~~

(Erase heading not required.)

Place	Date	Hour	Summary of Events and Information	Remarks and references to Appendices
Field.	Mar 10.		Watercarts of 32nd R.F.; D.190 R.F.A.; 11 Queens; 4th A.S.C.; 34th Batt R.F.A. have been drawing water outside this area without conforming to the proper rules of Carrying no Bleaching Powder: I have asked for reports in all cases concerned.	
			—	
			216 Co R.E. Army troops' billets & camp inspected thoroughly today & reported on. Also prisoners' guard camp La Clyte 25. As this latter situation is to be taken over as a Dressing Station it is necessary to have it put in a thoroughly sanitary condition. This section has taken the matter in hand, & as far as material is available will construct & improvise.	
			The chief difficulty is the water supply, which is obtained from a shallow well at 216 Co. Camp, & from a pump in a farm adjoining the prisoners camp.	
			It has been recommended that the water supply may be obtained	

2449 Wt. W14957/M90 750,000 1/16 J.B.C. & A. Forms/C.2118/12.

Instructions regarding War Diaries and Intelligence Summaries are contained in F. S. Regs., Part II. and the Staff Manual respectively. Title Pages will be prepared in manuscript.

WAR DIARY
or
~~INTELLIGENCE SUMMARY~~
(Erase heading not required.)

Army Form C. 2118.

Place	Date	Hour	Summary of Events and Information	Remarks and references to Appendices
			from watercarts of 124 Brigade Transport which are immediately opposite.	N.
Field.	Nov 11.		Water used by Y.M.C.A. @ La Clyte found unchlorinated. Reported to A.D.M.S.	
			Water from cart of "D" 189 found unchlorinated; reported.	
			More latrine seats required from R.E.	
			5 men of this section were reinoculated c̄ T.A.B. vaccine on 9/3/17)	
			The ventilation of huts in rest camps is still unsatisfactory. The suggestions that I sent to area commandant for a simple system of "louvring" in the huts has been dropped – owing to scarcity of timber, but nothing has been done in	

2449 Wt. W14957/M90 750,000 1/16 J.B.C. & A. Forms/C.2118/12.

Instructions regarding War Diaries and Intelligence Summaries are contained in F. S. Regs., Part II. and the Staff Manual respectively. Title Pages will be prepared in manuscript.

WAR DIARY
or
INTELLIGENCE SUMMARY
(Erase heading not required.)

Army Form C. 2118.

Place	Date	Hour	Summary of Events and Information	Remarks and references to Appendices
			a simpler way to increase the ventillation. The huts require a good cleaning generally & whitewashing, & this should be a regular routine work.	
			The question of manure disposal is becoming troublesome. The chief method of disposal is to the Belgian farmers, but now ~~that~~ they are not requiring so much for the land, & it is beginning to collect, & will have to be burnt; at present very little is burnt in this area, but as the weather improves steps will have to be taken to dispose of this manure more effectively.	W.

2449 Wt. W14957/M90 750,000 1/16 J.B.C. & A. Forms/C.2118/12.

Instructions regarding War Diaries and Intelligence Summaries are contained in F. S. Regs., Part II. and the Staff Manual respectively. Title Pages will be prepared in manuscript.

WAR DIARY
or
INTELLIGENCE SUMMARY

(Erase heading not required.)

Army Form C. 2118.

Place	Date	Hour	Summary of Events and Information	Remarks and references to Appendices
Field	Mar 12.		I reported theft of "area stores" lamp from public urinal during night to area commandant.	
			R.E. have definitely refused to supply me with more material for making flyproof latrine seats, owing to shortage of timber.	
			I spent the aft. lecturing at X Corps School of Sanitation BOESCHEPE.	
			I find that washing for the soldiers is done (by civilians) in places which are also used as cafés estaminets & in many cases the clothes are hung for drying in the actual café room. This practice is certainly liable to be a source of danger. In other cases drying is done in the civilians dining & living room, & I have seen it done in the bedroom.	

2449 Wt. W14957/M90 750,000 1/16 J.B.C. & A. Forms/C.2118/12.

Instructions regarding War Diaries and Intelligence Summaries are contained in F. S. Regs., Part II. and the Staff Manual respectively. Title Pages will be prepared in manuscript.

WAR DIARY
or
~~INTELLIGENCE SUMMARY~~
(Erase heading not required.)

Army Form C. 2118.

Place	Date	Hour	Summary of Events and Information	Remarks and references to Appendices
Field	Mar 13.		Water tested from cart D 189 RFA showed absence of chlorination: reported.	
			I reported circumstances re soldier's washing which I noted ~~on~~ 1/3/17, to APM & asked for authority to act in the matter: this he gave. Soldiers washing is only to be done according to D.R.O. 1215 in houses which have the ADMS permission & license.	
			I again asked the ADMS if it could not be arranged to have the huts in rest camps properly cleared out & whitewashed at least once during each period of occupation.	
			I thoroughly examined & inspected 3 of the rest camps here, namely Chippewa, Alberta & Ontario. In spite of my suggestions for ventilation very few of the huts have any windows at all. Where there are windows they are practically never opened, & are even	

2449 Wt. W14957/M90 750,000 1/16 J.B.C. & A. Forms/C.2118/12.

Army Form C. 2118.

Instructions regarding War Diaries and Intelligence Summaries are contained in F. S. Regs., Part II. and the Staff Manual respectively. Title Pages will be prepared in manuscript.

WAR DIARY
or
~~INTELLIGENCE SUMMARY~~

(Erase heading not required.)

Place	Date	Hour	Summary of Events and Information	Remarks and references to Appendices
			completely wedged up so that they will not open. I will try & have this rectified, by making it compulsory to have both door & window (where windows exist) opened & kept open for a period of at least 2 hours during the day. In the majority of huts the amount of air space for each man is only 80 cu ft – with no ventilation to replace the exhausted air. San. work normal.	H.V.

2449 Wt. W14957/M90 750,000 1/16 J.B.C. & A. Forms/C.2118/12.

Instructions regarding War Diaries and Intelligence Summaries are contained in F. S. Regs., Part II. and the Staff Manual respectively. Title Pages will be prepared in manuscript.

WAR DIARY

or

~~INTELLIGENCE SUMMARY~~

(Erase heading not required.)

Army Form C. 2118.

Place	Date	Hour	Summary of Events and Information	Remarks and references to Appendices
Field. (Renningheld)	Mar 14.		I had to remove a Horsfall destructor from CHIPPEWA Camp as it was too broken for use. Some of the parts have been used; remainder of iron I have asked Salvage to take.	
			—	
			Again sent to A.D.M.S. suggestions for improving the hygienic conditions of huts in rest billets. These suggestions were briefly:	
			a. Compulsory opening of doors & windows of huts after reveillé each morning.	
			b. Men's kit should be kept tidier.	
			c. Lighting of coke braziers should be forbidden during the day time.	
			d. More receptacles for food & refuse in huts.	
			e. Small ventilation holes to be drilled in the huts above the window & door – i.e. @ both ends, & kept permanently open.	

Army Form C. 2118.

Instructions regarding War Diaries and Intelligence Summaries are contained in F. S. Regs., Part II. and the Staff Manual respectively. Title Pages will be prepared in manuscript.

WAR DIARY

or

~~INTELLIGENCE SUMMARY~~

(Erase heading not required.)

Place	Date	Hour	Summary of Events and Information	Remarks and references to Appendices
			f. Removal of piled up earth from bases of huts, in such a way as to combine free ventillation c drainage.	
			—	
			5 more ranks of this section reinoculated c T.A.B. this morning.	[illegible]
			—	

2449 Wt. W14957/M90 750,000 1/16 J.B.C. & A. Forms/C.2118/12.

Army Form C. 2118.

Instructions regarding War Diaries and Intelligence Summaries are contained in F. S. Regs., Part II. and the Staff Manual respectively. Title Pages will be prepared in manuscript.

WAR DIARY
or
INTELLIGENCE SUMMARY

(Erase heading not required.)

Place	Date	Hour	Summary of Events and Information	Remarks and references to Appendices
Field.	Nov 15.		Spent the aft. lecturing @ X Corps School of Sanitation BOESCHEPE, on water. — 3 Billets of X Corps cavalry @ BOESCHEPE disinfected c Formaldehyde after suspected Scarlet Fever. Billet in Reninghelst likewise – (X Corps cyclist billet) — I was ordered to prepare & hand over all Sanitary contrivances &c in connection with Right Sector of this Div. in view of the fact that 124 Brigade is going back to rest. This I have done, & the necessary files are ready for handing over @ any moment! — I have been ordered also to give 2 lectures to the Field ambulances on Water & Conservancy; dates to be given later.	

2449 Wt. W14957/M90 750,000 1/16 J.B.C. & A. Forms/C.2118/12.

Army Form C. 2118.

Instructions regarding War Diaries and Intelligence Summaries are contained in F. S. Regs., Part II. and the Staff Manual respectively. Title Pages will be prepared in manuscript.

WAR DIARY
or
~~INTELLIGENCE SUMMARY~~
(Erase heading not required.)

Place	Date	Hour	Summary of Events and Information	Remarks and references to Appendices
Field (Remyfelst)	Mar 16		Investigation of one of the YMCA. huts here (@ Lallyte) shewed the following points:	
			a. Insufficient latrine & urinal accomodation - none was in fact provided for the troops.	
			b. No provision made for dealing with greasy water:	
			c. No incinerator: neighbouring camp one used.	
			d. Washing arrangements of utensils might be improved, particularly when there is a rush of men.	
			e. Water supply: supplied by the neighbouring brigades water carts. (Water has always given positive result to tests for presence of free chlorine when tested by this section).	
			Sample of water supplied for testing by 20 D.L.I. of this Div shewed gross contamination: more than 20 scoops of B.P. required per 110 gals. Water was condemned & supply boarded	

2449 Wt. W14957/M90 750,000 1/16 J.B.C. & A. Forms/C.2118/12.

Instructions regarding War Diaries and Intelligence Summaries are contained in F. S. Regs., Part II. and the Staff Manual respectively. Title Pages will be prepared in manuscript.

WAR DIARY

or

~~INTELLIGENCE SUMMARY~~

(Erase heading not required.)

Army Form C. 2118.

Place	Date	Hour	Summary of Events and Information	Remarks and references to Appendices
			up & labelled.	
			I drew up a report on Mummlidge camp, which is to be handed over shortly.	
			While a little has been done to improve the sanitation of the camp: a great deal still remains to be done, & if I had my way I would condemn the place as unfit for occupation by troops. Now that it is likely to be handed over to another division, possibly some attempt might be made to get it in a more sanitary condition. The R.E. & 124 Brigade who have occupied it all the time the Div. has been here have persistently refused to alter the men's huts for the better or exercise any disciplinary measures to prevent wooden sanitary structures from being pulled down & used for firewood.	
			I think it is worth while to add something about the type of hut used in this camp & in the Div area. There was	

2449 Wt. W14957/M90 750,000 1/16 J.B.C. & A. Forms/C.2118/12.

Instructions regarding War Diaries and Intelligence Summaries are contained in F. S. Regs., Part II. and the Staff Manual respectively. Title Pages will be prepared in manuscript.

WAR DIARY
or
INTELLIGENCE SUMMARY

(Erase heading not required.)

Army Form C. 2118.

Place	Date	Hour	Summary of Events and Information	Remarks and references to Appendices
			case is it as bad as in Hurrumbidgee camp, (which was designed by Colonial troops).	

— corrugated iron or felt over boards

8'4"

ground level

The huts are usually 24' x 16' & 8'4" high @ centre: usual no of occupants 25 giving an average air space of 77 cu ft per man.

In addition in only few of the huts is there any window, nor is there a ventilator. Along the perpendicular sides where these join the roof provision was evidently made for a space for ventilation but this has been blocked up in practically every case.

The floor level is below ground level: in this damp country of clay & mud the inference is obvious.

After a great deal of pressure (1) two ablution sheds were built by R.E. but these are not sufficient.

(2) Two new cookhouses are being built.

2449 Wt. W14957/M90 750,000 1/16 J.B.C. & A. Forms/C.2118/12.

Instructions regarding War Diaries and Intelligence Summaries are contained in F. S. Regs., Part II. and the Staff Manual respectively. Title Pages will be prepared in manuscript.

WAR DIARY
or
~~INTELLIGENCE SUMMARY~~
(Erase heading not required.)

Army Form C. 2118.

Place	Date	Hour	Summary of Events and Information	Remarks and references to Appendices
			In one hut in one of the camps which was pulled down, 192 rats were killed.	H.V.
Field (Reninghelst)	Mar 17.		There seems to be no regular system of drainage in this area. Here in Reninghelst the San. Sec. is employed men on street sweeping, & as fast as the streets are swept some civilian authorities come along & clear the ditches to a certain extent & pile the refuse on the road side & leave it there. Another thing Div. H.Q. do nothing about sanitation but leave it to the San. Sec. We have been able to do it up till the present, but the Camp Commandant is responsible for the discipline of Div. H.Q. & also the sanitation. If the proposed change of making San. Secs area & army troops comes about it will be a great deal of trouble for the camp commandant, as the whole of the sanitation of Div. H.Q. will be thrown on him.	

2449 Wt. W14957/M90 750,000 1/16 J.B.C. & A. Forms/C.2118/12.

Instructions regarding War Diaries and Intelligence Summaries are contained in F. S. Regs., Part II. and the Staff Manual respectively. Title Pages will be prepared in manuscript.

WAR DIARY

or

~~INTELLIGENCE SUMMARY~~

(Erase heading not required.)

Army Form C. 2118.

Place	Date	Hour	Summary of Events and Information	Remarks and references to Appendices
			It is pitiable to see the way Sanitation is ~~neglected~~ neglected by this division, particularly by Div. H.Q.	
			I reported a civilian slaughter house for allowing the viscera of a slaughtered animal to be thrown into open & uncovered for days - also other insanitary conditions.	
			I reported some civilians who were unauthorised to cook for troops for doing so.	D.V.
Field Ravigfelst	Mar 18.		A no. of tins of Bully beef - 57, were condemned by me as being bad - sides of tins were bulging & burst.	
			No authorities have approached me yet with regard to the handing over of the area occupied by the 24 Brigade, who are going out for three weeks rest.	D.V.

2449 Wt. W14957/M90 750,000 1/16 J.B.C. & A. Forms/C.2118/12.

Army Form C. 2118.

WAR DIARY
or
INTELLIGENCE SUMMARY

(Erase heading not required.)

Instructions regarding War Diaries and Intelligence Summaries are contained in F. S. Regs., Part II. and the Staff Manual respectively. Title Pages will be prepared in manuscript.

Place	Date	Hour	Summary of Events and Information	Remarks and references to Appendices
Field. Reninghelst	Mar 19.		Applied to A.D.M.S. to obtain permission to pull up some of the Pavé in Reninghelst to make a proper drain & soak pit for a Public urinal.	
			The method of work adopted by the civilians who are working under Corps Roads Officer is very objectionable. Road sweepers sweep all the refuse from the roads into the ditches, & the civilians who clean the ditches pile the rubbish & filth from the ditches on to the roads.	
			Sample of water taken from cart of "C" 187 R.F.A. tested shewed no trace of chlorination: Reported for necessary action.	
			No 4 Coy 41st Div A.S.C. was found to be using bad bleaching powder on the water cart: no trace of chlorine was discovered in the	

\

Army Form C. 2118.

Instructions regarding War Diaries and Intelligence Summaries are contained in F. S. Regs., Part II. and the Staff Manual respectively. Title Pages will be prepared in manuscript.

WAR DIARY

or

~~INTELLIGENCE SUMMARY~~

(Erase heading not required.)

Place	Date	Hour	Summary of Events and Information	Remarks and references to Appendices
			Bleaching powder. I reported this: the water ~~tank~~ cart carrying this B.P. was found insufficiently chlorinated in consequence. This I reported.	[illegible]
			———	
Field.	Mar 21.		Watercart of 34th Batt R.F.A. att'd this div. found as follows.	
			No water detail c cart.	
			Clarifier incomplete.	
			No stores box carried.	
			Reported this for necessary action.	
			—	
			Area commandant has refused permission to dig the pave as I suggested & offered an alternative site which is not so convenient.	
			—	
			The ~~[illegible]~~ ground immediately around the new Soldiers' Club here in [illegible] is kept v. dirty & I have asked the	

2449 Wt. W14957/M90 750,000 1/16 J.B.C. & A. Forms/C.2118/12.

Instructions regarding War Diaries and Intelligence Summaries are contained in F. S. Regs., Part II. and the Staff Manual respectively. Title Pages will be prepared in manuscript.

WAR DIARY
or
~~INTELLIGENCE SUMMARY~~
(Erase heading not required.)

Place	Date	Hour	Summary of Events and Information	Remarks and references to Appendices
			Camp commandant to try & arrange for the ditch which runs alongside of the ground to be kept in proper order.	
			Owing to the continued thefts of Lamps from the Latrines here I have had to arrange a picket for each system of urinals & latrines. These pickets will bring in the Lamps each eve when they come off duty.	
			—	
			One private of this section evacuated to C.C.S. on 19/3/17.	
			—	
Field ~~Mar 22nd~~	Mar 22nd		On instructions, I took over temporary duty with 84th SANITARY SECTION from CAPT VICKERS who proceeded on leave. I occupied myself in perusing the files in the Office and ascertaining the disposal and duties of the men of the Sanitary Section.	
			J.S. DOYLE. CAPT. RAMC	

2449 Wt. W14957/M90 750,000 1/16 J.B.C. & A. Forms/C.2118/12.

Instructions regarding War Diaries and Intelligence Summaries are contained in F. S. Regs., Part II. and the Staff Manual respectively. Title Pages will be prepared in manuscript.

WAR DIARY
or
INTELLIGENCE SUMMARY
(Erase heading not required.)

Army Form C. 2118.

Place	Date	Hour	Summary of Events and Information	Remarks and references to Appendices
Field ~~Mar 23rd~~	Mar 23rd		Visited the various camps of WESTERN ~~District~~ HD SECTION most of them are very damp but are kept well and in a Sanitary Condition under the circumstances.	
Field ~~Mar 24th~~	Mar 24th		On request of M.O. of 12th E. Surrey Regt I visited ALBERTA CAMP in reference to case of measles. I advised him as to isolation etc and had infected hut thoroughly disinfected. Received correspondence re Urine pit for Public Urinal opposite Church in RENINGHELST. Will see BELGIAN MISSION if it is possible to dig same inside church wall at lower end.	May 24th: HB Handed over files and map copy of area occupied by 124 BRIGADE to O.C. SANITARY SECTION of 16th DIVISION.
Field. ~~Mar 25th~~	Mar 25th		Ablution benches in ALBERTA CAMP discharge direct into Stream. Pump in well not in working ~~order~~ as the piping	Withdrew my own men from this district on orders from Major Thurston

2449 Wt. W14957/M90 750,000 1/16 J.B.C. & A. Forms/C.2118/12.

Army Form C. 2118.

Instructions regarding War Diaries and Intelligence Summaries are contained in F. S. Regs., Part II. and the Staff Manual respectively. Title Pages will be prepared in manuscript.

WAR DIARY
or
INTELLIGENCE SUMMARY

(Erase heading not required.)

Place	Date	Hour	Summary of Events and Information	Remarks and references to Appendices
			is much too short. I am having proper (Arko-breeze) filter built and erected and channels from the four ablution benches diverted to this filter. The matter should be finished in a few days.	
Field ~~March~~	Mar 26th		Had water tank at YMCA hut (LA CLYTTE Rd) fitted for Cover. Water in tank did not contain free chlorine. Measures taken to ensure proper Chlorination in future.	
			New labour battalion in OUDERDOM district (28th QUEENS R.W.SURREYS). Men are billeted in tents but ground is very sodden and duck-boards are badly wanted. Wooden flooring to each tent. Latrines are not suitable as they consist merely of a number of buckets with pole.	
			Ablution benches are satisfactory but soapy water discharged into stream. Sanitary Corporal stated he had ~~a~~ filter	

2449 Wt. W14957/M90 750,000 1/16 J.B.C. & A. Forms/C.2118/12.

Army Form C. 2118.

WAR DIARY
or
INTELLIGENCE SUMMARY
(Erase heading not required.)

Instructions regarding War Diaries and Intelligence Summaries are contained in F. S. Regs., Part II. and the Staff Manual respectively. Title Pages will be prepared in manuscript.

Place	Date	Hour	Summary of Events and Information	Remarks and references to Appendices
			under Construction. I Advised him as to provision of Fly-Proof latrines and other necessary precautions & detailed one of my Inspectors to super-intend the proper working of the Sanitation of the Camp.	
Field ~~[illegible]~~	Mar 27th		Visited DICKEBUSH in EASTERN SECTION, and district around and found the latrines Urinals (both public & private) and ~~Camp~~ billets in good Sanitary Condition. Water Supply very Satisfactory.	
			Some units in CENTRAL SECTION are somewhat slow in providing proper grease traps & Soakage pits and have promised to remedy same immediately.	

2449 Wt. W14957/M90 750,000 1/16 J.B.C. & A. Forms/C.2118/12.

Army Form C. 2118.

Instructions regarding War Diaries and Intelligence Summaries are contained in F. S. Regs., Part II. and the Staff Manual respectively. Title Pages will be prepared in manuscript.

WAR DIARY
or
INTELLIGENCE SUMMARY

(Erase heading not required.)

Place	Date	Hour	Summary of Events and Information	Remarks and references to Appendices
Field	May 28th		Estaminets & laundries in WESTERN and CENTRAL SECTIONS in a Satisfactory Condition and Complying with Regulations laid down as to washing vessels Etc.	
			Some laundries ~~were~~ not authorised to do washing and were informed of proper procedure to obtain permission to do so. A.P.M. also acquainted of these houses. They were Clean and Satisfactory.	
Field	May 29th		Samples from Some water-carts lately have not contained the necessary amount ~~of free chl~~ bleaching powder. The M.Os of the units have been notified and asked to take particular care in this matter.	
			Some of the Camps in WESTERN SECTION are not as well drained as they Should be, and existing drains in Some cases needed attention and clearing.	

2449 Wt. W14957/M90 750,000 1/16 J.B.C. & A. Forms/C.2118/12.

Army Form C. 2118.

Instructions regarding War Diaries and Intelligence Summaries are contained in F. S. Regs., Part II. and the Staff Manual respectively. Title Pages will be prepared in manuscript.

WAR DIARY
or
INTELLIGENCE SUMMARY
(Erase heading not required.)

Place	Date	Hour	Summary of Events and Information	Remarks and references to Appendices
~~Field~~ RENINGHELST	Mar 30th		Ground around SOLDIER'S CLUB not sufficiently drained. Kitchen in same club some feet below level of ground with the result that floor is very often flooded. Kitchen is also use to store everything including sacks of potatoes etc. I would suggest building of proper houses & storerooms for various stores. Kitchen not as clean as it should be. There being only a single flooring overhead, a considerable amount of dirt, sawdust etc filters down between the boards and is likely to mix with the food in preparation. I am communicating with the Adjutant on these matters.	
Field	Mar 31st		The question of fly-proof latrines for front-line & reserve trenches requires immediate action owing to near approach of warm weather. Whilst acting as temporary M.O. to 21st K.R.R.C. I reported this matter several times and find that the delay in procuring	

2449 Wt. W14957/M90 750,000 1/16 J.B.C. & A. Forms/C.2118/12.

Instructions regarding War Diaries and Intelligence Summaries are contained in F. S. Regs., Part II. and the Staff Manual respectively. Title Pages will be prepared in manuscript.

WAR DIARY
or
INTELLIGENCE SUMMARY

(Erase heading not required.)

Army Form C. 2118.

Place	Date	Hour	Summary of Events and Information	Remarks and references to Appendices
			Same is due to lack of material. The R.E's state and have recently stated that they have no timber with which to build same. There seems to have been plenty of timber for Soldiers' clubs and other recreation huts, but the question of the bodily health of the men evidently takes a back place. As Dysentery is one of the diseases which decimates a battalion very rapidly I would like to see a special effort made to procure the necessary latrines. These should be single-seaters as the difficulty of getting three & four seaters up to front line is considerable.	

84th SANITARY SECTION.
No.............
Date.............

J S Doyle
Capt R.A.M.C.
Acting O.C. 84th SANITARY SECTION.

2449 Wt. W14957/M90 750,000 1/16 J.B.C. & A. Forms/C.2118/12.

www.ingramcontent.com/pod-product-compliance
Lightning Source LLC
Chambersburg PA
CBHW080838010526
44114CB00017B/2330

* 9 7 8 1 4 7 4 5 2 0 2 2 5 *